PRAISE FOR
THE ESCAPE INDUSTRY

'Today it's so simple and inexpensive to travel, or to see the world virtually from the comfort of your armchair, that it's easy to forget that not so long ago travelling afar was the purview of the most adventurous and the elite. From the Ritz to Pan Am, Mark Tungate's brilliant book takes the reader on a grand tour of the history of the brands and experiences that have shaped the travel landscape we now take for granted.' **Claire Bridges, Founder, Now Go Create, and author,** *In Your Creative Element*

'Yesterday's world of travel – palatial hotels, elegant air transportation and class-act cruising – set standards of service and etiquette that have surprisingly survived to this day. But now guests and passengers require impeccable service and facilities in an atmosphere of "no-tie" freedom. Mark Tungate takes us on a fascinating journey through this evolution, via interviews with the proud heirs of the golden age of travel.' **Jean-Pierre Soutric, Senior Vice President Sales and Marketing, Oetker Collection**

'*The Escape Industry* shows why 21st-century nomads want to experience local culture after being globalized by brands for the past 50 years.' **Florian Wupperfeld, Founder, Leading Culture Destinations**

The Escape Industry

How iconic and innovative brands built the travel business

Mark Tungate

First published in Great Britain and the United States in 2018 by Kogan Page Limited

2nd Floor, 45 Gee Street	c/o Martin P Hill Consulting	4737/23 Ansari Road
London EC1V 3RS	122 W 27th St, 10th Floor	Daryaganj
United Kingdom	New York, NY 10001	New Delhi 110002
www.koganpage.com	USA	India

© Mark Tungate, 2018

ISBN   978 0 7494 7350 1
E-ISBN   978 0 7494 7351 8

British Library Cataloguing-in-Publication Data

A CIP record for this book is available from the British Library.

Library of Congress Cataloging-in-Publication Data

Names: Tungate, Mark, 1967- author.
Title: The escape industry : how iconic and innovative brands built the
    travel business / Mark Tungate.
Description: London ; New York : Kogan Page Limited, [2018] | Includes
    bibliographical references and index.
Identifiers: LCCN 2017026098 (print) | LCCN 2017035155 (ebook) | ISBN
    9780749473518 (ebook) | ISBN 9780749473501 (alk. paper)
Subjects: LCSH: Tourism. | Tourism–Marketing.
Classification: LCC G155.A1 (ebook) | LCC G155.A1 T786 2018 (print) | DDC
    338.4/791–dc23

Typeset by Integra Software Services, Pondicherry
Print production managed by Jellyfish
Printed and bound by CPI Group (UK) Ltd, Croydon, CR0 4YY

For my father, who charted the way.

CONTENTS

ABOUT THE AUTHOR

Mark Tungate is a British journalist based in Paris. He is the author of several books about branding and marketing, including *Fashion Brands: Branding style from Armani to Zara* and *Adland: A global history of advertising*. His articles have appeared in publications ranging from *Campaign* and *Advertising Age* to the *Financial Times* and *The Daily Telegraph*. He is a regular contributor to the ad industry intelligence site AdForum.

Alongside his writing, Mark is editorial director of the Epica Awards, an annual competition in which journalists who are specialists in their field celebrate excellence in design, advertising, PR and branded content.

Mark has lectured on advertising and branding at universities and conferences around the world.

ACKNOWLEDGEMENTS

This trip began in a restaurant. Over lunch I told my wife Géraldine that I was thinking of writing a book about travel brands. 'I want to call it *The Escape Industry*,' I told her. I could see from her expression that she liked the idea. 'And you're just the man for the job,' she said. So my first thank you goes, of course, to Géraldine, for the inspiration and encouragement she constantly provides.

Thanks also to all those who agreed to be interviewed for these pages. Their names appear in the text – but there were many others who made connections behind the scenes: Amanda Benfell, Michael Chefles, Brittany Cornejo, Natania Jansz, Anna Moss, Romina Tina Fontana, Brigitte Hogarth, Heloise Hooton, David Kijlstra, Kelly Lee, Ulrich Proeschel, Amanda Smith, Ian Wagasky. If I have forgotten anyone, please call me and I will apologize in person.

The book took so long to write that it actually went through two commissioning editors, so thanks are due to Jasmin Naim and especially Jenny Volich, who provided focus amid many distractions.

Finally, a big thank you to Helen Kogan and her team at Kogan Page, my loyal publisher.

Introduction

'The idea of travel.'

Imagine you're strolling down Broadway, New York, some time in the early 1920s. You hear a faint buzzing sound, merely irritating at first, like an angry gnat. But the sound grows louder. And louder, accompanied by the tortured whine of overwrought machinery.

Along with everyone else, you turn towards the noise. You look up, holding onto your hat as a gale screams between the skyscrapers. But the racket is in fact a small aircraft, flying so low that it looks set to crash onto the street. The entire crowd ducks as the spindly wooden plane skims overhead and roars down Broadway, trailing – or so it seems – a banner of demonic laughter.

The guy in the cockpit is Juan Trippe, the owner of an air taxi service out of Long Island – and the future founder of Pan Am. The stunt is being filmed by a friend of his for a silent movie. He'll receive a police summons for his barnstorming act, but it won't be the last time he goes out of his way to get noticed.

Inevitably, when you write about iconic brands, you end up writing about the people behind them. And the people who built the travel business were colourful characters, almost without exception. Travel is said to broaden the horizons, but people like Juan Trippe came with the bigger picture built in. Their ambition was to share it with us.

I've often stated that I'll only write books I want to read. So if you're looking for a conventional business tome – with tables and charts and appendices – you may as well close this book right now. Certainly, its aim is to explore the history and strategies of travel brands. But more than anything, it is a collection of inspiring business stories.

Talking of business, it's fair to say that business and leisure travel have evolved in different ways. As the book's title suggests, I tend to concentrate on the consumer side of travel – tourism, in other words – although the two worlds often overlap.

During the research process, I bumped into many unexpected facts, some of which jarred my perception of the travel industry. But that's the beauty of a project like this. I started out as a reporter, and in many ways I've remained one. I hope it doesn't sound too pompous if I suggest that my job is to discover things. Writing a book is a journey, too.

History and autobiography

I came to the travel industry at a pivotal moment. The business of travel is constantly evolving – mostly under the influence of technology, which has made the world ever smaller – but the change seems to have accelerated of late.

First came the low-cost airlines. These may have had their roots in the 1970s – with Southwest in the US and the short-lived Skytrain in the UK – but they proliferated after the deregulation of European skies in the 1990s. EasyJet, one of the most emblematic, launched in 1995. Barely five years later, the online booking revolution gave travellers an entirely new and efficient way of reserving tickets and securing cheap vacations. Both of these advances have been seized upon by what might be termed the 'mobile social generation', with their increased flexibility and mobility. Today, it's insanely easy to fly to a city on impulse and book a hotel on the spot, without making a single phone call. Actually, you need not bother with a hotel – you can rent an Airbnb apartment. At the same time, increased security prompted by the threat of terrorism has made flying more tedious and stressful.

Travel agents, airlines and hotels – the classic lynchpins of the travel experience – have all been impacted by this shifting situation. I've tried to explore their responses and solutions, as well as the methods they use to communicate with us. As in many other sectors, effective branding has become crucial in a field overcrowded with choice and colonized by digital players.

The creative director of a branding agency once told me that the perfect brand was 'a promise kept'. The promise was the sum of all the visual and promotional elements of a brand – the logo, the design, the advertising – but the trick was to deliver on that promise, which meant service. Travel companies are probably some of the most complained-about in the world. We invest so much emotion into our trip at the outset that they struggle to deliver on our expectations. Those that come even close can command immense loyalty. I've examined a few of them here.

But this is also a very personal book. For as far back as I can remember, I've loved to travel. Or perhaps I should say I've loved the *idea* of travel (which, by the way, is exactly what the industry's marketing experts are constantly trying to sell us). *Treasure Island* is probably to blame; to this day I'm convinced that no book that begins with a map can ever be entirely bad. I also adored that book because my father used to read it to me aloud; he did a perfect pirate accent.

Dad was a great fan of maps, which no doubt rubbed off on me. He kept a whole bunch of them in the glove compartment of his car – a lurking concertina of paper that would spring out if you opened the door too quickly. Many weekend road trips began with Dad poring over a map in search of a certain castle or haunted house. Later, writers ranging in quality from Alistair MacLean and Wilbur Smith to Ernest Hemingway and Graham Greene convinced me that the possibility of excitement and sophistication lay far beyond my doorstep.

As a result this book is studded with anecdotes, snippets from my travel experiences. I make no apology for them – they made the task of writing less arduous and besides, if you find them annoying, you can always skip over them. Since many of the quotes in this book come from original interviews with the people concerned – as I said, I'm essentially a reporter – the research process also enabled me to chat to some of my travel heroes. I particularly enjoyed talking to Mark Ellingham, creator of the *Rough Guide* series of guidebooks, which accompanied me on a number of memorable trips.

But if *The Escape Industry* occasionally resembles autobiography, it more often reads like history. When I started planning its contents, I was keen to find out how people travelled when leaving home really was an adventure, and who helped them on their way.

So to start our journey, let's turn a page back to the past.

Grand Tourists 01

'A man who has not been in Italy is always conscious of an inferiority.'

In the late spring of 1864, after a Channel crossing buffeted by south-westerly winds, a ship anchors in Studland Bay, Dorset. The bay is famously sheltered, protected by the curving arm of Ballard Down and the chalk cliffs at Handfast Point, which end in the snaggled teeth known as Old Harry Rocks.

Night is falling. A passenger, clad in a dark overcoat against the chill, emerges onto the deck to peer out at the bay he has not seen since his exile more than 20 years earlier.

Soon, the creak of oars. The passenger descends shakily into the smaller vessel and is rowed ashore. From there, a fast ride in a covered carriage to his destination – the great country house of Kingston Lacy. His steward, Seymour, shows him inside.

Perhaps they explore by the light of a single lamp – this is, after all, a covert visit. He shouldn't be here at all. Not even in England. If he is discovered, he will be arrested.

Lamplight flickers across the walls, finally allowing him to see his collection *in situ*. He has been sending these objects back from his travels, instructing Seymour by letter about exactly where to place them. Until now, he could only imagine the results.

Marble from Venice, sculptures from Verona, a pair of oil paintings by Bonifacio, which once hung in a palace on the Grand Canal.

His masterpiece is The Spanish Room. He thinks of it as The Golden Room, with its glittering coffered ceiling, the walls swathed with gilded and embossed leather. The doors are also exquisite: made of pear wood, with 12 panels depicting the months, executed to his own designs. On the walls are the paintings he collected during the Peninsular War in Spain, long before his disgrace: the beloved Murillos; the sketch for *Las Meninas* by Velasquez (or so he fervently believes).

The visitor is ailing, and this is the last time he will see his ancestral home. Soon he will return to Venice, where he will die at the age of 68.

His name is William Bankes. Collector, adventurer – and one of the very grandest of the Grand Tourists.

The allure of travel

My parents live near Kingston Lacy, and we often visit the wonderful old house when I go to stay with them. I've always been intrigued by the story of William Bankes, the inveterate traveller.

Bankes was forced to leave England definitively in 1841, having been caught 'in compromising circumstances' with a guardsman in Green Park. In those days such indiscretions led to prison, at the very least. But the self-exiled Bankes continued to explore and collect, furnishing his home with exotic wonders *in absentia*. The story of his surreptitious final visit is part of the legend of the house.

During his formative years, his tastes and travels were influenced by a wider movement that encouraged young men of a certain class to abandon the comforts of home and explore other cultures – essentially in Europe but sometimes beyond. Bankes made it as far as Egypt, where he arranged to have an obelisk shipped back for the gardens at Kingston Lacy. He referred to these activities as 'tourifying', borrowing a term coined by his friend Byron.

According to Anne Seba in her (2004) book *The Exiled Collector: William Bankes and the making of an English country house*, Bankes was rather contemptuous of the 'French–Italian track of earlier Grand Tourists'. Instead he set his sights on Portugal and Spain.

Then in his mid-twenties, Bankes set sail from Portsmouth on 20 January 1813 for the six-day voyage to Lisbon. The quality of his travels from that point on illustrates the challenges faced by early tourists, not to mention their determination.

In Portugal, Bankes slept in a monastery in the hills of Arrabida, a wild and isolated place despite its lush vegetation. Next he arrived in a Spain described by Seba as 'unsettled, dangerous, snake-infested and almost bankrupt', not to mention patrolled by gangs of ruthless bandits. The roads were little more than tracks and many of the bridges were out.

Incidentally, Spain was still at war. Aided by the Duke of Wellington and 60,000 British troops, the Spanish had been fighting the occupying French army since the 'Dos de Mayo' uprising against Joseph Bonaparte five years earlier. By the time Bankes arrived, the war was practically won, thanks to the British victory at Salamanca the previous July. But there were, as Seba puts it, 'pockets of resistance'.

In Spain, Bankes did not put up at a lavish hotel. He stayed with Wellington, a friend of his father's, as an *aide-de-camp* at the great man's headquarters – more or less a camp follower. He visited besieged Pamplona in disguise, where he claimed to have dined with the French commanding general, who sold him a Raphael.

These may be extreme examples, and Bankes was more adventurous than most – but it's fair to say that early tourism was an improvised and often hazardous activity.

In fact, tourifying could be terrifying.

The trailblazers

William Bankes was one of a long line of young Englishmen who had subjected themselves to the rigours of foreign travel in order to complete their education.

In his (1969) book *The Grand Tour*, Christopher Hibbert describes the 16th-century travels of Sir Philip Sidney, who would later become an ambassador. 'Journeys like this were often subsidized by the Queen herself, who was concerned to establish a body of young courtiers fit to represent her at foreign courts, or by colleges which were anxious to profit from the knowledge imparted at foreign universities.'

Sidney set forth for Paris in 1572, accompanied by 'a half-Italian tutor, three servants and four horses'. Having trekked around France, Germany, the Low Countries and Italy, with shorter visits to Poland and Hungary, he returned home a full three years later.

His itinerary seems to have set a pattern for tours to come. The phrase 'The Grand Tour' appeared in print for the first time in Richard Lassels' *Voyage of Italy* (1670). By the early 18th century, writes Hibbert, The Grand Tour had become 'accepted as a finishing school for a young gentleman of fortune'.

Or as another great tourist, Dr Samuel Johnson, put it: 'A man who has not been in Italy is always conscious of an inferiority, from not having seen what it is expected a man should see.'

Here we see the first glimmer of an idea that would later be fully exploited by the travel industry – the suggestion that those who have not seen enough of the world are only partly formed; that they are bound to ignorance by their narrow horizons.

It was a snobbish viewpoint, especially in Johnson's day. Foreign travel was undoubtedly the preserve of the elite.

The mid-18th century – the golden age of The Grand Tour – was an era of comparatively little conflict, making European travel somewhat less perilous than at other periods, although Britain remained sporadically at war with France. But according to Jeremy Black, author (in 1992) of *The British*

Abroad: The Grand Tour in the 18th century, another factor was equally important. Black refers to it as 'the consumer revolution of the eighteenth century'. He explains:

> There was an increase in the consumption of... non-essentials such as luxury furniture. An information revolution was one aspect of this development, with a massive growth in the production of books, newspapers and other printed material...[This] encouraged the development of different sorts of literature, including travel accounts. Authors, such as Tobias Smollett, and publisher-booksellers, produced such literature because they knew there was a market for it among those with the money to buy and the leisure to read.

This early travel writing was 'an important stimulant to the growth of foreign travel'. 1749 saw the publication of one of the very first guidebooks: *The Grand Tour*, by Thomas Nugent. It covered France, Italy, Germany and the Netherlands, although Italy was considered by far the most prestigious destination, with its classical Roman sites and Renaissance art.

The sheer cost and effort of tourism meant that many trips were made only once in a lifetime. Writes Black: 'Having gone abroad once, most, although by no means all, British tourists did not cross the Channel again.'

There was also the problem of infrastructure. Even on the Channel crossing to France, there was little resembling a regular passenger service. Embarking on the shortest route from Dover to Calais – which took three to six hours, depending on the weather – travellers were forced to rely on 'the packet boat that carried the royal mail and could take paying passengers', or private arrangements with the captains of merchant ships. These vessels were unstable and the winds hostile, causing delays and sickness.

Braver passengers opted for the longer route from Brighton or Southampton to the ports of Le Havre, Dieppe or Cherbourg – which were closer to Paris. (When Britain was embroiled in one of its habitual wars with France, tourists crossed from Dover to Ostend.)

After a wave-tossed and vomit-splashed crossing, travellers were often required to transfer from their ship to a rowing boat or fishing vessel before they could reach the shore. They were charged a guinea for this service – to put that sum into context, the entire Channel crossing may have only cost half a guinea. Sometimes they were obliged to pay twice as much to be let off the vessel as they had forked out to board it. This was when travellers got an inkling of how rapidly their finances might evaporate while they were abroad. Although the notion of mass travel lay far in the future, an entire economy had sprung up around the objective of separating tourists from their money.

When they finally reached dry land – drenched, exhausted and wretched – they had to deal with the customs officials.

Christopher Hibbert describes the tourist who, having looked on in alarm as his bags were tossed onto the quay, 'was asked to pay what he considered exorbitant fees to bare-legged porters, both male and female, who carried these bags to the customs house'. There, according to a young servant, the tourists were delivered into the hands of 'the most shocking sharks I ever saw', who did not hesitate to 'put their hands into our pockets and then felt down our sides, even to our ankles, for contraband commodities'. Of course, if they found something that displeased them, a bribe induced temporary blindness.

Passports for travel in France could also be acquired, if travellers had not obtained one from the French consul in London prior to their trip (the modern passport system did not emerge until the First World War).

With this indignity behind them, tourists sought an inn at which they would spend their first night on foreign soil. The most celebrated Calais *auberge* of the late 18th century was the Hôtel Dessin in rue Royale. Such was its reputation, writes Hibbert, 'that the rich young man would think of staying nowhere else'. By providing superior yet costly accommodation, a fine supper and crucial services – such as securing carriages, changing money and extending credit – the enterprising Monsieur Dessin had become a rich and influential man. He promoted his establishment as 'the inn of kings', eagerly listing the procession of monarchs and notables who had stayed there.

Having survived the crossing to France, an expensive dinner of seafood washed down with champagne, and quite possibly a sleepless night, the Grand Tourists were ready to move on to their first important destination – Paris.

Travel and arrival

The great city was not an easily achieved goal. Although the roads in France were reasonably good, travelling on them was either expensive or arduous.

Lynne Withey gives a detailed account of the options in her (1997) book *Grand Tours and Cook's Tours: A history of leisure travel, 1750 to 1915*. The wealthiest travellers simply acquired a private coach, horses and a driver for the duration of their trip. Others preferred to 'rent a carriage... and travel "post", which meant hiring horses and driver at designated stations spaced along the main roads at intervals of six or seven miles... Most posting stations doubled as inns, offering travellers the convenience of dining while waiting for fresh horses to be harnessed to their carriage.'

But this solution was not without its challenges. Travellers often found that horses and drivers had been reserved in advance by 'some prince or nobleman who would be along shortly' – and of course they complained about being overcharged.

Two other vehicles that made the journey to Paris were criticized as overloaded and lumbering: the *carosse*, which like an English stage-coach carried six passengers; and the larger *coche*, which could take 16 occupants. Once their cumbersome baggage was stashed aboard, in large wicker baskets strapped fore and aft, the *coche* struggled to achieve more than a walking pace.

A quicker and cheaper option was the *diligence*, which resembled an ungainly cross between an elongated coach and a seaside tourist train on wheels. It was essentially 'three coaches hitched together with a platform across the top for luggage and additional passengers'. Carrying up to 30 people, these conveyances travelled daily from Calais to Paris, a journey of three to four days. They were crowded, noisy and jarring – pricier coaches had springs, but the operators of the diligences considered suspension a luxury.

On arrival in Paris – and having again suffered at the hands of customs officials, this time at the gates to the city – travellers fended off touts offering their services as valets and made their way to their accommodation. Hotels certainly existed: among the most reputable, Christopher Hibbert lists the Imperial and the Anjou in Saint-Germain, the Picardie in nearby rue Mazarine and the Hôtel du Dauphin in rue de Teranne (a street of which I can find no trace).

However, in a shadowy early version of Airbnb, many tourists preferred to rent furnished rooms – in Paris as well as in Florence and Rome, where they expected to spend several weeks. Writes Withey: 'The fashionable quarters of these cities were filled with spacious town houses, whose owners were often happy to rent part of their homes to visitors.'

Of course, visitors to Paris were disproportionately concerned with fashion. Parisian dress was more flamboyant than the London style, and in order to be accepted in polite society, a visiting tourist was required to transform himself. (The largest percentage of travellers were male, although there were several adventurous women tourists – such as the great travel writer Mariana Starke, who spent six years in Italy at the end of the 18th century and returned after the Napoleonic Wars to research a series of influential guides.)

Having decked himself out in a 'Frenchified' powdered wig, a long velvet coat – in a vivid colour – lined with white satin, matching breeches, a brocaded waistcoat, white silk stockings and slender pumps with gold or even diamond buckles, and griped bitterly about the expense of doing so,

DC Public Library

Author: Tungate, Mark,
1967-
Title: The escape industry :
how iconic and innovative b
Item ID: 31172094752359
Date charged: 11/13/2019,
20:13
Date due: 12/4/2019,23:59

Thank you for using the
DC Public Library

a man was ready to visit Versailles. Even if he lacked the connections to be presented to the King and Queen, he could at least wander the public rooms and admire the art. A true gentleman was also expected to carry a sword, but these could be rented at the palace.

Literally putting themselves in the Parisians' shoes did not make British visitors to the city any more empathetic. Predictably, they found Paris crowded and filthy, and its citizens gaudy and arrogant. Then, as now, the Paris tourist scene could be fairly cleanly divided into two groups: visitors who complained about the city's hostility, and locals who complained about the tourists.

Paris has never been the utopia first-time visitors envisage. Before the Revolution, its muddy thoroughfares were cluttered with carriages and cabriolets careering at breakneck speed, threatening to mow down the unwary. 'After the Revolution,' notes Christopher Hibbert, 'the streets were just the same.'

It was a place of indolence and chaos, grandeur and horror. Understandably, once they had ticked off the required sights, the tourists were ready to move on – to Italy, the focal point of their trip.

Italy and beyond

Once again, the price of access to the sublime was misery – also known as the Alps. Crossing its crags and passes was 'a horrid necessity', writes Hibbert, who informs us that the most popular tourist trail of the 18th century led over Mount Cenis. He quotes the poet Thomas Gray, who believed the peak pushed 'the permission mountains have of being frightful rather too far'.

Just how frightful becomes apparent when we learn how tourists made the crossing. First, at the foot of the mountain, the traveller's coach was dismantled and packed onto the backs of mules. The tourist, swaddled in furs, was then transferred to a sedan chair 'with long poles which porters grasped or rested on their shoulders as they leaped from rock to rock. The chair had no floor which, as Mariana Starke discovered, was very uncomfortable when the porters put it down for a rest and she was left sitting in the snow, clutching for warmth a little lap dog and a heated bag of semolina.' This was often followed by a scary (or exhilarating) descent by sledge.

By the early 19th century, roads had begun to appear – notably the famous Simplon Road, built through the pass of the same name on the orders of Napoleon, initially to carry artillery pieces. But the road was long, treacherous and often blocked by avalanches – and the post-houses were notoriously spartan.

In fact, the tourists could only breathe easily when the mountains were at their backs, and they were trotting across the gentle Plain of Lombardy. At last, the real journey had begun.

Italy was a profusion of riches. The first major stop was Turin, which tourists found agreeable, if unremarkable. It was as if they had already projected their minds forward – to Florence and Rome – and were therefore unable to concentrate on their immediate surroundings. They could also sidestep to Venice, but strangely enough, given the city's later status as one of the world's most romantic destinations, their opinion of it was mixed. Venice was said to be in decline: it was muddy, malodorous and full of brothels and gambling houses.

But its Carnival was a formidable tourist magnet. The event in February swelled the city's population by an additional 30,000, according to Hibbert, who cites streets packed with 'lawyers, knaves and pickpockets; mountebanks, old women and physicians: strumpets bare-faced… a jumble of senators, citizens, gondoliers and people of every character and condition'.

Padua and Bologna offered more sedate pleasures: the former boasted the church of St Justina, designed by Andrea Palladio (hence the architectural term 'Palladian'), while the latter was renowned for its palazzos and frescoes.

Far more prominent on the tourists' itinerary was Florence. 'With its lovely setting straddling the Arno, it was one of the most popular of European cities, especially with British visitors,' Lynne Withey writes. Some of the visitors stayed, and there was a sizeable British community by the early 19th century. Apart from the city's obvious charms, this was partly the result of acquired – or learned – taste. 'Eighteenth-century tourists had been educated to admire Renaissance painting as the pinnacle of artistic achievement,' observes Withey. And while tourists were bringing Italian paintings back to Britain at that time, there were no major collections to rival those of the Uffizi or the Pitti Palace. Jeremy Black points out: 'Whereas French cooking and Italian opera could be sampled in London, it was necessary to visit Italy to appreciate, to any degree, Italian art and architecture.'

Not that the opera was overlooked in Florence. In fact it was considered something of a naughty pleasure, derided by religious conservatives back in England as a morally dubious import, enjoyed only by languid aristocrats who liked watching flute-voiced *castrati* and men dressed as women. This ambience of faintly illicit entertainment explains the gossipy social dimension of the Florentine opera, where groups could be observed playing cards in their boxes.

But it was in Rome that tourists found the emotional core of their journey, 'both reality and symbol of what was desirable about foreign travel', as Black puts it. Here the tourists bagged their biggest game, in the form of the antiquities they sketched, made diary entries about and ticked off in their new guidebooks. Seeing the sights that today come with long queues and ticket booths was more of an adventure back then: they were often half-buried in the rubble of the centuries, notes Hibbert. 'The Palatine Hill was overrun with gardens and weeds; twice a week there was a market in the Forum... and the Coliseum was let out to citizens who kept sheds for their animals there.'

The luckier tourists arranged to be presented to the Pope. Pius VII received them in the Vatican gardens, where he was 'unaffected and entertaining', even though it had been made clear that visitors must kneel to kiss his foot. Those who wished to avoid this humiliation might choose instead to visit the Catacombs, an eerie labyrinth of bones, which featured sculptures and frescoes alongside its more macabre attractions. The English, particularly, loved the Villa Borghese, a palatial home that already looked like the art gallery it would later become.

In fact, writes Hibbert, the Romans did all they could to make the English feel at home. 'There were English coffee houses where English journals could be read, English inns where English cooking could be enjoyed, taverns run by Englishmen where English students met. The expensive Albergo Londra was always full of English guests; while the elegant apartments at Casa Guarneri, near the Spanish Steps, were occupied by a succession of English tourists.'

Although Italy was the sentimental locus of The Grand Tour, tourism did not begin and end there. Along with the educational aspects of travel, a parallel industry was growing up to cater to those who came to the Continent for their health. Decorous English spa towns like Bath and Tunbridge Wells were popular destinations for the rich and gouty in the 18th century; as well as providing health-giving mineral waters, they were places to flirt, gamble and dance.

Those who wished to ail in style also travelled to the appropriately-named Spa, in Belgium, familiar to film buffs as the place where the eponymous hero of Stanley Kubrick's *Barry Lyndon* falls for a beautiful countess. Grandiose and glamorous, Spa also had a noted casino; in fact, the link between gambling and taking the cure was so strong that Monte Carlo was initially conceived as a health resort.

Monaco was the furthest-flung destination on the strip of coastline that the English had taken to calling the French Riviera, more properly known as the Côte d'Azur. Wintering in warmer climes was thought to combat tuberculosis, and Tobias Smollett had written approvingly of Nice in his 1766 work *Travels in France and Italy*. This useful bit of publicity translated into flocks of English visitors: not for nothing is the town's seafront walkway called *La Promenade des Anglais*.

Towards modern tourism

You might get the impression from the above that only Europeans were interested in broadening their horizons. But by the early 19th century the United States also had a nascent travel industry, and some of its sights were far more dramatic than anything the Continent had to offer.

Niagara Falls had first been 'discovered' by a European expedition – led by the French explorer Robert de LaSalle – in 1678. As Lynne Withey reports, it 'lured travellers from a remarkably early period, when getting there meant a long journey by horseback or private carriage', and the only accommodation was a local fort.

The effort was rewarded with a stupendous vision: 'Two massive cascades nearly 180 feet high… the third largest in the world in terms of power and volume of water.'

But, Withey adds, 'experiencing Niagara Falls transcended the merely visual. Visitors heard the Falls long before seeing them… For a generation accustomed to finding God in nature, Niagara offered physical evidence of God's power'.

Many travellers required little more in the way of encouragement. By the early 19th century, Niagara was hemmed in with souvenir shops and hotels. 'As early as the 1830s, many visitors complained that Niagara was becoming overcrowded and too commercial,' Withey reports.

Niagara was the highlight of a route that emerged as the North American version of The Grand Tour, 'a loop from New York City up the Hudson to Albany, with stops in the Catskill Mountains and at Saratoga Springs and Ballston Spa, across upstate New York to Niagara Falls, and then back to the Hudson, perhaps by a slightly different route'.

As usual, writers sold the dream of exotic travel: Washington Irving and James Fenimore Cooper 'were best known for the distinctly American settings of their enormously popular novels and stories', including the Catskills and the Mohawk Valley.

It took a while for infrastructure to catch up with desire. Before the 1820s, paved roads were rare – carriages either rattled over corrugated ruts or sank axle-deep in gloop – and inns were equally few and far between. But while road construction lagged, Americans were early entrants to the age of steam, launching the first steam-powered ship – the *Clermont* – in 1807. By 1812 it was possible to steam from Pittsburgh to New Orleans. These riverboats evolved into luxurious vessels, as white and ornate as floating wedding cakes.

Railroads emerged later, but with impressive speed. The first stretch of the Baltimore and Ohio railroad was completed in 1830; just 10 years later 'the United States had nearly twice as much track in operation as all the nations of Europe combined'. Work on the first transcontinental railroad, which would slash the cross-country journey time from six months to six weeks, began in 1860. It was finished in only nine years, thanks to the toil of thousands of Chinese and Irish labourers working in extremely harsh conditions. Nitro-glycerine was used to blast a path through the Sierra Nevada; men died in explosions, rock slides and avalanches. An outbreak of small-pox claimed more lives. As accurate records were not kept, estimates of the number of fatalities range from less than 200 to more than a thousand.

Steam, as we know, shrank the world. The Liverpool and Manchester Railway – the first timetabled passenger train service in Britain – opened in 1830. The SS *Great Western* (SS as in 'steamship'), designed by Isambard Kingdom Brunel, made its first transatlantic crossing in 1838 (see Chapter 6, The battle for the high seas).

With the emergence of steam travel, the scene was set for the rise of the mass tourism industry. One man did more than any other to make foreign destinations accessible to everyday citizens.

His name was Thomas Cook.

Tour highlights

- In the 18th century, it became fashionable for young men to take a 'Grand Tour' to complete their education. A travel and accommodation infrastructure slowly grew up to serve them.

- An 18th-century consumer revolution saw an increase in the consumption of luxury goods and published materials. Writers sold the dream of exotic travel.

- People travelled for their health to spa towns, which were also associated with gambling, gossip and dancing.

- Steam shrank the world and made it easier for travellers to traverse the vast distances of the United States.

The enterprising 02
Mr Cook

'*Advertising is to trade what steam is to machinery.*'

Saturday morning in a rain-swept London suburb, at some point during the late 1970s. A small boy drags his mother into a travel agent, the words 'Thomas Cook' visible in cheerful red lettering across its façade. Although his family has no intention of taking an exotic holiday – at this point, the furthest afield he has travelled is Wales – he proceeds to pillage the rack of glossy travel brochures. Later on, as raindrops patter on the window of his bedroom, he pores through the images of Cairo and the Caribbean, daydreaming about the adventures he might have there.

The boy, of course, was myself. Later, when I was old enough to travel abroad on my own, the same name appeared on the travellers' cheques I took with me: Thomas Cook. Until recently, I had never given much thought to the man behind the brand.

When I began my research, many aspects of his character surprised me. Except one: in common with all personalities who become brand names, Thomas Cook was a marketing genius.

The great arranger

On Monday 5 July 1841, a boisterous crowd gathered on the platform of Campbell Street Station, Leicester. To judge by their bright eyes and excitability, one might have assumed they were intoxicated. Nothing could have been further from the truth, at least in the conventional sense of the term; none of them had touched a drop. Indeed, along with their guide, they actively campaigned against the evils of alcohol.

Raised in a deeply religious household, Thomas Cook had learned to read from the Bible and had been a Baptist preacher before taking up a slightly more lucrative trade as a carpenter. He had also been taught the rudiments of printing by his mentor and father figure (his own father had died when he was three), the Reverend H Joseph Foulkes Winks. From Winks, Thomas learned that print, in the form of tracts and journals, was a more efficient way of spreading 'the word' than declaiming from a pulpit. In the 19th century, his printing skills gave him the kind of advantages that somebody who can write code has today. As Jill Hamilton notes in her (2005) biography *Thomas Cook: The holiday maker*, he once stated: 'Advertising is to trade what steam is to machinery.'

With Cook, the holiday brochure as dream vector was born.

Both intolerant of sloth and keen to aid his fellow man, Cook had been naturally attracted to the Temperance movement, sparked in England by Joseph Livesey, who had founded the Preston Temperance Society in March 1832. Its members were required to sign a pledge: 'We agree to abstain from all liquors of an intoxicating quality, whether Ale, Porter, Wine, or Ardent Spirits, except as Medicines.'

Alcohol was undoubtedly a problem – or a solution, depending on your point of view. At the height of the Industrial Revolution, workers put in long hours for pitiful wages. They were poor, browbeaten and exhausted. When payday came, booze offered a short cut to happiness. As Hamilton puts it: 'For a large number of people, the only refuge from depression and misery was the bottle. A copper or two... could buy oblivion.'

Meanwhile, families went hungry and wives were struck. Thomas Cook signed the Pledge on New Year's Day 1833. From that moment on, much of his time was devoted to the Temperance movement. More tracts were printed – but he also sought ways of distracting the masses from the temptations of alcohol. One in particular occurred to him. Steam was indeed driving all kinds of machinery – including trains, a new and alluring form of transport.

Leveraging the competition for passengers among the privately-owned railway companies, Cook wrote to the secretary of the Midland Counties Railway Company and effectively asked if he could borrow a train. Ostensibly, the purpose of the return trip from Leicester to Loughborough was to attend a quarterly Temperance meeting. In fact, Cook had organized a pleasure trip.

More than 500 people responded to his notices, posters and handbills. Almost as many showed up to observe the train's departure and watch its progress from bridges and embankments. A brass band tooted the train off – another parped it into its destination. Cook wrote: 'All went off in the best style... and thus was struck the keynote of my excursions, and the social idea grew on me.'

Thomas had divined that travel was as effective as alcohol at blotting out the anxieties of daily life. As more Temperance trips were organized, he refined his formula: an educational or exciting journey, promoted via extensive advertising, for a low fare delivered by the negotiation of a group booking. He soon abandoned carpentry for a dual career as printer and 'excursion agent'.

According to Hamilton, Cook revelled in the details of these voyages, fretting over what he called the 'arrangements'. 'For him "arrangements" was a cherished word – arrangements for banners, arrangements for bands, arrangements for posters and arrangements for dignitaries.'

He transported travellers in their hundreds to Liverpool, North Wales and distant Scotland. The last nearly cost him his reputation, as passengers who had booked a steamship excursion were under the impression that their ticket included a cabin. Unfortunately, overbooking meant that many were forced to spent the night on the chilly and rain-swept deck. They were perhaps the first package tourists to discover that the reality of a trip does not always live up to the description in the brochure.

There were more tours to come, but in a sense they were all rehearsals for Cook's ultimate destination – the Holy Land.

En route for the Orient

For the time being his eastward progress was delayed by another opportunity. In 1850, in London, work began on the structures that would house the Great Exhibition, a spectacular showcase of 'Britain's domination in arts, sciences, industry, commerce, armaments and medicine'. The highlight of this manifestation of Victorian power was a huge pavilion of iron and glass, a 'crystal palace' 108 feet high and more than a third of a mile long.

Cook was one of the operators charged with transporting visitors to the exhibition, receiving a cut of ticket sales as well as the accommodation he had pre-booked in London. When the Great Exhibition opened in May 1851, the ringing of a metaphorical cash register could almost be heard above the brass band.

It was for the exhibition that Cook launched his magazine, *Cook's Exhibition Herald and Excursion Advertiser*, which later became simply *The Excursionist*. Still rolling off the presses at the start of the Second World War under the name *The Travellers' Gazette*, 'it provided page after page of itineraries, fares, lists of hotels, testimonial letters, articles about tours, advertisements and editorial comment'.

With wealth came a faint lightening of Cook's austere persona. As Hamilton puts it: 'Materialism was, just a little, tingeing his idealism.' In 1852 this manifested itself as a large and comfortable home next to the new Temperance Hall in Granby Street, Leicester.

Two years later, he finally sold off his printing business to become a full-time tour operator. He now began to plan trips to 'The Continent', notably to the Universal Exhibition in Paris. However, as the company's own website notes (www.thomascook.com/thomas-cook-history/), most of the cross-Channel services refused to work with him 'and the only route he was able to use was the one between Harwich and Antwerp. This opened up the way for a grand circular tour to include Brussels, Cologne, the Rhine, Heidelberg, Baden-Baden, Strasbourg and Paris, returning to London via Le Havre or Dieppe. By this route, during the summer of 1855, Thomas escorted his first tourists to Europe'.

Next he conquered Switzerland, taking a party of 60 people to Geneva on an initial fact-finding tour. Subsequent visits were so successful that he soon crossed the Alps, organizing his first Italian tours in the summer of 1864.

Perhaps inevitably, a provincial existence in Leicester became out of step with his growing success, and by the end of the decade he was installed in what Hamilton describes as 'a charming Georgian townhouse' at 59 Great Russell Street in Bloomsbury, London, from which he would henceforth direct his 'arrangements'.

He toyed with the idea of tours to the United States, and indeed his son John Mason (who had previously kept his distance from his father's business, preferring to start his own career as a printer) took 'an exploratory group from New York to Washington, Niagara, Chicago, the Mammoth Caves of Kentucky and the deserted battlefields of Virginia'. But the sheer distances involved seem to have dampened the company's ambitions.

In the meantime, Cook kept an eye on the progress of the Suez Canal, due to open in 1869. As if he could no longer resist the draw of the region that had fascinated him since childhood, he organized a tour to the Nile and Palestine a full year before the event.

Several strands of Thomas Cook's life came together during that first tour, on which he escorted a group of 60 or so travellers. His impetus, as ever, was religious: 'Thomas believed that faith would be intensified and deepened by people visiting the source of their creed,' Hamilton writes.

She also points out that Egypt and the Holy Land were largely alcohol-free. 'Thomas, who had spent nearly 30 years fighting to suppress the use of alcoholic beverages, saw his convictions made real in Muslim countries.'

But even Cook proved susceptible to the glamour of foreign travel. He fell hard for Egypt: 'the magnificent panoramas with ruins, the tranquillity, the Nile busy with feluccas, the palm trees, the minarets and the mosques'. So excited was he that he suddenly took it upon himself to dive into the Nile. He was snatched by an undertow and might have drowned had a boatman not reached out to him with an oar.

His first glimpse of Jerusalem was one of the peak moments of his life. 'Arriving at biblical sites he had visualized since childhood was an intense experience... Thomas longed for thousands to share his own wonder of standing on the Mount of Olives – from where the earthly form of Jesus was last seen by man – and feel the windy gusts while viewing Jerusalem.'

By this time it had become obvious that Cook's son would eventually take over the family firm – indeed, the company was now officially named Thomas Cook & Son. But John Mason disliked the way his father mixed faith and commerce, fearing that some travellers might be put off by the evangelical aspects of the enterprise. Not only that, but Cook put his money where his mouth was: he purchased a building for the mission school in Jaffa and helped fund similar establishments in Bethlehem and Jerusalem. John Mason would have preferred to re-invest the money in the business. The pair had an abrasive relationship throughout their lives.

Meanwhile, Egypt was becoming the key to the company's future, the motor that would transform it into an unassailable global brand. When Thomas Cook attended the official opening of the Suez Canal on 16 November 1869, his presence was noted by the Khedive (effectively the Viceroy of Egypt under the Ottoman Empire). The following year, Thomas Cook & Son was named the sole agent for passenger traffic on the Nile. 'After visiting the Pyramids and the Sphinx, tourists would float down the Nile... between Cairo and Aswan listening to one of the specially recruited "experts" telling the history of the monuments.'

After profiting from the 1870–71 Franco-Prussian war by selling 'circuitous tickets which allowed travellers to reach the South of France and the Italian Mediterranean resorts by bypassing the belligerent countries', the Cooks turned their gaze once again to the United States. This time, however, the traffic flowed in the opposite direction: John Mason brought a group of US freemasons to Paris shortly after the end of the conflict. It was one of his many contributions to the business, and set the scene for a slow and turbulent succession.

New departures

Thomas Cook's inaugural Round the World Tour in 1872 was his last great commercial adventure. The 29,000-mile, eight-month journey was, as Hamilton notes, an 'enlarged version of the grand tour', including the United States, Japan, China, India and Egypt. But when he returned home via the Suez Canal, Cook glimpsed something that must have both lifted and distressed him: the future of his company.

'In Egypt,' Hamilton writes, 'Thomas saw that John Mason had established the reputation of Thomas Cook & Son as one of the top tourist operators in the world.'

Given the unfortunate rivalry between father and son, Thomas may not have entirely appreciated his son's latest innovations. Thomas Cook & Son branch offices had sprung up across the globe; in 1873 John Mason oversaw the opening of a massive new headquarters at Ludgate Circus. This incorporated a waiting room for clients, its own post and telegraph offices, a reading room, and daily weather bulletins from Europe and the Middle East (one imagines something both impressively modern and delightfully quaint, as if conceived by Wes Anderson). It was less a building than a statement, sending out a message of impregnability, reliability and global reach.

The company's website and Hamilton disagree about the author of two of the most important developments in travel history: 'Circular Notes' and 'Hotel Coupons'. Circular Notes were vouchers that tourists could exchange for cash when they arrived at a destination – in other words, an early form of travellers' cheques. Similarly, travellers could pay for meals and hotel rooms in advance, allowing them to travel with easily replaceable coupons rather than tempting wads of cash. The site clearly states that these were initiated by Thomas – Hamilton writes that they were 'perfected by John Mason'. The truth, as always, no doubt lies somewhere between the two; in later years, Thomas Cook's portrait appeared on the cheques.

John Mason certainly understood the importance of guide books to the company's image, hence the introduction of *Cook's Continental Time Tables and Tourist's Handbook*. It was positioned as the definitive guide to 'railway, diligence and steamship routes across Europe'.

John Mason Cook officially took charge of the company at the start of 1879, following his father's 70th birthday. Thomas Cook – who had almost single-handedly built the package tourism industry over the past 40 years – took himself off to an entirely grudging retirement at his new home in Leicester, a red-brick villa called Thorncroft.

Two tragedies subsequently occurred. First of all, the death in 1880 of his 34-year-old daughter Annie (a barely documented presence in his life, although she apparently helped him organize tours to France and Italy) in a freak accident: she drowned in the bath after being overcome by fumes from a faulty gas water heater. Three and a half years later, having succumbed to depression, Cook's wife Marianne passed away. Although Cook had spent much of his life far from her side, he now found it difficult to live alone. 'The long dark candle-less nights of his youth returned; reluctantly he caught up with all the sleep missed in those years of backbreaking labour.'

These events had little impact on the tireless energy of John Mason and the expansion of Thomas Cook & Son. In Egypt, the company was now one of the pillars of the economy, branching out all over the country from its offices next to Shepheard's Hotel in Cairo. In Europe, John Mason actually bought the funicular railway that trundled visitors up to Mount Vesuvius. In a speech quoted by Hamilton, he takes full credit for the company's success: 'In 1865 the whole personnel of the business consisted of Thomas Cook, myself, two assistants and one messenger... In 1880 we had a staff of 1,714 permanent salaried members... we have 45 distinct banking accounts... 84 offices... and in addition 85 agencies.'

Thomas himself rallied a little, although his sight was now fading. Deciding he wanted to see the Holy Land one final time – to Cook, tourism had always been a sort of pilgrimage – he persuaded four companions (including his neighbour Mr Glasgow and a 'staunch Temperance supporter, Miss Lines') to travel with him by train to Venice, by boat to Alexandria and Jaffa and finally to Jericho, Jordan, Palestine and Jerusalem. In a somewhat eccentric twist, he returned home with a pretty young Syrian schoolteacher, Labeebeh, who had 'expressed a strong desire to see England'.

Raise an eyebrow if you will, but it seems his motives were characteristically Christian, combined perhaps with an unconscious desire to replace his daughter. Labeebeh stayed for six months, sharing insights into Syrian culture as a guest of honour at Temperance halls. She was present at Thorncroft for Cook's 80th birthday – shortly afterwards she sailed for Jaffa aboard the SS *Britannia*.

Thomas Cook died of old age on 18 July 1892, less than a week after struggling to the polls in Leicester to vote for the local Liberal candidate. The *Leicester Chronicle* provided an epitaph of sorts: 'The total blindness which overcame him did not affect his spirits or prevent him from making an excursion to the Holy Land.'

At the end, he was remembered as the ultimate excursionist.

Cook after Thomas

Travel appears to have proved as fatal to John Mason Cook as inertia had to his father. Making arrangements for a trip to Palestine by the German Emperor Wilhelm II in 1898 – and presumably having embraced the ideas of Temperance to a certain extent – he ignored the widespread theory that it was better to drink wine while abroad, and instead sampled the local water. He contracted dysentery and was dead within a year.

However, the Cook line had not yet ended: John Mason's sons Frank Henry, Ernest Edward and Thomas Albert now took over the business, seeing it through an era that saw 'the introduction of winter sports holidays, tours by motor car and commercial air travel'. Thomas Albert died in 1914, but his brothers remained at the helm until 1928, when they sold the company to Belgium's *Compagnie Internationale des Wagons-Lits*, operators of luxury trains, including the Orient Express (see Chapter 5, The Return of the Orient Express).

The start of the Second World War marked the beginning of a long and turbulent period for the company. When the *Wagons-Lits* headquarters in Paris were seized by occupying forces, Thomas Cook's assets in Great Britain were requisitioned by the British government. The firm was initially sold to the company's four main railway companies – but after the war, it became part of the nationalized and state-owned British Railways. However, as the company's website admits, 'its pre-eminence was now being challenged by new travel firms that were able to undercut Cook's prices and offer cheap package deals'. In 1972 it was sold to a consortium of Midland Bank, Trust House Forte and the Automobile Association.

The 1970s saw the introduction of its Money Back Guarantee Scheme and a soon-to-be familiar logo – the words Thomas Cook in flame red. These appeared on an expanding network of high-street shops, boosted in the late 1980s with the acquisition of three retail chains: Frames, Blue Sky and Four Corners.

There followed a long series of acquisitions, mergers and consolidations far too dull to go into here. I refer you to the website for the labyrinthine details. But in summary, Thomas Cook was acquired in 2001 by C&N Touristic AG, one of Germany's largest travel groups, which merged with MyTravel Group in 2007 to form Thomas Cook Group plc. In 2011 Thomas Cook merged its UK travel and foreign exchange businesses with those of the Co-operative Group and the Midlands Co-operative Society, creating 'the UK's largest retail travel network of over 1,200 shops'.

Then, in 2013, an axe fell.

'Don't just book it...'

It is one of the most memorable British advertising taglines of all time. 'Don't just book it, Thomas Cook it.' In fact, the slogan answers two of the greatest copywriting challenges: it hooks itself effortlessly into the brain, and it contains the name of the brand. (See also 'Have a break, have a Kit-Kat'.)

The line was introduced by the agency Wells Rich Greene in 1984 and used until 1993. It was then resurrected in 2009, when Thomas Cook conducted a poll of 2,000 people 'and found that when prompted with the first half of the line, 60 per cent could finish it… [T]he joy of the slogan is its versatility. It says nothing specific but suggests that buying a holiday or flight from Thomas Cook is superior to "just" booking it with someone else'. ('Slogan Doctor', *Management Today*, 3 March 2009.)

But in 2013, the new management decided that the slogan had run its course. The replacement? 'Let's Go!' I'll let the reader decide whether it does the job as effectively. The line was also accompanied by a new logo, described as a 'sunny heart'.

'Although it's one of those famous advertising lines, it doesn't represent the company we want to be,' said Thomas Cook's then marketing and e-commerce director Mike Hoban of the old slogan. 'Firstly, it's an English phrase which only works with the Thomas Cook brand, but we are an international group of companies and we needed to come up with something that unites the group.'

He added that 'Let's Go' fulfilled those and a number of other require-ments. 'Firstly, it encapsulates our promise to the consumer, ie let's go and have a great holiday. For our people it's a call to action and reminds them that we are in a service business, and it's also a phrase which speaks to our owners and our shareholders in the City.' And the sunny heart? It evoked warmth and emotion and worked for any type of holiday. 'Then, the type in metallic grey reflects a hi-tech, digital Thomas Cook.' ('Say farewell to "Don't just book it…"', www.travelmole.com, 1 October 2013.)

Like every company with pre-internet roots, Thomas Cook has been obliged to adapt to the digital era. In the travel sector, this means confronting a world where travellers are their own agents, booking flights online, researching hotels via TripAdvisor or even eschewing hotels altogether in favour of Airbnb and its growing number of competitors. How has Thomas Cook responded?

Mathias Brandes, group head of external communications, emphasizes that service is the key that differentiates Thomas Cook from online travel agents. 'It's all about truly knowing our product and being able to make recommendations, because the offer online is overwhelming. If you picture a family of four who go on one major holiday a year, for two weeks in the summer, that is a big economic and emotional investment. You need good advice. Which is why personal contact within our stores remains important.'

But of course Thomas Cook is well aware of the importance of what could be called 'impersonal contact' – commentary about the brand and its offering via social media. 'We monitor social media and have a dedicated customer care team responding to comments on Twitter,' confirms Brandes.

The company has also harnessed technology in a more proactive fashion. At the end of 2014 customers were invited to share their photos of Thomas Cook vacations on social media platforms. These images would then be integrated into a wider marketing campaign. It was a conscious step away from conventional travel advertising, which sells dream destinations, to a more authentic approach.

Another technological advance pointed the way to the future of travel marketing. The company began rolling out virtual reality headsets in selected stores in the UK, Germany and Belgium. These allowed customers to 'experience', for example, the swooping exhilaration of a helicopter flight over New York, or to stroll around a hotel. 'It almost literally allows you to try before you buy,' says Brandes.

At least until online travel agents offer apps that connect with users' own headsets, bringing the VR experience into homes, the device gives travel agencies a useful edge.

Moving past a scandal

For all Thomas Cook's efforts to highlight its transparency and trustworthiness, in 2015 it found itself in the midst of an image crisis. The issue dated back to 2006, when the company was embroiled in a tragic accident that bore a ghostly echo of the fate that befell its founder's daughter more than 125 years earlier. Two English children, Christi and Bobby Shepherd, aged seven and six, died of carbon monoxide poisoning while on a Thomas Cook holiday at a hotel on the Greek island of Corfu. Their parents, having passed out, came to in hospital. An investigation found that fumes from a faulty gas water heater in a neighbouring outhouse had leaked into the bungalow where they were staying.

After a trial on the island in 2010, the manager of the hotel and two others were sentenced to seven years, but two Thomas Cook employees were exonerated.

However, an inquest jury in the UK in 2015 returned a verdict of unlawful killing and said that Thomas Cook had 'breached its duty of care'. This would have been bad enough, were it not for the comportment of the Thomas Cook management during the inquest, widely reported by the media. CEO Peter Fankhauser told the inquest he felt deeply sorry for what had happened but said there was no need for the company to apologize 'because there was no wrongdoing by Thomas Cook'.

While an outright apology during the inquest might have been tanta-mount to admitting culpability, it appeared that the company had allowed its legal advisors to dictate its response to the tragedy. As a result, it appeared cold and lacking in remorse.

In addition, it emerged that Thomas Cook had received compensation of £3.5 million from the hotel concerned, as opposed to the £350,000 received by the family. In yet another twist, without consulting the family, Thomas Cook announced that it would pay £1.5 million to UNICEF. The family and the media perceived this as an ungainly stab at absolution.

Finally, while announcing the group's first-half results on 20 May 2015, CEO Fankhauser apologized. 'I am deeply sorry, as a father myself, about the tragic deaths of Bobby and Christi Shepherd in 2006 on a Thomas Cook holiday. It is absolutely clear that there are things we as a company should have done better over the past nine years, in particular how we have conducted our relationship with the family.' ('Thomas Cook apologizes over Corfu gas deaths', www.bbc.com, 20 May 2015.)

Subsequently, Fankhauser met with the parents face-to-face and offered what their lawyer described as a 'sincere and heartfelt apology'. Thomas Cook also said it would meet the costs of the inquest into the children's deaths and make a 'financial gesture of goodwill' to the family. The family asked Thomas Cook to demolish the bungalow where the tragedy occurred and build a children's playground. At a press conference, Christi and Bobby's mother, Sharon Wood, said it was time to 'accept we cannot change the past and that it may be time to look to the future'. ('Thomas Cook makes "sincere and heartfelt apology" over children's deaths', *The Guardian*, 21 May 2015.)

Setting aside the emotional aspect of the tragedy, it was, as they say, a 'teachable moment'. What should Thomas Cook have done? Experts cited by *PR Week* clearly felt that the crisis could have been alleviated, if not avoided ('Our expert panel assesses the company's handling of the tragedy', www.prweek.com, 20 May 2015).

Julian Pike, head of reputation management at law firm Farrar & Co, said:

> From the outset, Thomas Cook should have made the family its priority, irrespective of the legal advice or insurers' requirements... A company of Thomas Cook's size and importance could be expected to have had well-rehearsed crisis management plans, with a holiday fatality being an obvious risk. It should have been programmed into the company how it should look to prevent such a tragedy – eg regular checks on accommodation – and how to respond to such an eventuality with humility.

Stuart Leach, managing director of crisis and litigation at PR consultancy Bell Pottinger, observed:

> When the extent of liability is yet to be determined the lawyers will advise you to say nothing to prejudice the case. It is the media advisor's job to not be ruled by this but to engage with the media and use language in a way that protects reputation and avoids prejudicing any proceedings. To do this it is vital for the media advisors and lawyers to work together, with both working to achieve the best outcome.

Whatever the thousands of people who signed up to boycott the company on a dedicated Facebook page might have wished, it is hard to eradicate a 170-year-old brand. News cycles are short, the gaze of the media (and therefore the public) moves on.

The *Financial Times* reported that Thomas Cook's share price had wobbled in the wake of the inquest. The paper also quoted an anonymous 'investment banker' who said the company's 'legacy of shops' was 'dragging them down'. The article added: 'The company's weakness is that it remains a high-street business in an age when more and more people are making their travel bookings online.' ('Turmoil over apology adds to Thomas Cook's woes', *Financial Times*, 20 May 2015.)

Yet the company had recovered from its precarious financial position the previous year, with improved turnover and reduced losses. Bookings were also ahead. In addition, Thomas Cook had been buoyed by its strategic partnership with Chinese travel concern Fosun, the owner of Club Med, which took a 4.8 per cent stake in the company for £92 million in 2015. The pair were due to invest in new hotels.

Thomas Cook will remain a relevant name in the travel business. And whatever happens in the future, nothing can dislodge its founder from his place in the history books as the pioneer of package tourism.

Travel, meanwhile, means different things to different people. And some travellers require an altogether different class of experience. So let's pack our Louis Vuitton bags and check into a grand hotel.

Tour highlights

- Thomas Cook, an ardent supporter of the Temperance movement, saw 'pleasure trips' as a way of distracting workers from the temptations of alcohol.

- A skilled printer, like the evangelists of the Grand Tour he used the written word to sell the allure of travel. He could be said to have invented the travel brochure.

- Cook's company also pioneered travellers' cheques and pre-paid coupons that could be exchanged for meals and hotel rooms.

- Today's Thomas Cook uses a blend of personal contact and social media to inform and influence travellers overloaded with information.

Legendary havens: the rise of the grand hotel

03

'Your problem is our problem.'

A few years ago I found myself stranded at the Alvear Palace Hotel in Buenos Aires. There can hardly be a better place to be a castaway. It was built in the 1920s by a wealthy businessman who wanted to evoke the flamboyance of his favourite Parisian hotels. Black-clad porters in top hats bow you through the revolving doors into a Belle Époque fantasia. The marble-floored lobby swirls with Persian carpets beneath delicate Louis XV and Louis XVI chairs, upholstered in ruby velvet. Chandeliers twinkle above; the walls gleam with gold leaf. In the lobby bar, the polished wood, smartly ranged bottles and cocktail shakers promise evenings of urbane gossip.

I was told that a famous writer of tango songs lived full-time in the hotel: I imagined him subsisting on red wine and melancholy, slipping unremarked into the restaurant toward the end of the evening. It was, in short, an ideal spot for daydreaming.

It was April 2010. I had been invited by Leading Hotels of the World (LHW), of which the Alvear Palace is a member, to give a talk at a conference about luxury branding. I can't remember if I charged a fee. I should not have done: LHW flew me business class to Argentina and booked me into a suite at the hotel.

The morning after I had given my speech and was about to pack my bags, I got the news: an Icelandic volcano with an unpronounceable name (*Eyjafjallajökull*) had erupted, filling the atmosphere with debris and disrupting flights around the world. Including mine, which I learned via e-mail was grounded 'indefinitely'.

I sought out the hotel's manager and told him that there was no need for me to stay in the suite – I would find a cheaper hotel and pay my own way from now on. He smiled. 'Sir, your problem is our problem. You will stay with us as our guest for as long as is necessary.'

I stayed an extra two nights. It felt like forever – in a good way.

A couple of other improbable things happened during my time at the Alvear Palace.

Spotting me at breakfast one morning, the manager came over to say hello. I remarked that I usually liked to swim first thing, but the pool did not open until 11am. He said: 'What time would you like us to open it for you?' Shamelessly, I took him up on his offer, and at 9am the next day I had the pool to myself.

That evening, in the lobby bar, the organizers of the conference arrived to whisk me into town for dinner. I had not yet finished my drink, and jokingly told the barman I would be back for it later. When I returned to my room, shortly before midnight, there was my dry martini, sitting on the desk – topped up, just cold enough, and surrounded by dishes of nuts and olives.

Why am I telling you all this? Because now, if anybody ever asks me to define a grand hotel, I often cite the Alvear Palace.

A brief history of grand hotels

'To speak of grand hotels,' writes Jean d'Ormesson, the great French journalist and voyager, 'is to speak... of legendary havens for exotic travellers... or, if you will, the romance between wealth and poetry, of dwellings where sheer splendour carries the day in a frenzied modern world.' (From the introduction to David Watkin's *Grand Hotel: The golden age of palace hotels, an architectural and social history*, 1984.)

But where do they come from, these sublime establishments? How did we get from hostelries and taverns to such vast marble edifices? Most historians agree that the boom period of the grand hotel was concurrent with the birth of the industrial age, when steam not only created the new rich, but got them moving.

'These are images from another era,' d'Ormesson continues, 'one that stretched from the Industrial Revolution to World War II. Before that time, most grand hotels were in fact mere inns, or else they still functioned as private homes in the hands of aristocratic families soon forced, by the tide of history, to give them up.'

Paradoxically, there was something democratic about the early grand hotels. In another contribution to the book mentioned above, the architectural historian David Watkin writes: 'Conventional histories of western architecture concentrate up to the mid-eighteenth century on two building types: the church and the palace. Thereafter the types increase rapidly, but several of them – the opera house or theatre, the library and the museum – were in fact the attributes of the palace designed to cater for a prosperous middle class.'

In this respect, Watkin considers the Opéra in Paris, designed by Charles Garnier and completed in 1875, a cousin of the grand hotel, its cavernous lobby the setting for 'an elaborate social ritual as spectacular as anything that is likely to take place on stage'.

Indeed Le Grand Hotel (now the InterContinental Paris le Grand Hotel) opened in 1862 on the same square as the Opéra. Inaugurated in great pomp by Empress Eugénie, wife of Napoleon III, it was a machine for stylish living, with 800 rooms across four floors.

But Watkin puts the true birth of the grand hotel somewhat earlier in time, and in a less likely place: '[I]t was democratic America, entirely lacking in royal palaces, that first developed the grand hotel. The earliest major American hotel was the City Hotel in New York, erected in 1794–96, with 73 rooms on five floors.'

The City Hotel was still within 'the tradition of the European inn'. But other architects dreamed bigger. Benjamin Latrobe (1764–1820) envisaged a giant hotel complex that would incorporate a theatre and assembly rooms. While his project 'was clearly foreseen as part of a new social way of life', it was never realized.

A version of his social experiment came to life in the spa town of Baden-Baden, Germany, under the aegis of the architect and town planner Friedrich Weinbrenner (1766–1826). Weinbrenner's hotel, the Badischer Hof, cheekily converted a former Capuchin convent into a lavish resort. It 'boasted a ballroom with a moveable stage, a library and a reading room, sitting rooms, 48 bedrooms, 11 water closets, extensive stables and a bathing establishment'. Watkin suggests that in the 'noble design' of the establishment, with its decorative columns, Weinbrenner sought to imply that 'a secular building can be as magnificent as an ecclesiastical one'.

Perhaps that is why we feel so wicked in grand hotels – their hedonism is subversive.

In Britain, of course, grand hotels followed the railways. The Midland Hotel in Derby (1840), the Victoria Station Hotel in Colchester (1843), the ornate Great Western (1854) at Paddington in London – one imagines them blooming alongside the rapidly extending tracks like exotic flowers. They strove for magnificence, referring to Italian and French Renaissance styles. The Great Western 'contained a Royal waiting room for the use of Queen Victoria when travelling to Windsor'.

For a full immersion into the world of the great railway hotel, by all means visit the former Midland Grand (today the St Pancras Renaissance London

Hotel) at St Pancras station. I might refer to it as an eccentric Victorian pile – Watkin describes it as 'a paradigm of the extravagant romanticism of England's Gothic Revival'. The rooms themselves offer the rather bland comfort that might be expected of the Marriott group; but the exterior and public areas are a glorious confection of pink brick and tile, curly iron and frivolous archways. It's as if Hogwarts has been turned into a five-star layover. Even its architect, Sir Gilbert Scott (1811–78) described it as 'possibly *too* good for its purpose'. Once again, it is more cathedral than hotel – a shrine to the new religion of leisure travel. Thomas Cook would have approved.

Grand hotels also performed a civic branding function, attesting to the wealth and influence of a city. 'Often they were wallpapered in nationalism,' observes an article in *The Economist*:

> King Alfonso XIII of Spain built a Ritz in Madrid to keep up with London and Paris. When the rebuilt Waldorf Astoria opened in New York in 1931 in the depths of the Depression, Herbert Hoover called it 'an exhibition of courage and confidence to the whole nation'. As the Cold War began Joseph Stalin planned the vast Hotel Ukraina in Moscow as a symbol of Soviet might.

> 'Be my guest', *The Economist*, 31 December 2013

The opening of a grand hotel might coincide with a great exhibition: such was the case of the Langham in Portland Place, London, which opened in time for the International Exhibition of 1865. The Paris Exhibition of 1878 gave rise to the Hotel Continental in rue de Rivoli.

By now you may have concluded that the mid-19th century saw a frenzy of grand hotel construction – and you would not be far wrong. The period had its peak, according to Watkin, from the 1880s to the 1920s. 'At the climax of this development, around 1900, the chief resorts with gigantic palace hotels... were to be found in Switzerland... the South of France... Normandy... the French spa towns... and the German ones. The fabled Brenner's Park Hotel in Baden-Baden counted among the many places where Edwardians recuperated from their rich and copious dining.'

Londoners had to wait until 1889 for the arrival of a name indelibly associated with the world of the grand hotel: César Ritz. Having managed hotels in Lucerne, Monaco and Nice, Ritz was installed as the manager of the new Savoy, designed for the theatre impresario Richard D'Oyly Carte, who saw a ready market of tourists flocking to his shows. The hotel had all mod cons in the American fashion, with 'fireproof construction... electric light throughout [and] six lifts'. Ritz deserves a chapter of his own, so we'll leave him at the Savoy for now, awaiting the arrival of his wonderful chef, Auguste Escoffier.

The construction of grand hotels naturally faltered during the First World War – although they formed the ideal backdrop for espionage and clandestine transactions – and the style never again attained its 19th-century grandeur. The future of hotels was industrialization: a corporate template to cater for the jet-borne business class.

But fortunately the buildings themselves still exist. And if we're very lucky, we occasionally get to stay in one.

The Leading Hotels of the World

There are many luxury hotel groups – certainly too many to profile in detail here. The cluster at the top end includes Belmond (the former Orient Express group), Dorchester Collection, Faena, Fairmont Raffles, Firmdale, Four Seasons, Mandarin Oriental, Oetker Collection, One&Only, Peninsula, Relais & Chateaux, Ritz Carlton, Rocco Forte, Rosewood Hotels, Shangri-La, Six Senses, Small Luxury Hotels of the World (SLH), St Regis & Luxury Collection and the Taj Group. This list is by no means exhaustive.

Each of them has a subtly different positioning, but their appeal can be summed up by the word 'experience'. For their guests, the hotel is an integral part of the trip, if not the entire point of the journey. The buildings themselves are landmarks. And of course, when somebody in the outside world asks one of their guests where they are staying, it no doubt gives them a brief frisson of satisfaction to respond with a prestigious name.

Which is just as well, because hotel groups tend not to own hotels. Either they manage their establishments for a fee, or franchise out their brand names. While the hotels in each group may vary somewhat in character, they reap the benefits of a collaborative approach, from shared booking sites to promotional campaigns and high awareness among travel agents and tour operators.

The organization that perhaps best captures the essence of the 'grand hotel' in the classic sense of the term is one I mentioned earlier: The Leading Hotels of the World (LHW). In fact, it's not really a group at all – it's an exclusive club.

Richard McGinnis, director, France and Benelux, explains: 'Unlike other groups, this is not a management company or a chain, it's a membership organization.' Members pay an annual fee, which varies according to their income and number of rooms:

It's for hotels that wish to stay independent while benefiting from an infrastructure of 23 offices around the world. Our job is to produce bookings and revenue for the hotel owners. There is no branding in their rooms, apart from our membership directory, which is obligatory. The result is that when you stay at the Alvear Palace, for example, you are one hundred per cent immersed in the Alvear Palace. There is no sense that you could be staying in a similar hotel in another city. At the same time, our aim is to create an irreproachable brand – a label of quality. As such, being part of Leading is a very strong positioning device for an independent hotel.

LHW was founded in 1928 by a group of aristocratic European hotel owners who wished to tap into the growing market of wealthy American travellers. 'At the time, their establishments were the paradigm of the grand hotel,' says McGinnis. 'But at the start of the season they were forced to set up shop in the ports of Le Havre and Southampton in the hope of luring customers directly off the transatlantic liners. Finally they set up a joint booking office in New York, which became the first central reservations service.'

The descendants of those founders still own the group today. Technically the shareholder hotels are due an annual dividend, but they invariably choose to invest it in the business, according to McGinnis.

What launched as The Leading Hotels of Europe became The Leading Hotels of Europe and Egypt in 1930, when a European hotelier asked if the establishments he ran there could become members. Despite this slight change, the strategy remained the same, as the group's website notes: 'The Manhattan office of Leading Hotels sent employees to New York's piers to catch Americans as they headed to the docks to board transatlantic cruises, offering to book luxury hotel rooms in Europe for their arrival.'

While travellers crossed the Atlantic in style, the Leading Hotels agents would telegraph ahead to ensure that this life of cosseted opulence continued seamlessly when they disembarked. The first brochure distributed by Leading Hotels includes a telling description not only of the hotels, but also of their guests: 'A luxury hotel is one which can offer its guests beautiful and luxurious apartments, and irreproachable cuisine, and perfect individual service; such amenities of life, in fact, as they enjoy in their own homes from their own servants.' ('LHW Celebrates 85 Years', www.lhw.com, 18 November 2013.)

If the war years were lean times for Leading Hotels, the 1950s saw not only a revival of transatlantic travel, but an expansion of the international travel market as a whole, with sleek airlines replacing the lumbering steamships. Says the group's website:

Between 1955 and 1972, passenger numbers more than quadrupled... In 1971, it was determined that the company should expand its scope and attract new members from around the globe. The decision to include more non-European hotels was dictated by the ever-growing need to satisfy the increasing demand to travel to other continents. But it was not until 1978 that the company acquired the official name: The Leading Hotels of the World, Ltd.

The website notes that technological innovation has always been one of the group's selling points when it comes to attracting members. In the early days, agents hunched over room availability charts provided by the hotels and organized bookings via telegraph and later telex. By 1974, this had evolved into a computer- and satellite-based reservation system. 'Almost all of Leading Hotels' business came from travel agents until the mid-1970s, when the company obtained a WATS [wide area telephone service] line, otherwise known as a toll-free phone number. It was considered cutting edge to have a toll-free 1-800 line for both travel agents and direct consumers.'

The group's most iconic marketing tool – its directory, found in all Leading hotel rooms – listed 116 hotels in 23 countries in 1975. It also revealed that the style of the grand hotel had survived two world wars and the swinging sixties without changing a jot:

> Seemingly minor things, such as the guest's aversion to different colours or kinds of flowers, may, if known to the hotel, make the difference between a satisfied and an exceptionally satisfied client. On the other hand, in due deference to the dignified atmosphere of these deluxe hotels, it should be borne in mind that certain generally accepted standards of appearance, attire and behaviour are expected.

Ladies' 'pant-suits' were acceptable in Continental hotels, but banned in the bars and restaurants of London hotels. Gentlemen were expected to wear jackets and ties in restaurants and bars 'except during the daytime at some resort hotels'. Those of 'an extreme avant-garde appearance' were unwelcome – and they could not buy their way in. The directory warned: 'Wealth alone is not the criterion for acceptance.'

At the time of the group's 85th anniversary, both its chairman Andrea Kracht and CEO Ted Teng provided useful insights into the attitudes that separate a grand hotel from a mere place to lay one's head.

Kracht is the proprietor of the Baur au Lac hotel in Zurich. He noted: 'I believe that a keen sense of our common history is at the heart of what makes us Leading Hotels of the World... For example, Baur au Lac was founded by my ancestors 170 years ago... This shows that our connection with history doesn't stem from an obsession with the past, on the contrary, it is a core part of who we are and it drives our vision of what we want to become.'

Building on this, Teng added: 'Multi-generational family ownership of a hotel enhances the guest experience. Families invest in their hotels for the long-run, not just short-term profits. Rather than a three-to-five-year exit strategy, they are looking at three-to-five-generation investment.'

Long-serving staff and regular customers come to feel as if they are a part of this family. 'Family owners tend to hire managers who are from the area and have a deep and true understanding of the location. And, of course employees are more likely to stay at the same hotel longer thus providing consistent direction and continuity.'

Now the group embraces more than 400 hotels in 80 countries. And to use its own words, 'each celebrates the culture of its destination, rather than trying to mask it with corporate-mandated sameness'. Indeed, its advertising tagline at the time of writing is 'Remarkably uncommon'. Among its most legendary members are the Ritz and the Bristol in Paris, the Negresco in Nice and the Mamounia in Marrakech.

New members are regularly accepted, says Richard McGinnis:

> It usually begins with an e-mail or a phone call. In our environment, it's all about the personal touch; this is a small world so everybody knows everybody. I'm often the first contact, but I hand the property over to our membership department in New York. They do an in-depth analysis. Apart from the obvious factor of suitability, the kinds of question they're asking are, 'Is this a destination where we can produce revenue for them?' We don't want to disappoint our members.

In addition to its directory and website, LHW promotes the brand through traditional and digital advertising. For instance, it has a longstanding relationship in the United States with *Departures*, the quarterly magazine (published by Time Inc) available exclusively to American Express Platinum card holders. And despite its somewhat old-fashioned values, the brand is fully present on social media. Users of Instagram and Twitter can follow Leading Hotels and post pictures and tweets of their experiences, with the hashtags #LHWtraveler and #uncommontravel.

In fact, the group's hotels – like other grand hotels – have something of an advantage in the cluttered media landscape in that they stand out, whether content is created in-house or guest-generated. Their history, architecture, Michelin-starred chefs and spectacular grounds all inspire storytelling and, let's face it, bragging.

Back in 2011, the group redesigned its directory to reflect the fact that much of the information it contained was now available on its website. So that year's edition devoted 23 pages to family histories of some of the hotels' owners. More recent versions (and I have the bible-sized tome sitting in front of me) incorporate factoids and snippets of history. For instance, I can tell you that the La Casetta restaurant at the Hotel Eden Roc in Ascona, Switzerland, 'played an important role during the secret surrender negotiations during World War II'. And that Michael Jackson wrote song lyrics on the walls and bed sheets of the Presidential suite of the Hotel D'Angleterre in Geneva (one wonders what the housekeeping service thought). Details, perhaps – but they add to the mystique of the location.

This strategy has continued into the digital world. In an interview with the travel industry website Skift, CEO Ted Teng confirmed:

> Marketing is all about storytelling. I think that customers, with social media, are telling the stories today. Our brands can no longer think that they have control over how they tell the story. I see a lot of companies in the social media space with their brand Facebook page and tweets and all that. That's fine. That's a component of it. I think the most important part of social media is what your customers are saying about you, not what you're saying about yourself.

> 'Leading Hotels of the World CEO on Branding the Independents', www.skift.com, 7 January 2015

Reputation matters in the hotel business – and not just for 'ordinary' customers. As *The Economist* points out: 'Trade and diplomacy take place in hotel chains, as much as in boardrooms and the United Nations General Assembly. The negotiations in November 2013 over Iran's nuclear programme were held at the InterContinental Geneva. Hotels are where people plot takeovers and debate global warming.'

For places that might seem outwardly trivial, grand hotels are surprisingly important.

A tale of Four Seasons

Isadore Sharp, the Canadian businessman who founded Four Seasons Hotels, does not come from remotely the same background as many of his luxury-loving guests. Now in his 80s, Sharp is an industry legend – Steve Jobs is said to have been inspired by his focus on irreproachable service when conceptualizing the Apple stores.

'Issy' Sharp started out as a real estate developer and architect. His father came from an even more humble background – forced to leave Poland in 1920 to escape the pogroms, Sharp senior emigrated to Toronto, where he transformed his skill as a plasterer and home renovator into a construction and real estate concern. Young Issy progressed from helping dad out over the summer to working at the company full-time.

He designed and built his first hotel (Motel 27) in Toronto for a family friend. But in the meantime, according to Jean-Pierre Soutric – who worked for 20 years in sales and marketing roles for Four Seasons before moving on to the Oetker Collection – Issy had spotted a niche:

> He started out from scratch with one hotel that he put together with a group of friends in the worst neighbourhood of Toronto – the red-light district. But he had a vision: as he'd travelled across Canada on various construction projects, he had stayed in many hotels – and he found most of them uncomfortable. He told himself that he was going to create the perfect hotel: great beds, effective sound proofing, plumbing that didn't look as if it came from the last century, air conditioning, swimming pool… and above all, nice folks to look after the guests. That seems like a given today, but 55 years ago it was not the case. He was the first to professionalize the notion of good service.

The Four Seasons Motor Home opened in 1961. Buoyed by its success, Sharp built other hotels – but in 1974, when costs at a Vancouver establishment spiralled out of control, nearly bankrupting the company, he began moving out of the real estate, asset-based side of the business, and into management.

Today, Four Seasons operates its hotels:

> … on behalf of real estate owners and developers, who typically call this office in Toronto with nothing but a patch of land and a cheque-book. Four Seasons participates in the design of the property and runs it, with nearly total control over every aspect of the operation, from the number of bell staff to the thread count of the sheets. For its efforts, the company generally earns 3 per cent of the gross and approximately 5 per cent of profits, and owners must also chip in… [with] funds for global sales, marketing and reservations.

'Pillow fights at the Four Seasons', *The New York Times*, 28 June 2009

Because Sharp insists on a high ratio of staff to guests, profit margins are said to be lower than at rival groups. But over the years, as Four Seasons has climbed from its modest beginnings to its current luxury positioning, Sharp has insisted that those 'nice folks' are central to the success of the brand.

'In the past,' says Jean-Pierre Soutric:

> … if you went to a luxury hotel in Paris or Venice, you were treated with deference only if you were obviously famous or wealthy. Everyone else was generally made to feel unwelcome. They were sitting on traditions that were

decades out of date. Our modern approach no doubt comes from our North American heritage. When Four Seasons came to Europe, starting with London in 1970, it brought that energy, while remaining respectful of local cultures.

Like Leading Hotels of the World, the group encourages each hotel to retain its distinct character. 'When you wake up in Tokyo, you want to feel as if you are in Tokyo,' observes Soutric. 'So you don't need to be consistent in terms of room size or décor. But you do need to be consistent in terms of service.' Indeed, the group furnishes its hotel staff with a list of around 120 quality standards. 'You tend not to memorize them all; but you definitely know the ones that are relevant to your job.'

These include simple notions like making eye contact and not filtering phone calls. At the end of the day, though, great service is hard to systemize. 'It all comes down to finding the right people,' Soutric says. 'When you're filling a role at the hotel, let's say it's a chef, or a maître d'hôtel, you could see two people. One could be the perfect technician – faultless. But he's a little moody. He doesn't smile. Not a people person. The other might be minutely less skilled, or less experienced, but he's open and charming. He's the right guy.'

Not only that, but it can't look forced. 'People can tell when it's fake – you have to engage in a genuine way. And that's all about personality. It's ironic that the most crucial thing about the hospitality business is the most intangible.'

Soutric compares a luxury hotel to the famous 'Kelly' handbag from Hermès:

If you see one of those bags sitting on a table, it's just a bag, right? But when you know the history – when you know that it was named after Grace Kelly – it takes on another dimension. And then when you see the woman who is wearing the bag, how stylish and elegant she is, it takes on a further dimension. That for me is the essence of luxury branding. The product is just the starting point. People make brands.

He also points to something he calls 'the moment'. This could be the time you're drinking a sun-downer on the terrace of a hotel with your companion, when the waiter informs you that there is a spare table at the restaurant with a magnificent view of the bay. Installed at the table, you proceed to have one of the greatest evenings of your life, purely because the waiter somehow divined what you needed.

'That's the moment – it's indelible, you never forget it. To give you another example, from a Four Seasons hotel in Istanbul. You go up to the top floor, you step out onto the terrace, and there it is, right there: the Hagia Sophia. It's incredible. That moment, that experience. That's what people come for.'

Which is why, like Leading Hotels of the World, Four Seasons does little in the way of conventional advertising. It is, however, equally at home in the digital and social worlds. In June 2015 it launched a mobile app, a digital concierge that 'enables guests to check in, check out, order room service, request a car from the valet or turndown service from housekeeping, and… ask for personal items like toothbrushes, earplugs, and razors without having to speak to a soul'. ('The Four Seasons Launches A New Do-Everything App', *Condé Nast Traveler*, 9 June 2015.) Needless to say, it strives for faultless functionality and beauty, with glamorous images drawn from the group's hotels.

'As a society, in the digital age, we've become more individualistic,' Soutric observes. 'Which is fine with the luxury hotel business, because we're all about catering to individual needs. We want their experience to feel something like magic.'

Nostalgia versus innovation

One of the grandest hotels I know is by no means the biggest. The Grand Hôtel Nord-Pinus (from the Latin name for pine tree) in the southern French city of Arles has just 26 rooms, yet it has all the right ingredients.

Dating from the 1920s, it sits at the very centre of town, lording it over a café-filled square. It has had legendary patrons – Picasso, Jean Cocteau and any number of toreadors have gathered in its small bar. Its young proprietor has combined antique furniture, oriental touches and Provençal textiles with mid-century modern pieces. And you're always welcomed like royalty by Christina, who runs the front of house.

But what makes the Nord-Pinus so special is that it is more than just a hotel. It is a hub, a focal point for the town. Most importantly, although the place is timeless, it is always changing. When I last visited with my wife, we arrived to find it home to a pop-up restaurant headed by young British chef Harry Cummins, while Gwladys Gublin from the Experimental Cocktail Club in Paris was mixing up a storm in the bar.

If you ask Rouslan Lartisien – co-founder with his brother Ivan of the premium booking service Grand Luxury Hotels – innovation is one of the key characteristics of a 21st-century grand hotel.

'Take for example the Peninsula in Hong Kong,' he says:

They have an internal IT department of 100 people. They've completely reinvented in-room technology, with tablets that control the different elements – air conditioning, lighting, TV and so on – from one device. They worked for months to create something totally intuitive. Because I think we've all been in the position where you can't find the light switch, or you have to call reception to find out how to work the air conditioning.

He adds that the Peninsula was one the first hotel groups to provide free internet – which should have been a given long ago. 'And now they provide an internet-based telephone service, so guests don't get overcharged for international calls. The video-on-demand service is entirely free of charge, by the way. In short, they've understood that technology is crucial to a new generation of guests.'

Grand Luxury Hotels appeals to the younger rich: 'golden boys and girls,' as one envious industry rival puts it. But technology isn't everything. They also follow fashion, and they're susceptible to brands, Lartisien says, 'Whether it's a well-known interior designer like Jacques Garcia or a famous chef like Alain Ducasse.'

The reason many clients book via Lartisien's site (even though they pay the same price for their room as they would have done by booking through the hotel) is that it offers the little extras that make their trip special. A car at the airport, a bottle of champagne in the room, a bouquet of flowers – all these can be organized by the site's 'guest experience managers', often at a fraction of the price charged by the hotel itself. These customers feel entitled, and they enjoy experiences that confer status, but at the same time they have an eye for a good deal.

Like their parents – and even their grandparents – many well-heeled travellers are looking for authenticity and character. The Ritz in Paris opened in December 2015 after a lengthy refurbishment. It may have better Wi-Fi and discreetly augmented in-room technology, but most guests will stay there simply because there is no other place like it on Earth.

One of Rouslan Lartisien's consultants at Grand Luxury Hotels, Emmanuel Isaia – a well-known French luxury connoisseur, globe-trotter and travel blogger – shares this view:

For me the term 'grand hotel' designates a building that has a history – and a history that has been carefully preserved. The Connaught in London is a good example of a hotel that has maintained the allure of the past, while skilfully adapting to modern times. The younger generation is attracted to the minimalist and designer aspect, while the more traditional customers appreciate the antiques and the landscape paintings.

The hotel's own website captures this contrast perfectly:

Every room and suite at the Connaught has been carefully refurbished by legends of the interior design world, Guy Oliver and the late David Collins. Each space reflects a distinctively 21st-century coming together of classic elegance and contemporary style, yet one which remains sensitive to the enduring symmetry and simplicity of the building's original Adam-style interiors. Bespoke modern furniture sits comfortably alongside antique pieces.

The co-branding aspect mentioned earlier is also taken care of: the restaurant by top chef Hélène Darroze has two Michelin stars; the spa is run by Aman Resorts, which has its roots in Asia and is known for streamlined elegance and an ethical approach – for instance, in the use of local building materials.

But Isaia's favourite grand hotel remains the Cipriani in Venice, to which he returns with his partner for one weekend every autumn. 'The first time we arrived, we noticed that the clientèle had little in common with guests you might see at ordinary hotels. That's to say, it wasn't a clientèle of one-time visitors, but a clientèle of habitués.'

The Cipriani is the kind of place, he says, where one dresses for dinner. Where you might see an elderly gentleman rise to kiss his wife's hand when she comes down to breakfast; where fabulous jewels are 'actually worn, rather than being shown in a display case'.

But as much as the guests define a grand hotel, so do the staff. 'I'm talking about people who have worked there for thirty years,' says Isaia. 'While there will always be newcomers, the familiar faces form part of the mythology of the hotel. Take the Cipriani's head barman, Walter Bolzonella – he was taught to make a Bellini [the iconic Venice cocktail, a mixture of prosecco, syrup and peach] by Giuseppe Cipriani, the founder of Harry's Bar and the hotel, when Walter was 18 years old.'

Bolzonella has been at the Cipriani since 1978. 'He's a star,' says Isaia. 'And yet, every time we arrive, he recognizes us, he chats with us, he remembers what we like to drink.'

A grand hotel, to summarize, has the right mixture of history and personality. To put it another way, it has 'a sense of place'.

One thing its guests can be sure of is a warm welcome. Rouslan Lartisien believes that 'personalization is fundamental' in the luxury hotel sector, even though he finds some groups have let it take second place to technology and branding:

By personalization I mean the very first time you stay there, if you pass a member of the staff in the corridor, they address you by name. I find that much more astonishing than being able to open the curtains via iPad. If I arrive in my room and I find something I particularly appreciate – a type of wine, or the flowers I love – without having asked for it, that is going to leave an indelible memory. It's what makes the exception.

High-end hotel groups have sophisticated customer relationship management (CRM) operations that enable them to note requests like hyper-allergenic pillows, meal preferences or the temperature at which guests set the air conditioning. These are flagged when they next make a reservation. But finally, it's the human touch that counts.

'Everyone has CRM,' says Matthieu Goffard, press attaché at the Ritz in Paris. 'It's a technique, whereas a hotel should be an experience. We are not a chain, so nothing is standardized. Every member of staff can make a difference. We listen to our guests – and we know they love being recognized by our personnel.'

In that respect, the grand hotel has barely changed at all. Which brings us back to Christina at the Nord-Pinus, whom we see once a year but think of as a friend. As we check in, she tells us what's new at the hotel and around town. She makes us feel mollycoddled and precious. There are many other hotels in Arles, but we will never go to them. This is our place, and it's personal.

Tour highlights

- Grand hotels emerged with the Industrial Revolution to serve a new wealthy and mobile leisured class.

- Often family-owned concerns, their appeal is based on history and continuity. Staff members and customers also become members of the extended 'family'.

- Many grand hotels are now part of management groups, enabling consistent quality standards and collaborative sales and marketing operations.

- Irreproachable service and 'magic moments' lie at the heart of the luxury hotel experience.

- With their status-conferring surroundings and accent on personalized service, grand hotels are surprisingly at home in today's narcissistic digital and social era.

- The perfect 21st-century grand hotel strikes a delicate balance between nostalgia and innovation.

From rags to Ritz

04

'You are going to teach the world how to live.'

It would be easy to think of the Ritz in Paris as a lovely but old-fashioned establishment – a portal to a more refined past. But in fact the hotel's opening in 1898 signalled the end of one era and the start of the next. César Ritz conceived of his hotel as a truly modern destination: the first grand hotel of the 20th century.

As Tilar J Mazzeo points out in her (2014) book *The Hotel on Place Vendôme*, one of the main subjects of debate on the hotel's glittering opening night – 1 June 1898 – was the Dreyfus Affair. This notorious episode began with the discovery that someone had been passing French military secrets to the German Embassy in Paris. The French counter-intelligence service, known as the Statistics Section, had discovered that the Germans were communicating with a spy code-named 'Dubois'. Based on the flimsiest of circumstantial evidence, and largely because he was Jewish in an army with barely concealed anti-Semitic leanings, Captain Alfred Dreyfus was framed, convicted of treason and scuttled off to Devil's Island.

By the time the Ritz opened its doors, new evidence had been unearthed – and it appeared that the spy was in fact a major with an aristocratic family name: Ferdinand Walsin Esterhazy. The military, however, stood by Esterhazy and obstinately refused to clear Dreyfus. The writer Emile Zola protested with his famous *J'accuse* letter, published in the newspaper *L'Aurore*.

French society was divided: aristocrats and nationalists in support of the military, artists and intellectuals rallying behind Dreyfus (*les Dreyfusards*). One might have thought that Ritz would have favoured the aristocracy. But almost instinctively, he seems to have realized that the coming century belonged to the opposing group. While plenty of aristocrats would stay at the Ritz, its legend was built on the names of artists, writers and performers: Marcel Proust, Jean Cocteau, Picasso, the fashion designer Gabrielle 'Coco' Chanel; the US reporters who gathered there during two world wars and the authors whose words immortalized it, such as F Scott Fitzgerald and Ernest Hemingway (who considered the Ritz a proxy for paradise).

In short, César Ritz and his hotel redefined glamour.

The perfect partnership

Like many of those who make it big in the luxury business, César Ritz was a dreamer and a chancer, with more than a touch of the ringmaster. He was, wrote the late Hugh Montgomery-Massingberd (in *Grand Hotel*, cited in Chapter 3) 'in theatrical terms… a brilliant director and producer, who set the stage for star performances by the *clientèle*'.

In the beginning, the fact that his name should come to define opulence and sophistication was unimaginable: he was born in Switzerland, the youngest of 13 children, into a family that owned a smallholding – not even large enough to be termed 'a farm' – on the slopes of the Alps. He entered the hospitality trade at 15, as a sommelier at a hotel in Brig, a small resort town at the foot of the Simplon Pass. Things got off to a rocky start: not only was he dismissed from the post, but he was told that he 'would never make a true hotelier'. At least one account (cited in Gubler's 2008 book *Great, Grand & Famous Hotels*) suggests that he then spent a couple of years learning how to be a locksmith – a craft that perhaps came in handy later, given some of the goings-on at his hotels.

But you can't keep a good chancer down, and in 1867 César finally packed his bags and headed to Paris in time for the World Exhibition, when he was certain there would be work for waiters with even the most rudimentary skills. At the age of 18, he was working as a bellhop at the Hotel de la Fidelité. Legend has it that he had an affair with a Russian aristocrat, who smoothed out his rough edges and taught him how to behave in society. But the romance was discovered – and Ritz was fired yet again.

Wily and tenacious, César survived the dark winter of 1870–71 – the height of the Franco-Prussian war – when Paris was besieged and then occupied by the Prussian army. During his stint as a waiter at one of the city's finest restaurants, the Voisin, the situation became so desperate that the zoo was raided for meat – hence the appearance on the menu of 'elephant trunk in sauce chasseur'. This effort was not enough to save the establishment.

César waited out the conflict at a downmarket café, but by the time France had made peace with Germany, in 1872, he had bobbed to the surface again – this time as a waiter at the restaurant of the Hôtel Splendide in the Place de l'Opéra. It was here that Ritz noticed a group of newcomers who were to help him carve out his destiny: wealthy Americans, who had arrived in Paris hungry for French fashion, cuisine and culture. César gave them wine – very expensive wine.

Sidling up to him, the restaurant manager said, 'The Château-Lafitte 1848 is going extraordinary well.'

One imagines a conspiratorial smile from Ritz. 'I have recommended it,' he replied. 'I have made it clear to my clients that it is the surest antidote to the doubtless poisonous waters of the Seine, sir!'

Ritz charmed them all: Cornelius Vanderbilt, JP Morgan, Jay Gould, John Wanamaker… these were the power brokers of the new world, and they followed Ritz as his star rose. He had a talent for making influential friends: while working in Vienna during the World Exhibition of 1873, he met Albert Edward, Prince of Wales, who would also become a supporter.

Having made something of a name for himself, Ritz returned to Switzerland in an entirely new guise – as the manager of the Grand Hotel National in Lucerne. Now he began to put into place some of the innovations that would forge his legend. 'Ritz shrewdly noted the needs and tastes of both the "old" and "new" groups,' according to Montgomery-Massingberd, 'whether it was ice-water for the Americans or Egyptian cigarettes for Albert Edward, Prince of Wales. [He]… banned heavy furnishing materials in favour of washable fabrics, and replaced wallpaper with paint.' Later, he insisted that each hotel bedroom should have its own bathroom – still a rarity at the time. As one journalist was to put it: 'Many distinguished people saw their first real bathroom in a Ritz hotel.' ('César Ritz', *The Spectator*, 11 November 1938.)

At the National in Lucerne, he 'refurbished the cheerless building, repainted bedrooms, reorganized staff and renewed the restaurant menu'. He also ensured that the guests were diverted with a constant stream of balls, regattas and parties. The owner of the hotel, Baron Pfyffer, rewarded César with a job for the summer season at the Grand Hotel Monte Carlo.

In these sunny surroundings, César met two of the most significant figures in his life: Marie-Louise Beck, the daughter of hoteliers, who became his wife – and the visionary chef Georges Auguste Escoffier, who became his creative partner.

Ritz and Escoffier recognized one another right away: both were 'perfectionists and innovators' who 'rebelled against convention and were supported by the winds of social change'. Just as Ritz had devised the most perfectly flattering pink lampshade by comparing it to his young wife's cheeks, so Escoffier banned groaning buffets and banqueting tables and replaced them with *à la carte* meals served as separate dishes to smaller, more intimate groups. In other words, he introduced the modern dining experience.

Now a man of means, Ritz began to make investments, first acquiring the Restaurant de la Conversation in the spa town of Baden-Baden, then a hotel in the same resort, the Minerva.

He was busy revamping the Hôtel de Provence in Cannes when he was approached in 1889 by Richard D'Oyly Carte. The theatre impresario had heard that Ritz was skilled at catering to the modern tastes of rich Americans; what better person to run the new Savoy in London, a hotel designed for precisely that target market? With an early touch of the arrogance that was to prove his undoing, Ritz wrote in his diary that D'Oyly Carte wanted 'the clientèle I can give him', not only the aristocrats, but 'the best of the theatre and opera crowd… the Vanderbilts and the Morgans… the Rothschilds. He wants to make his hotel the Hotel de Luxe of London and the world'.

Once again, Ritz brought Escoffier with him – and for the first time in history, dining out at a hotel became not only acceptable, but fashionable:

> In London, it was considered 'absolutely immoral' to dine out in public on Sunday nights… Ritz did everything he could to abolish these attitudes. With the support of the press and even members of parliament, he introduced Sunday evening dinners… Conspiring with some of the leading lights of female society, Ritz and D'Oyly Carte paved the way for ladies to attend dinners after the theatre and late in the evening. Sunday night dinner became the highpoint of the week and after theatre suppers became all the rage.
>
> 'The Savoy', www.famoushotels.org, 4 September 2014

Ritz divided his time between his new post and investing in hotels across Europe, applying to each his exacting standards of hygiene and décor. Even when he was not financially involved in a new establishment, he was in great demand as a consultant.

Embroiled in these various business dealings, Ritz began to neglect his duties at the Savoy. In addition, the kitchen budget under Escoffier escalated to alarming proportions. D'Oyly Carte may have been a man of the theatre, but he was also a businessman with his eye on the margins. And here the sparkling story of César Ritz becomes somewhat tarnished. After an internal audit, it was found that Ritz and Escoffier had been wining and dining potential investors in their next big London venture – the Carlton Hotel – at the Savoy's expense. They had also been lavishly entertaining the hotel's staff. Goods destined for the Savoy had somehow been delivered to Ritz's private home in Hampstead. The total bill came to more than £6,000 – almost £500,000 today. In addition, Escoffier was found to have been taking financial 'gifts' (some might say 'commission', others might infer 'bribes') from his preferred suppliers. ('The master chef who cooked the books', *The Daily Telegraph*, 2 June 2002.)

Despite their genius, Ritz and Escoffier had become a liability – D'Oyly Carte was forced to let them go. It is perhaps indicative of Ritz's power and connections that the matter was settled out of court.

As anybody who has ever been fired knows, getting pushed out of a job at a certain age often impels you to put into action a plan that has been in the back of your mind for years. In the case of César Ritz, this meant opening his own hotel.

'Where fashion sits...'

Whether or not Madame Ritz shared her husband's enthusiasm for the entrepreneurs of the steam age, she was equally partial to dropping names. Her account of the opening night of the Hôtel Ritz in Paris is studded with titles. In her (1938) book *César Ritz* she writes of 'Comtesse de Pourtalès, looking like a stately swan in a gown of trailing white; Princess Lucien Murat and the Vicomptesse Léon de Janzé, and Comtesse Salverte...'. Their celebrity has faded with time, but we still recognize the self-effacing figure of Marcel Proust, 'small, dark and nervous-looking'.

It was left to one of Ritz's financial backers, Henry Higgins, to capture the significance of the soirée. He told the hotelier: 'Kings and princes will be jealous of you, Ritz. And they will copy you. You are going to teach the world how to live.'

Ritz did not lack investors, from the South African diamond and gold mining magnate Alfred Beit to the wine merchant Alexandre Marnier-Lapostolle, who was obliged to Ritz for having suggested the brand name 'Grand Marnier'.

As in all such cases, location was key. The building itself, a splendid 18th-century townhouse (*hôtel particulier*) with a façade by the architect Jules Hardouin Mansart, had been the private residence of several aristocratic families before briefly becoming home to a financial institution, Crédit Mobilier. It had all the grandeur and gravitas that Ritz required. Its address was 15, Place Vendôme, and as Tilar J Mazzeo writes: 'It was not by chance that the Hôtel Ritz was established in the heart of the new Parisian couture district at the very moment that the French were inventing modern fashion. The shops touting the names of design and luxury were clustered around the Place Vendôme and to its west along the rue du Faubourg Saint Honoré.'

Later, the hotel expanded into an adjoining building on rue Cambon, and the two sides were linked by a long hallway lined with vitrines displaying luxurious baubles. Regulars referred airily to the 'Cambon side' of the hotel when they were organizing rendezvous.

Ritz adorned his establishment with all the modern innovations he'd finessed over the years: electric lighting, fast elevators, en suite bathrooms, uncluttered interiors, built-in cupboards rather than wardrobes (Ritz had an almost pathological hatred of dust), brass beds instead of wooden – while retaining an atmosphere of spectacle and indulgence. He was exacting with staff but strove to work miracles with guests; he may have invented the term 'the customer is always right'.

And the customers repaid him. The very word 'Ritz' became a symbol of contemporary chic. 'Why don't you go where fashion sits?' suggested the songwriter Irving Berlin in 1927, 'Puttin' on the Ritz.' At around the same time, the word 'ritzy' entered the lexicon.

But César had not finished imposing his new template on the hotel world. Almost concurrently with the opening of his Paris establishment, he was finalizing the Carlton in London, in part to avenge his experience with D'Oyly Carte at the Savoy. The hotel was named after the historic residence of the Prince Regent (later crowned George IV) around the corner, but that was its only concession to the past: the Carlton had an exotic palm court on the ground floor and telephones in every room.

Inspired by the hotel's and his own royal connections, in 1902 Ritz began planning a series of lavish events to celebrate the coronation of his favourite client, Albert Edward, the Prince of Wales, as Edward VII. But when Edward fell ill and the coronation was postponed indefinitely, Ritz plummeted into deep despair that led to a nervous breakdown. He had been spreading himself too thinly, for years now, and something had to give. Weakened and increasingly eccentric, with violent mood swings – he would have been diagnosed as bipolar today – he never fully recovered.

Yet he was still to put his stamp on another hotel: this time the London incarnation of the Ritz, built from scratch to resemble a Parisian apartment block and opened in May 1906. All the familiar elements were there, from the palm court where taking tea at the Ritz became an institution, to the built-in storage space in the bedrooms. There were heated towel rails in the bathrooms; hot water was in constant supply.

When the Carlton was demolished after the Second World War, following bomb damage, the Ritz reigned supreme as the hotelier's legacy to London.

Hotel fully occupied

César Ritz did not so much die as gradually withdraw from life. Starting in 1905, he began selling his shares in various hotels around the world. Then he relinquished the management of his other properties, one by one, ending with the Paris Ritz – perhaps his most beloved hotel – in 1911. Officially retired, he moved into a Swiss sanatorium, and then another, at Küssnacht, on the shore of Lake Lucerne. It was here that César Ritz, in 1918, having changed the very idea of what a grand hotel should be, definitively checked out.

The brand associated with his name, however, had a curious afterlife. The Ritz hotels in London and Paris are connected by their shared origins and membership of The Leading Hotels of the World, but they are owned by entirely different people. They also have nothing whatsoever to do with the Ritz-Carlton hotel group, which is based in the United States.

How did that come about?

Ritz and Escoffier had established restaurants under the Ritz-Carlton name on two cruise ships shortly before the First World War, but they were short-lived. Meanwhile, in order to expand into the United States, they allowed businessman Albert Keller to initiate a chain of Ritz-Carlton hotels as a franchise. By the 1920s there were a handful of these across the States. The chain declined during the Depression until, finally, only the Boston establishment remained.

After a long series of manoeuvres, the Ritz-Carlton Boston and the brand name that went with it moved into the hands of the developer William B Johnson, in 1983. He teamed up with an experienced hotelier, Horst Schulze, who grew the Ritz-Carlton company into the respected group that it is today. It has been part of the Marriott group since 1998.

Famously, Ritz-Carlton places an intense focus on CRM and service. Its staff are encouraged to think of themselves as 'ladies and gentlemen serving ladies and gentlemen'; they are issued with 12-point credo, including: 'I am empowered to create unique, memorable and personal experiences for our guests' and 'I own and immediately resolve guest problems'.

This is not just hot air: each member of staff has permission to spend up to US$2,000 to solve a guest's problem, without recourse to a superior. As Adam Toporek points out in his (2015) book *Be Your Customer's Hero: Real world tips and techniques for the service front line*, this makes perfect sense in the light of the fact that 'the average Ritz-Carlton customer will spend US$250,000 with the Ritz over their lifetime'. (For more on the Ritz-Carlton group, see my own 2009 book, *Luxury World*.)

The result of this is that, despite its somewhat schizophrenic existence, the Ritz name is still associated with luxury, quality – and irreproachable service.

After its founder's death, the original Ritz in Paris continued to thrive under the steerage of Madame Ritz. Even the Second World War and the Occupation could not extinguish the hotel's glamour. While other establishments were requisitioned as administrative centres by the Nazis, the Ritz remained a hotel – an uneasily neutral Switzerland in the heart of Paris, to paraphrase Tilar J Mazzeo.

Naturally, it became the opulent backdrop to scandal, evasion and betrayal. The fashion designer Coco Chanel shuttered her boutique but spent the war years ensconced at the Ritz with her Nazi lover, Baron Hans Gunther von Dincklage, an intelligence officer. Conversely, the barman, Frank Meier, became a conduit for messages left by the German Resistance: according to Mazzeo, he played a supporting role in a plot within the German military to assassinate Hitler.

In 1944, as victory neared and allied troops closed in, many of the US reporters who had enjoyed the hotel's hospitality before the war saw it as their ultimate goal on the long road back to Paris. The most colourful of these was of course Ernest Hemingway, who took it upon himself to 'liberate' the Ritz. Screeching to a halt outside the hotel in a borrowed truck with a mismatched crew of US army irregulars and resistance fighters, he burst into the lobby fully armed, contrary to all the rules of neutrality governing the press. Having made his entrance, he quickly requisitioned the bar. Since the writer long ago achieved brand name status, it is fitting that the bar on the Cambon side is now officially known as the Bar Hemingway.

The Ritz entered the post-war years in the charge of Charles ('Charley') Ritz, who during his father's lifetime had shown far more interest in soldiering and fly fishing than the hotel. Nevertheless, as Marie-Louise Ritz grew frail he gradually assumed more responsibility, becoming president in 1953. Following his mother's death in 1961, he was free to shake some of the starch out of the place, loosening up its atmosphere in order to make way for a new generation of colourfully-attired guests. Writes Mazzeo: 'Charley insisted that the world was changing. They needed to keep pace with it. Life was more casual now. Stuffy formality was out-dated.'

But if the Ritz had once been the place 'where fashion sits', the fashionable had moved on. Rooms lay empty; a chill wind whistled down the glass-lined corridor leading to the Cambon side, where the glamorous figures who had once propped up the bar – 'Papa' Hemingway, his friend and rival the photojournalist Robert Capa – were nowhere to be seen, the victims of chance and their own oversized lives. Financial collapse loomed.

Charles Ritz died in 1976, and the last frail tendrils of that lost era died with him. The Ritz squatted in the Place Vendôme like a dusty bauble in an antique dealer's window: an undervalued prize ready to be snapped up by a sharp-eyed collector.

His name, as you know, was Mohamed Al-Fayed, an Egyptian businessman who had, according to Mazzeo, 'visited the palace hotel as a boy and... vowed that he would someday own it'. His dream came true for the bargain price of US$20 million. However, he spent 10 years and a reported US$250 million renovating the hotel, without closing its doors for a single day. Among other things, he added a swimming pool and a cooking school, evoking the legend of Escoffier. The Ritz regained its prestige – and in August 1997, its notoriety, when Diana, Princess of Wales stepped out of the hotel with Al-Fayed's son, Dodi, and into the chauffer-driven car that would take them to a fatal crash beneath the Pont de l'Alma. The Ritz has a habit of inserting itself into both the brighter and darker moments of history.

Fourteen years later, the hotel was wavering again. César Ritz had envisaged it as the world's most modern hotel, but any guest who tried to connect to Wi-Fi there could attest that this was no longer the case. One hotel consultant commented: 'The façade and rooms are one thing but the nuclear core of a palace hotel is out of sight, in the kitchen or the basements where the new electronics and computer systems are stored.' ('No room at the Ritz as Al-Fayed's fading hotel closes its doors', *The Independent*, 19 October 2011.)

This core would have to be overhauled. For the very first time, the Ritz closed its doors.

The renaissance of the Ritz

In June 2016, the Ritz in Paris re-opened after only the second major refurbishment in its 117-year history. The facelift took over three years and is said to have cost more than €200 million. It was partly inspired by an influx of new luxury hotels – the Mandarin Oriental, the Peninsula and the Shangri-La – into Paris. More worryingly, the French Tourism Ministry had declined to give the Ritz its highest designation: 'Palace'. And if the Ritz is anything at all, it is a palace.

The overhaul was largely about fundamentals: the plumbing, the air conditioning, the technology. The classic Ritz touches – like the peach bath towels that the hotelier thought were easier on the eyes than white – remained in place. The decorators were instructed to respect the original interiors. Even the staff were assured that their old jobs would still be available if they chose to return. Fundamentally, the Ritz has not changed. The hotel may have better Wi-Fi, but most people will come simply because there is no other place like it on Earth.

'The Ritz makes people dream,' says Matthieu Goffard, the hotel's press attaché. 'The word itself has become a mark of excellence, of prestige and a certain French *art de vivre*. People who pass in front of the hotel's wrought iron doors can't help wondering what goes on behind them, what kind of people might be staying there.'

Mostly, he says, they're not staying on business:

> It tends to be a place for celebrations: honeymoons, birthdays. It has a magic about it. Many of our regular guests come from the worlds of fashion or film. Historically we've attracted a lot of American guests, and that is still the case. I think they like it here because they are looking for a classically 'Parisian' experience, which they might not find at the Peninsula or the Park Hyatt, for example.

Their age range is fairly broad, but they have a certain discernment and a sense of their own status. They have not been lured by traditional advertising – the Ritz does not countenance such things. It would rather, for example, team up with US *Vogue* for a 16-page fashion shoot starring Kate Moss, as it did in April 2012. Later that year, in July, *Vanity Fair* ran a 12-page article entitled 'A legend as big as the Ritz'. Such projects remind customers of the hotel's mythic status. Journalists are attracted by the Ritz, and Matthieu keeps them furnished with stories: 'We have of course adapted to the modern world – we're present on social media. But we remain discreet. We try to communicate in an elegant, understated way. So that's why – no advertising.'

One does not have to stay at the Ritz to get a taste of it. Those on a modest budget simply have to pluck up their courage, walk through the imposing front door, and take that long crystalline corridor to the Bar Hemingway. Not inexpensive, but still an affordable luxury.

It's notable that Colin Field, barman at the Bar Hemingway since 1994, remained an employee of the Ritz during its long closure. In fact, he toured the world's grand hotels giving cocktail masterclasses and keeping the Ritz aura alive while the building itself was brought up to date. 'Colin is one of our finest ambassadors,' Goffard confirms. 'He bumps into clients everywhere he goes.'

In fact, as with Walter Bolzonella at the Cipriani, it seems that the head barman is often a link between a grand hotel and the rest of the world; a comforting figure in a daunting environment.

Not that everyone is daunted, mind you.

'I think the younger generation are less self-conscious about entering establishments like the Ritz,' Goffard says. 'In fact there are many ways you can experience the hotel without being a guest. Not just the bar or the restaurants, but also the spa and the cooking school.'

Parisians and visitors, individually and in groups, can choose from a selection of classes at the École Ritz Escoffier, ranging from 'ateliers' of one to four hours (costing around a hundred euros) to professional courses lasting several weeks (and costing several thousand).

'In a way, the hotel is a self-contained world,' says Goffard. 'It is like a resort in the middle of the city – you could quite easily stay here for a week without ever stepping outside. Of course, you probably would not wish do to that, as you're no doubt here to see Paris. But there's so much to do here that it is quite feasible.'

Like other Paris monuments, the Ritz is imposing, but not inaccessible. If one day you're passing, don't hesitate to follow in Hemingway's footsteps. Make your way to the bar, hoist one of Colin's cocktails, and feel as if you've made a success of life.

Tour highlights

- César Ritz built his brand name through connections – with charm and impeccable service, he attracted clients and friends who followed him from establishment to establishment.

- Discerning rather than snobbish, Ritz understood that the new generation of wealthy American tourists were just as important as the traditional, aristocratic patrons of the grand hotels.

- Later, he adopted and befriended the racy, bohemian community that would create the art, literature and fashion of the early 20th century.

- A stickler for cleanliness, Ritz insisted on paperless walls, washable materials and built-in cupboards, combined with the antiques and noble materials that created a palatial environment.

- Ritz also realized that to be 'in fashion' meant embracing novelty and innovation.

- Long after the reign of Ritz, his name remains a byword for luxury – and for service beyond the call of duty.

The return of the Orient Express

05

'The train of kings and the king of trains.'

On a beautiful Paris afternoon, a line of railway carriages with a familiar royal blue and cream livery gleams in the spring sunshine. For the moment they are empty, but the usual gaggle of mismatched characters, thrown together by fate and the train's legendary allure, wait to board.

'D'you think it's haunted?' a small boy asks his mother.

'A ghost?' she says, amused. 'The ghost of the Orient Express?'

Nearby, a man in tortoiseshell glasses shuffles his feet and surreptitiously jots the exchange in his notebook. He is by no means the first writer to have stepped aboard the train – although he is certainly among the least famous.

When at last the visitors are able to file onto the carriages, it looks as though the previous occupants have left in a hurry. In one sleeping compartment, a casually draped fur and a phonograph. On a table in the restaurant car, a typewriter, a stub-filled ashtray, a gin bottle and an empty glass. It is as if the train really is haunted: more Mary Celeste than Orient Express.

The other problem is that the train will remain stationary. In fact, the carriages are moored on a windswept concrete plaza outside the Arab World Institute. They are the centrepiece of an exhibition about the historic train, and the role it played in linking Occident with Orient. This is not a journey – it is a museum exhibit. The carriages are not even hooked up to the locomotive, which stands aloof from them on a dais at the entrance to the museum, looking imperious but faintly lost, like an interloper at a cocktail party. As well it might: its only connection with the train is the fact that it appeared in Sidney Lumet's film version of *Murder on the Orient Express* (1974).

As the film demonstrates, the Orient Express was not so much a mode of transport as a cultural phenomenon – one of the greatest travel brands ever to have existed. The opening scenes of the movie capture some of its magnetism. The last passengers scuttle aboard, the heavy doors banging like rifle shots. A whistle blows. A great lamp opens its bright white eye at the front of the locomotive. Emerging from its slumber, the train begins to move. Ponderously at first, in clouds of steam, hissing with effort. The pistons rise and fall. A little faster now. Then faster still, urged on by the soundtrack. Finally it is flying along, trailing exhilarating gusts of music and a silken scarf of steam. The film has an all-star cast, but this is the blockbuster draw.

The exhibition at the Arab World Institute in 2014 attempted to define the factors that gave the Orient Express its remarkable, epoch-bridging status. And also, perhaps, to answer the question: 'Was it really as glamorous as it sounds?'

Mister Pullman and Monsieur Nagelmackers

The father of the Orient Express, a Belgian engineer named Georges Nagelmackers, made sure several journalists were aboard the train for its inaugural voyage on 4 October 1883. Women were not invited, and the men were advised to pack pistols. This last detail may have been an example of Nagelmackers' flair for showmanship.

Like many great stories, that of the Orient Express begins with conflict. (It is told in great detail in the catalogue of the exhibition above: *Il Était Une Fois l'Orient Express*, published by Éditions Snoek in 2014.) Born in Liège into a wealthy family of bankers, Nagelmackers trained as a civil engineer. He became smitten with a cousin, but his love remained unrequited – and in any case his family strongly disapproved of his choice. He was dispatched to the United States in the hope that travel and adventure would dissipate his ardour.

Travel meant the railroad – and Nagelmackers developed a new passion for the comfortable Pullman sleeping cars in which he toured the United States for 10 months. The Belgian saw a business opportunity: there was nothing like this in Europe. He contacted the maker of the carriages, George Pullman, to suggest a partnership. Already fabulously wealthy – to the extent that he had built and essentially ruled over an entire town for his factory employees, with houses, stores, parks, churches, theatres and a library – Pullman declined. This time, fortunately, Nagelmackers was not so easily deterred from his goal.

In 1873 he founded Georges Nagelmackers & Company, which quickly became the *Compagnie Internationale des Wagons-Lits* (CIWL). Its logo:

two heraldic lions supporting an interlaced WL. His adviser on technical matters was an American Civil War veteran and inventor, Colonel William d'Alton Mann, who had previously patented the 'Mann Boudoir Car'. The enterprise was necessarily based in Belgium, bearing in mind the financial backing of Nagelmackers' family, not to mention the support of a very special friend of his father's – Leopold II, the King of Belgium. The future king of trains was already the train of kings.

Georges established his administrative headquarters in Paris. In the coming years his company would be split into three parts: administration, construction and, crucially, the *Compagnie Internationale des Grands Hôtels*. This was charged with establishing and operating the luxury hotels in which Orient Express passengers would stay, to ensure that their accommodation matched the standards of opulence set by the train itself. Some of these hotels became legends in their own right: the Riviera Palace in Nice, the Avenida Palace in Lisbon and, perhaps most famously of all, the Pera Palace in Istanbul.

For now, though, all that lay in the future. Having obtained through his royal connections the first sleeping car concession in Belgium, Nagelmackers began convincing railway operators across Europe to attach his company's *wagons-lits*, lounges and restaurant cars to their trains. By 1878, as he told his shareholders, his services had become almost indispensable:

> The circulation of our cars has spread so far, their usefulness is so widely accepted, and our international relations have developed to such an extent, that it has become difficult for a railway operator to do without us if it wishes to establish a sleeping car service on its network… even the operators most hostile in principle to our enterprises today recognize the need to use our cars.

> CIWL Annual General Meeting, 12 March 1878
> (quoted by *Les Rails de l'Histoire*, the magazine of the AHICF,
> the French Railway History Association, November 2013)

The next step was evident: the creation of trains entirely composed of CIWL carriages. The first of these left the Gare de l'Est in Paris for Vienna 'early in the evening' of 10 October 1882. Transporting 40 travellers, it made the 1,364-kilometre (848-mile) journey in just under 28 hours, at a speed of 48.7 kmh (30.2 mph) – roughly six hours faster than existing services. The story of the *train éclair*, the 'lightning train', made only a few lines in *Le Figaro*, which nonetheless reported that its passengers had found 'the beds perfect and the food excellent'.

The lightning train was a blueprint for the Orient Express.

By rail, river and sea

By March 1883, the project had built up steam. Nagelmackers informed his shareholders that he had signed agreements with every major railway operator from Paris to the Black Sea: he was ready to launch the *Train Express d'Orient*. Haulage would be the responsibility of the operators; the CIWL would provide, service and maintain every element apart from the locomotives: sleeping cars, restaurant cars, lounge cars and, more prosaically, baggage cars.

That summer there were weekly test runs – amounting to what might be termed a 'soft launch' today. On 7 June, *Le Figaro* reported that 'the first departure of... the luxury train from Paris to Constantinople... was accomplished in perfect order. Eyes were particularly drawn to the brilliant uniform of the train conductor, based on that of the *staatsbahn autrichienne*. Not only were all the cars full, but it was necessary to turn a certain number of passengers away.' (Quoted in *Les Rails de l'Histoire*, details as above.)

A discreet background hum of excitement could be detected. On 3 August, based on what seemed to be an official press release from the CIWL, *Le Figaro* and *Le Gaulois* published identical reports: 'All departures from Paris, and most of the return journeys from the Orient over the past 15 days, took place without a single empty seat.'

Finally, on 3 October, the great announcement appeared – once again in *Le Figaro* and *Le Gaulois*. A 'special inaugural train', containing only invited guests, would leave Paris the following evening, to arrive at Constantinople on 8 October.

In truth, the railway network of the day could not take a steam train all the way to Constantinople – the initial route of the Orient Express was somewhat circuitous. After passing through Bucharest, the train would stop at Giurgiu, a small Romanian port on the Danube. A steam ferry would take the passengers across the river, to Rustchuk (today called Ruse) where they would take another train to Varna beside the Black Sea. A steamship would then deliver them, 15 hours later, to Constantinople – bringing the total journey to 80 hours. This was still 30 hours faster than existing services. And in the end, the journey sounded even more romantic than a straightforward A to B run.

Nagelmackers certainly pulled out all the stops to ensure that the inaugural voyage carried more than a whiff of intrigue. Hence his insistence that the men should carry guns, and that the ladies should stay at home. He also made a show of the fact that there would be a medic on board – one Dr Harzé.

The journey was practically a press junket: the French and overseas reporters aboard included Henri de Blowitz of *The Times*, Georges Boyer of *Le Figaro*, and Jules Tréfu of *Le Gaulois*.

Blowitz provides a richly detailed description of the train's departure. Bearing a smart folded invitation containing a miniature route map, a time-table and his carriage and seat number, he arrives at the Gare de l'Est at nightfall to find it aglow:

> A profusion of electric lights are scattered throughout the station. Employees at the entrance indicate the platform where the Orient Express is standing. A good number of people have come to see off the departing passengers and, since most of them are making the journey to the Orient for the first time, it is not without a little emotion, mixed with a great deal of joy, that they part... At the moment the whistle blows, the Orient Express offers from the exterior, where I pause for an instant before bounding for the footplate... a very modern and arresting tableau.

Inside the train, he finds the conductors of the sleeping cars, 'the bright lights lending their brown uniforms a reddish glow', attempting to deliver luggage and packages to the right compartments but being forced to 'walk sideways or on the tips of their toes' amid passengers blocking the corridors and crowded around windows.

Not a single theatrical detail has been overlooked – Blowitz notes that the curtains of the restaurant car have been 'coquettishly raised' so that those who remain on the platform can see exactly what they're missing. Comparing its brightly lamp-lit interior to that of a banqueting hall, he writes that it 'lends an extraordinary radiance to the entire scene', with its seven ranks of evenly ranged tables 'for four diners on the right, and for two on the left', dressed with gleaming white tablecloths and artfully folded serviettes. The crystal wine glasses and decanters, the clarity of the water in the carafes, the 'silvery helmets' of the champagne bottles, all of these combine to 'throw a dazzling light over the crowd both outside and within'.

Handkerchiefs are waved, the guards on the platform command the spectators to step back – and at 7.30pm the inaugural Orient Express pulls sedately out of the station.

From train to icon

How did the Orient Express become a legend? As suggested earlier, this evolution was partly down to the personality of Nagelmackers himself. In *Il Était Une Fois l'Orient Express*, Martine Chantereau writes: 'His intelligence, his obstinacy, his education, his innate sense of public relations, diplomacy and the use of the media and advertising, enabled him to accomplish an extraordinary endeavour.'

In a portrait by the photographer Paul Nadar, the master of the *wagons-lits* cuts an imposing figure: the very model of a captain of industry in his tails and waistcoat, with his ramrod posture, lush beard and wide, almost fervent gaze. One hand is thrust into his pocket, the other clutches a cane, grey top hat and white gloves.

These dandyish touches were not, it seems, affected for the picture. By 1900, the CIWL headquarters at place de l'Opéra in Paris was essentially a deluxe travel agency for the very rich. Nagelmackers acquired a château at Villepreux, near Versailles, to which he invited celebrities, politicians and social gadabouts, transporting them by private train to hunting parties and picnics. It was one of the first houses in the region to be lit with electricity; a freshwater spring in the gardens filled the bottles on his trains. His son eventually married the daughter of Davidson Dalziel – who happened to be president of the English arm of the Pullman Company. Hence the rival concerns were at last united by family ties.

Another important ingredient was what might be referred to as 'the fantasy of the Orient'. With its roots in *The Thousand and One Nights*, a collection of Middle Eastern folk tales translated into French by the archaeologist Antoine Galland in the 18th century, the ideal of an alternative, fantastical realm – a world of domes and spires, of veiled beauties and whirling dervishes – inspired a chain of writers and travellers, from Chateaubriand (*Itinerary from Paris to Jerusalem*, 1811), to Gérard de Nerval (*Voyage en Orient*, 1851) and Pierre Loti (*Aziyadé*, 1879). Flaubert's *Salammbô* (1862) is set in Carthage, but it is a cornucopia of exotic imagery; the writer himself had travelled in North Africa and the Middle East, and sojourned in Beirut and Istanbul.

Artists were equally drawn to the Orient, particularly the concept of the harem: the paintings of Ingres writhe with voluptuous odalisques, notionally the sultan's concubines, although the word apparently derives from the term 'chambermaid'. Eugène Delacroix and Félix Ziem also captured oriental fables, architecture and landscapes.

In the 19th century, the Orient was Romantic with a capital R: fashionable, dangerous and erotic.

But this world was real. The Ottoman Empire had at that point existed for more than 500 years, with Istanbul at its heart. The Orient Express offered passengers the chance to experience for themselves what many suspected to be an alien and decadent society. For more enlightened travellers, it banished fantasy and brought two seemingly opposing cultures closer together.

If the train had existed merely at the whim of writers and romantics, however, the chances are that it would have gone out of business very quickly. The Orient Express was also a symbol of the Industrial Revolution – its speed was one of its great advantages, which is why it was eventually supplanted by air travel, and deluxe rail voyagers morphed into 'the jet set'. As Robert Halleux writes in *Il Était Une Fois l'Orient Express*:

> While it may have become the train of aristocrats, spies and courtesans, the Orient Express was above all a vector for expansion, the train of engineers. Along its route, Budapest, Bucharest, Belgrade and Salonika were all equipping themselves with running water, gas, electricity and tramways, while emerging countries, rich in natural resources, were venturing into heavy industry. At the end of the line, Constantinople, the Levant and Egypt were swiftly modernizing.

Nagelmackers died in 1905, exhausted both financially and physically by his venture. But the Orient Express, already on its way to becoming iconic, refused to die with him. The suspension of the service at the start of the First World War should have put an end to the story – but a new version of the train emerged in 1919, with the opening of the Simplon Tunnel through the Alps. The Simplon-Orient-Express called at Lausanne, Milan, Venice, Trieste and Belgrade, before dividing at Nis into trains to Istanbul on the one hand and Athens on the other.

The 1920s were perhaps the apogee of the literary and cinematic Orient Express – the version of the train we daydream about today. Art Deco styling, velvet-upholstered seating, mahogany panels set with crystal engravings by Lalique, journeys in the company of Josephine Baker and the notorious arms dealer Basil Zaharoff. These carriages transported passengers into the ruins of the Ottoman Empire and the foundations of the new, secular Turkey of Kemal Atatürk.

One Orient Express train became stuck in a snowdrift in Thrace for six days in 1929 – an incident that would inspire Agatha Christie, who was not aboard for that particular voyage, but had certainly enjoyed others. *Murder on the Orient Express* was published in 1934. The train will be forever associated with Dame Agatha, but many other writers have sent their characters along its rails. Graham Greene gathered a host of dissolute and desperate characters together for *Stamboul Train* in 1932; Ian Fleming booked James Bond onto the Orient Express for the agent's climatic battle with the brutal spy 'Red' Grant in *From Russia With Love* (1957). The film versions of these tales – and many others beside – took the myth to another dimension.

We should not forget advertising, of course, and the posters that promoted the Orient Express in the early 20th century still add a touch of exoticism to many living-room walls today: by artists such as Jean de la Mézière, Jacques

Touchet and Maurice Barbey, they were often inspired by the works of Ziem and Delacroix. They tend to play on the poetry of place names, the long list of destinations spooling across the image, rapping into the mind like the clatter of wheels over rails.

The Orient Express survived the Second World War, and lumbered gamely beyond the Iron Curtain – where its luxurious cars were uncoupled and replaced with more egalitarian, spartan carriages – but the era of the great train was coming to a close. At one point three different routes were served by trains named 'Orient Express'. They died out one by one. The Simplon-Orient-Express clung on until 1962, when it made way for the Direct Orient Express, something of a misnomer as it was slower than its predecessor. By 1971, the CIWL had stopped running trains, instead leasing or selling its carriages to operators. (A vestige of the company still exists today as Newrest Wagon-Lits. It offers catering and other on-board services to several railway companies, with 90 per cent of its income deriving from France and the remainder from Austria, Portugal and Canada. The corporate travel service Carlson Wagon-Lit Travel owes its name in part to the travel agency side of the business.)

The Orient Express in the true sense of the term stopped running in May 1977.

There is still a Venice-Simplon-Orient-Express, a nostalgic service run by a luxury hotel group. On board, honeymooners and wealthy vacationers do their best to recreate a lost world.

The Orient Express reborn

What if you could actually take the Orient Express? Not a museum on rails, but a fully-functioning contemporary luxury train, as relevant to our times as the original Express was to its passengers.

Thanks to the French national railway company – the SNCF – that may soon be possible.

At the time I met him – shortly after the exhibition mentioned at the start of this chapter – Patrick Ropert gloried under the title of executive chairman of the Orient Express. How that came about was a story in itself.

'In 2010, when I took up the post of communications director of the SNCF, I discovered while researching our history that we actually owned the Orient Express brand – it had been deposed immediately after the original train's last journey in 1977. So in fact it was part of our portfolio,' he told me.

He pointed out that French railways had always played a key role in the train's history. 'Nagelmackers created the concept – the *wagons-lits* – but he needed people who knew how to operate trains, how to connect carriages with locomotives and so on.'

The brand stayed in suspended animation until 2001, when it was licensed to what became the Orient Express group; under the agreement, the UK-based group could exploit the name for a chain of hotels and a luxury train.

'When I understood that we possessed the brand and began thinking about what we could do with it, how we might develop it, I started discussions with the English group. The result was, in short, that we decided not to continue our journey together.'

The hotel group changed its name to Belmond, but retained permission to operate its train – a strictly nostalgic, vintage experience – under the name Venice-Simplon-Orient-Express. As for the SNCF, Ropert said, 'We have ambitions for the brand. We are going to create a new universe that puts the train in a contemporary context.'

During our conversation, it dawned on me that this was more than a marketing challenge; it was a combination of business project and passion. 'We have re-established the Orient Express as a company and now we're going to develop the activities of that company.'

For now, he admitted, only a tiny sliver of those activities had been realized:

First we needed to understand the history of the brand. Of course we knew it had enormous potential – it has an inescapable magic, but we wanted to find out where that came from. So as well as working with lawyers to protect the brand, we also began working with a group of railway historians [the AHICF, mentioned earlier]. We asked them to plunge into the archives, to unearth documents and stories for us. Strangely enough, nobody had really done that – the mythology existed independently of any reality. So the exhibition came out of that, as a sort of first step, to revive and locate the naissance of the myth.

In parallel to the exhibition, during Design Week in Milan, the plan to resurrect the train itself was revealed. 'We spoke to designers, architects and engineers about our project, to solicit their advice and gauge their reactions. So in Paris and Milan both the historic and the contemporary aspects took form.'

The interior design of the new Orient Express was unveiled for the first time at that point. Ropert showed me the draft design for the *voiture-bar*. It did indeed look sleek and contemporary, while making subtle references to the original. 'We wanted to reinterpret the codes of Art Deco in a contemporary fashion. The train will be entirely of today, but the nobility and richness of the materials will be remarkable. We've kept touches such as the engraved glass.'

Next he turned to the restaurant:

What we've tried to do here is create the possibility of encounters. In the 1920s and 30s, there were several luxury trains in the world – but only one became a legend. And when we tried to work out why, one element in particular struck us: on this train there were many interesting encounters, and many stories about those encounters. So we've tried to create a sort of moving café terrace. Because when you're sitting on the terrace of a Parisian café, if you feel like it, you can fairly easily start a conversation with your neighbour.

And the *wagon-lit* itself – the bedroom suite? 'Here, of course, our goal is the opposite – to create intimacy. But also a sense of airiness, of depth of field, in what is inevitably a restricted space. So we took inspiration from a New York loft, where your eye is drawn to the exterior. We enlarged the window as much as we could. The desk is at the same level as the view. You live surrounded by openness.'

Finally came the salon, the social nerve centre of the train, which would offer panoramic views of the passing landscape. Here one will be able to read, take tea, chat or flirt, depending on one's humour.

This was still a dream on paper, however. Many of the designers who would bring the project to fruition had yet to be recruited. 'It should be the work of artisans – with a dose of invention,' underlined Ropert. 'Lalique invented a style with his glasswork; we must source that capacity for innovation today.'

In tandem with the exhibition, the SNCF launched a handful of what might be called teaser products for the train. One of these was a vanity case in 'Orient Express blue' co-created with Moynat – a trunk-maker founded in 1849 and now owned by Louis Vuitton. Says Ropert: 'Why only one piece of luggage? Because when you rebuild a brand like the Orient Express, you must be prudent; it has an enormous heritage and in order to respect the myth we must remain exclusive. By the way, look as hard as you might, you won't find an Orient Express logo on the valise. It merely alludes to the train.'

The second, less obvious, spin-off was a set of highly luxurious bedding sold at the posh Bon Marché department store in Paris under the Orient Express brand name. Snuggle into your sheets at home as if you're speeding to dreamland in an opulent sleeping car. There was also a lamp, designed to reflect the style of those that lit the restaurant car tables as the train rushed through the night.

This image raised another question: given the historic and geopolitical role of the Orient Express in connecting two cultures, where would the new Express go? Would passengers still be buying tickets for Istanbul?

'For the moment we're not sure,' Ropert told me:

> But I think the train itself will be the central experience, not the destination. The experience could be, perhaps, boarding without knowing your eventual destination. Or knowing that you are heading for Istanbul, but with unexpected stops along the way. You may also find the train at the other end of the world, because for a specific event it has been transported, let's say, to the United States. If you think of the inauguration of the original train, it was the beginning of a great adventure. Our challenge is to capture that spirit today.

Tour highlights

- Georges Nagelmackers, the creator of the Orient Express, used a combination of diplomacy and press relations to turn his train into a phenomenon.
- With a flair for theatricality, he packed the inaugural Express with journalists and urged them to carry pistols.
- He cultivated a fashionable personality and invited celebrities to travel on his private trains, or to parties at his château.
- Wealthy 19th-century romantics were attracted by the fantasy of the Orient; but the Express was also a rapid route to business opportunities in emerging markets.
- Reality and fiction combined to make the Orient Express one of the most iconic brands in travel history.
- Today, at least two different companies are using the romance that surrounds the name to sell products and services.

The battle for the high seas

06

'Size, power, luxury and sophistication.'

A few weeks ago, as my plane toiled across the Atlantic to New York, I tried to imagine a transatlantic liner making a parallel voyage far below. Our routes would have been similar – towards the treacherous waters off Newfoundland – but while I was flying in clear blue skies, high above the bergs and the fogs, my notional liner would have been exposed to constant danger.

The word 'liner' is important. During the golden age of the great ocean liners, in the 19th and early 20th centuries, the notion of 'cruises' barely existed. Liners travelled from A to B, like my aircraft. A cruise ship meanders around like a curious tourist, a mode of transport that is also a destination in its own right.

The book I was reading as I jetted over the Atlantic was *The Ocean Railway* (2004), by Stephen Fox (although I prefer its US title: *Transatlantic*). As I read deeper into Fox's tales of ingenuity and courage, I felt even more relieved to be in my flying metal tube: cocooned, cosseted and only a couple of hours from land. The passengers who made the first scheduled transatlantic crossings were genuine adventurers, travelling under sail on 'packet' ships.

The 'packets', as their name suggests, were primarily developed to ship goods and mail, with a few paying passengers aboard to boost profits. The first 'line' was founded in 1817 by a group of New York textile importers led by one Jeremiah Thompson. Ships had crossed the Atlantic before, of course, but in a haphazard manner. As Fox puts it: '[A] ship owner might advertise a ship's day of departure, but the captain would then wait until enough cargo and passengers had been loaded, and wind and weather seemed favourable, before weighing anchor.'

As a merchant dealing in often urgently-awaited goods, this was unacceptable to Thompson. He required a fleet of vessels 'sailing on known dates between established ports, and locked into an unchanging departure schedule for the foreseeable future'.

Thompson's ships, with a signature black ball painted on their fore topsails, sailed from New York to Liverpool. The first two ships of the Black Ball Line left New York in January 1818. Soon the line was running 'with the regularity of a horse-drawn mail coach'.

Rival lines rapidly emerged – the Red Star, the Blue Swallowtail – kicking off a nautical arms race as they battled to build ever bigger and faster vessels. The occasional weather-blessed 22-day crossing soon shrank to a regular 20-day voyage. It was inevitable that the lines would begin experimenting with a fascinating but daunting new technology: steam.

Brunel's last laugh

There had been other steamboats before Isambard Kingdom Brunel embarked on his great transatlantic feat. In the United States, the engineer John Fitch had trialled a 45-foot paddle boat on the Delaware River as early as 1787; this later evolved into a regular (although short-lived, due to financial difficulties) service between Philadelphia and Burlington, New Jersey.

Another name wreathed in steam was that of William Symington, an engineer and inventor from South Lanarkshire, Scotland. The same year that Fitch launched his paddle steamer, Symington patented his 'atmospheric engine' (named after the use of condensed steam and atmospheric pressure to drive its pistons). He trialled steamboats for various patrons before Thomas, Lord Dundas – governor of the Forth and Clyde Canal Company – provided serious backing. Symington's most famous steamboat bore the name of one of his patron's daughters: *Charlotte Dundas*. On 28 March 1803 it towed two loaded barges down the canal for eighteen and a half miles (albeit in nine and a half hours). In the end, though, the Canal Company rejected this new technology, fearing that the steamboat would have difficulty navigating the canal's locks and that its turbulent wake would 'injure the banks'. The plan ran out of steam.

Nevertheless, the *Charlotte Dundas* presaged a burst of steamboat innovation – including US inventor Robert Fulton's paddle steamers – and within a couple of decades the vessels were a familiar sight on the rivers of Europe and the United States.

Crossing the Atlantic, however, was quite another thing.

As almost every British schoolboy knows, Isambard Kingdom Brunel built the Great Western Railway, the iconic 117-mile route from London to Bristol. Or rather, as Fox puts it, the engineer 'surveyed the route... and then planned every detail of its construction, from the locomotives and the rolling stock down to the lamp-posts and stations'.

He was worldly, charismatic and rather European – his father, Marc, hailed from a northern French farming community. Short and dapper under the stovepipe hats he affected to give himself some loft, Brunel chuffed around like a steam train under a swirl of cigar smoke. He had 'blazing dark eyes' and used his hands when he spoke. He constantly pushed for better, more modern, more spectacular.

His transatlantic steamship started out as a joke. When a member of the Great Western board of directors complained at a meeting about the cost and length of the line, Brunel retorted: 'Why not make it even longer, and have a steamboat go from Bristol to New York?'

Another director, the sugar refiner Thomas R Guppy, took him up on the bet, and they soon teamed up with Christopher Claxon, 'a semi-retired Royal Navy officer', and Bristol shipbuilder William Patterson. Spurred on by the news that expatriate US businessman Junius Smith was also planning a transatlantic venture, the team 'planned and built the largest steamship yet, the first designed for regular crossings of the North Atlantic'.

Brunel was not a shipbuilder, and the design of the ship was largely the work of Claxton and Patterson. But he was the driving force behind the project, its spirit and its incarnation. The result was the SS *Great Western*, powered by giant paddle wheels, 'the biggest and most up-to-date steamship in the world'.

The décor was luxurious. The saloon was festooned 'with columns that imitated palm trees' and 'door panels five feet high' which featured painted vignettes of landscapes, the arts, science and leisure activities 'all in the rococo manner of Louis XV'. The staircase to the cabins below 'had a bronzed and gilded ornamental railing'. It was as if the decorators wanted to imply that the harsh Atlantic could not only be vanquished, but ignored.

Brunel's rival Junius Smith had barely progressed with plans for his own steamship, so in order to win the race across the Atlantic, Smith cut corners: he leased a Channel steamer and 'sent her on a risky, shortened passage from Cork, on the southern coast of Ireland', which knocked a day off the journey. Fox dismisses the voyage as 'a heedless, dangerous publicity stunt'. And while the *Great Western* set sail for New York a full four days behind the *Sirius*, she arrived only 12 hours later than the rogue steamer, on 23 April 1838 – a voyage of fifteen and a half days, 'the fastest crossing ever from England to America'. The Great Western Steamship Company would continue to operate its transatlantic service until 1846, often breaking its own record.

Junius Smith did eventually launch his own steamship, the *British Queen*. While bigger and more powerful than Brunel's vessel, she also proved to be slower. However, for her maiden voyage on 12 July 1839, a number of influential passengers were on board – including a man named Samuel Cunard.

Cunard's luck

At first they were the Kunders, a family of German Quakers who emigrated to America in the 17th century – supposedly on the strength of a bag of gold coins, possibly pirate treasure, that the men of the family had unearthed while ploughing a field. By the time Sam was born, on 21 November 1787, the family name had been buffeted through Conrad and Cunrad before stabilizing as Cunard.

Sam's father, Abraham, a carpenter and builder, had settled in Halifax, Nova Scotia, and married the daughter of Irish immigrants, Margaret Murphy, who later turned out to be an alcoholic. Sam, their oldest boy, grew into a sober and hard-working young man who kept a tight lid on his emotions. 'Living in a harbour town dominated by its waterfront commerce, he naturally turned to ships and shipping as the main mediums of his business activities,' writes Fox. He quit school early to trade in fish, vegetables and other goods – earning enough to buy his first suit at the age of 14 – but eventually got a proper job 'as a clerk in the naval dockyard's engineer department'. At the age of 21, in 1809, he persuaded his father to join him in the firm of A Cunard & Son, 'ship agents and general merchants in the West Indian trade'.

When Great Britain and the United States went to war in 1812, Sam Cunard turned the conflict to his advantage, trading in 'flour, meal, corn, pitch and turpentine', as Halifax had become a flourishing entrepôt for the British navy. 'By the end of the war [the Cunards] were buying not just cargoes, but the ships themselves,' notes Fox.

After the war, Sam won a royal contract to carry the mail on his sailing packets between Boston, Halifax and St John's. When his father Abraham died in 1824, the name of the enterprise was officially changed to Samuel Cunard & Company.

Backed by local authorities and stockholders, he launched his first steamship – the *Royal William*, from a Quebec shipbuilder – in 1830. The paddle steamer was due to ply the route from Halifax to Quebec, but the enterprise quickly ran into trouble: having spent a season hemmed in by ice at Quebec, the ship had barely started operating again when she was quarantined due to a cholera epidemic. Too few voyages, not enough cargo and even fewer passengers led to angry questions from the stockholders. The *Royal William* was sold at a loss in early 1833.

But Sam Cunard had learned from the experience – from that time on, he never adopted technology until it had proved its worth. This sense of prudence allowed Cunard to steal a march on Brunel's Great Western Steamship Company, which had ploughed a fortune into a highly advanced vessel called the *Great Britain*. The 3,400 ton ship – the largest in existence – had a revolutionary iron hull and was powered by screw propellers rather than paddle wheels. But the lengthy construction period and sheer cost of the project almost sunk Great Western before she was completed. The *Great Britain* finally entered service in 1845, and for a while she was the most impressive ship on the seas. But when she ran aground in September 1846, Brunel's company never recovered from the lost business.

Another key factor in the Great Western Steamship Company's demise was the fact that the British government had decided to grant its transatlantic mail contract to Sam Cunard.

At the age of 51, having kept a close watch on the steamer services from the British Isles to the United States, Cunard considered that a transatlantic shipping line 'was a logical extension of his lifework'. Previously managed by the Post Office, the transatlantic mail service was now handled by the Admiralty – the organization that oversaw the Royal Navy – via contracts with private shipping companies. The Admiralty's tender was for a monthly service. Cunard boldly proposed a weekly run. In the end, the Admiralty awarded him a contract for a twice-monthly service.

Cunard had promised the Admiralty that his ships would be 'plain and comfortable'. The first four – the *Acadia*, the *Caledonia*, the *Columbia* and the *Britannia* – were built by the Clyde shipyards and Fox describes them as 'austere beauties, sleek and black, with just a few ornamental touches of gold and red in the paddle boxes and smokestack'. Charles Dickens travelled on the *Britannia* in January 1842. The great writer was unimpressed by the spartan accommodation, the 'clanking and blasting' engine and the endless rolling of the ship. 'At dinner, Dickens noticed the most coveted seats were those closest to the door.'

Nevertheless, Cunard's audacity had paid off: the British and North American Royal Mail Steam Packet Company was up and running. Understandably, from the beginning 'it was known more simply as Cunard's line or the Cunard Line'.

For a while, as he ate up his competitors at the same pace as his ships traversed the Atlantic, it looked as if the Cunard Line would have the transatlantic route to itself. There was an extremely delicate period when Cunard – having ploughed his personal fortune into the project – was forced to beg and borrow to pay off his debts, selling property and calling in favours. But eventually 'the Cunard Line steamed towards solvency on its unmatched reputation for safety and order'. Indeed, reports Fox, 'for the first 75 years of the line's history no passenger in its North Atlantic traffic ever died from a shipwreck', while its rival lines – as you'll see – notched up several tragic accidents. It looked as though the Cunard luck, which had begun with a cache of treasure in a field, was set to hold.

Lines across the Atlantic

Cunard could not expect to rule the seas forever, of course, and competitors emerged. The first of these was the Collins Line, founded in 1850 by Edward Knight Collins, who had already established a reputation in the United States with his Dramatic Line packet service. The American was another of the travel industry's showmen, 'with an intuitive flair for public relations'. He treated the press to 'lavish food and drinks when celebrating ship launchings and maiden voyages', and they obligingly wrote up his exploits.

His relationship with the *New York Herald* newspaper under its swashbuckling owner James Gordon Bennett sums up his approach. Finding that the *Herald* did not give his business sufficient coverage, Collins dramatically increased the number of advertisements he placed in the paper – and coverage duly improved. By the time Collins was setting up his own steamship line, 'he had the biggest, least inhibited American paper in his corner'.

The new Collins Line ships upped the ante in almost every respect. Even their names sounded epic: the *Atlantic*, the *Arctic*, the *Pacific* and the *Baltic*. Luxury was back in fashion; their saloons sparkled with 'table tops of Italian marble, gleaming inlaid wood panelling, ornate mirrors and bronze work... plush Brussels carpets'. There was a barber shop and a clutch of bridal suites. Cabins were steam-heated. 'The Americans had rethought the whole concept of a transatlantic steamship, pushing it ahead by giant bounds in size, power, luxury and sophistication'. Once again, the cost of the exercise was underpinned by funding from the government, which had awarded Collins a bi-weekly mail contract.

The Collins Lines ships proved swift and serious competitors to the Cunard vessels. However, they gobbled coal at a ferocious rate and their sheer speed meant that their wooden hulls required frequent repairs. By January 1852, Collins was forced to go cap in hand to Congress and ask them to double their subsidy to US$858,000 a year. His backers grudgingly agreed, with the proviso that they could halve funding with only six months' notice if the Collins Line was seen to underperform.

In September 1854, in fog-shrouded waters off Newfoundland, the *Arctic* smacked into a smaller ship, the French SS *Vesta*, which plunged its bow like a narwhale's horn into the *Arctic*'s wooden hull. The *Arctic*'s captain shook her free by reversing her engines, but now she had a gaping hole below the waterline. In the knowledge that the *Arctic*'s lifeboats could only take about 40 per cent of the passengers aboard, he made a dash for land. But his speed only accelerated the rate at which water gushed into the ship. The *Arctic* sank 15 miles from shore. The wreck killed 350 passengers – including Collins' wife and two of his children, who had been travelling to join him.

Just over a year later, on 23 January 1856, the *Pacific* steamed out of Liverpool – and was never seen again. Stephen Fox reports that the mystery was not solved until a full 135 years later, when divers found her bow section 'about 12 miles north-west of the island of Anglesey'. Clearly, her journey had hardly begun when disaster struck – possibly a boiler explosion, although the details remain obscure.

The Collins Line did not survive these twin catastrophes. Its fifth ship, the *Adriatic*, was launched in April 1856, but had barely completed her sea trials when Congress notified Collins that it planned to reduce its funding. The *Adriatic* made only a single voyage before the Collins Line was wound up, 'in a puddle of tragedy, unpaid debts and ill feelings'.

The key difference between liners and cruise ships is that many of the people who crossed the Atlantic then were not doing so for leisure – they were on business, or they were visiting family, and there was simply no alternative. For some, it was a matter of life or death. The dirty open secret of the transatlantic lines was that much of their profit did not come from wealthy customers in luxurious staterooms, but from emigrants packed like sardines below decks.

The Inman Line typified this approach. William Inman – a businessman from a solid Lancashire merchant family – had been intrigued by the *Great Britain* and the potential of iron-hulled, screw-propelled ships. A propeller took up far less space than a paddle wheel, allowing for more cargo, and an iron hull meant fewer repairs. Inman was a partner in a packet ship line owned by Richardson Brothers, led by John Grubb Richardson. The Richardsons were Irish Quakers from Belfast. In 1850, Inman persuaded them to buy a new screw-propelled ship, the *City of Glasgow*. She was joined the following year by the *City of Manchester*.

The Richardsons had been following the plight of the Irish during the Great Famine (1845–52), when an aggressive potato fungus destroyed not only the livelihoods of those who grew the crop, but led to mass starvation, disease and death among a dependent population. Millions fled the country, with the United States their most common destination. Like refugees today, many fell victim to 'brokers and runners' – the equivalent of people traffickers – who sold them places on leaky old-fashioned sailing packets. For weeks on end they slept on planks, were unable to bathe and fell victim to cholera and typhus. The womenfolk were preyed upon by the crew. Many of these 'coffin ships' never reached safe harbour.

The Inman Line – under the impetus of John Grubb Richardson – began to make room for emigrants in 'steerage' on its liners. The trip took only two weeks, it cost little more than a place on the sailing packets, and although they were crammed into rows of bunks, the passengers stood a far greater chance of surviving the ordeal. Fox writes that emigrants were 'good business for Inman too', as the 300 steerage passengers on each ship 'ate the cheapest food obtainable... and did not expect – or receive – the constant attention of the stewards scurrying among the first- and second-class cabins on the upper decks'. Inman tellingly referred to them as 'the safest cargo'.

Sam Cunard, protective of his line's reputation for safety, was initially wary of taking on emigrants, maintaining that there would never be enough lifeboat space for hundreds of passengers in steerage. But when Cunard's new screw-propelled ship, the *China*, took to sea in 1862, she had space for no less than 770 emigrants – showing that Cunard was prepared to steal an idea or two from Inman.

Cunard's other great competitor was the White Star Line. The original White Star vessels were sailing ships transporting British prospectors to the Australian gold rush in the mid-1840s. But when the company later diversified into the transatlantic route, it over-invested in steamships, found itself unable to repay its debts, and quickly went bust. Enter Thomas Ismay, a shipbuilder from Cumberland, who snapped up the White Star name and flag for just a thousand pounds. The new line came into shape during a game of billiards at the home of a Liverpool merchant named Gustav Christian Schwabe. Ismay had been invited to the soirée along with Schwabe's nephew, Gustav Wilhelm Wolff. As they played, Schwabe proposed a simple deal: he would fund the White Star Line if Ismay awarded the shipbuilding contract to his nephew's company, Harland & Wolff, located in Belfast.

The White Star Line rose to prominence with some of the most impressive ships ever built, 'of revolutionary designs that made them more comfortable and luxurious than anything else on the ocean,' according to Stephen Fox. These included the *Oceanic*, which when it launched in 1870 was 'the first modern ocean liner', slender yet tall, with a promenade deck on the roof, cabins double the size of any others at sea, and taps with running water. White Star also built the ill-fated *Titanic*, part of its bid to compete with Cunard on size and grandeur rather than speed. Is there anybody who does not know that she was the largest ship afloat at the time, and that she sank on her maiden voyage? Rather than going into detail here, I refer you to the piles of books on the subject, not to mention James Cameron's Oscar-laden film from 1997.

But White Star had survived tragedy long before the sinking of the *Titanic* in 1912; in March 1873 the steamship *Atlantic*, running low on coal after traversing a storm, diverted to Nova Scotia rather than continuing to New York, and ran aground off Cape Prospect. Holed and taking on water, the ship sank first at the stern, and then rolled mightily onto her starboard side, spilling passengers into the sea. Others drowned below decks; most of those who made it into lifeboats or onto a nearby rock perished from cold. At the final count it was estimated that some 585 people died in the wreck.

The fact that White Star survived this disaster would suggest that transatlantic passengers had begun to view shipwrecks much in the same way that we see air crashes today: isolated incidents that make headlines but, with any luck, only happen to other people.

As for Cunard, the line's luck finally ran out in 1915, when the *Lusitania* – a lavishly modern vessel, carrying 1,257 passengers – was hit by a German submarine torpedo off the coast of Ireland. Eighteen minutes after impact, the *Lusitania* was at the bottom of the sea; the death toll was 1,201. For Stephen Fox, the sinking of the *Lusitania* was more significant than the *Titanic* disaster, which was 'an especially horrific accident'. But the *Lusitania* 'was sunk on purpose, with evil intent, as an act of war'. For more on the tragedy and the intrigue that surrounds it, I highly recommend Erik Larson's excellent (2015) book *Dead Wake: The last crossing of the Lusitania*.

Cunard retained some of its pride with the *Mauretania*, 'the greatest steamship ever built', unsurpassed, writes Fox, in 'technical innovation, speed, beauty and longevity'. When she was finally retired in 1934, she had steamed through 27 years and 2.1 million miles.

In the end, it was not so much luck that counted against Cunard as technology and the economy. At the beginning of the 1930s the Great Depression began to bite, along with competition from new entrants from Germany, Italy and France. With both Cunard and White Star struggling, the pair merged in 1934. After operating for a brief period as Cunard White Star, the company reverted to its Cunard Line brand name in 1950.

By then, of course, it was far more convenient to cross the Atlantic by plane. The great transatlantic liners were steaming against the tide.

From crossings to cruises

Joel Shahar was cruise sales manager aboard the *Queen Elizabeth 2* between 1999 and 2003, completing three world cruises. Now an academic and lecturer on the tourism business, Shahar still has fond memories of travelling on 'such an iconic ship'. The *QE2* was the last British-built liner, and perhaps symbolizes more effectively than any other vessel the shift in emphasis from crossings to cruises.

Shahar's job was to sell another cruise to people who were already on board. Their resistance was, understandably, low. 'Easiest job I've ever done,' he chuckles.

Even in Shahar's day, a voyage on the *QE2* retained a vestige of golden-era glamour. 'Dressing up for dinner two or three times a week was still an important part of a Cunard Line cruise. Bear in mind that there was no crime on board; you were in a very cosseted environment. Women could and did wear furs and diamonds.'

There was even a class system, of sorts. Passengers staying in the most expensive cabins dined in the Queen's Grill; those staying in the grade below had to 'make do' with the Princess Grill.

The *QE2* embarked on her maiden voyage from Southampton to New York in May 1969. To an extent she was a compromise: her larger predecessors, the *Queen Mary* and the first *Queen Elizabeth*, were both anachronistic and costly. To maintain its heritage and continue providing a transatlantic service ('Some people can't or simply won't fly,' observes Joel Shahar), Cunard spent US$80 million on a smaller, nimbler ship that would replace the two more cumbersome vessels. Even so, she weighed in at just over 70,300 tons and could carry 1,777 passengers.

The *QE2* was able to combine the best of both worlds: over the course of a year, her typical itinerary might include 30 transatlantic crossings, a world cruise lasting about 80 days, numerous shorter cruises out of Southampton and New York, and even several 'party' cruises (www.QE2.org.uk). Joel Shahar says: 'It's a myth that cruises attract only the "blue rinse" brigade. Obviously the world cruises skewed older because it's quite difficult for most younger people to step out of their lives for three months. But transatlantic crossings attracted a far wider variety of passengers – and generally speaking, today there are as many different types of cruises as there are people.'

The *QE2* stopped traversing the Atlantic in 2004 – replaced by the *Queen Mary 2*, which still plies that route – to become a full-time cruise ship. She was retired three years later, a stately reminder of the past amid the modern world of hi-tech floating skyscrapers. As I write she lives on, parked in a Dubai dock after being acquired by a United Arab Emirates conglomerate, her fate undetermined.

The Cunard Line brand still has a splash of old-world British charm. Nevertheless, since 1998 it has been owned by the Carnival Corporation, one of the twin behemoths of the cruise industry along with Royal Caribbean.

These have their spirits anchored far away from the rain-washed UK shores, in Miami, where the cruise business really got started in the early fifties.

The true pioneer of the cruise industry was a guy called Frank Fraser, who until that point had made a living running dusty freighters between Miami and the Caribbean – even during the war, when his small tubs were considered a waste of a good torpedo. As Kristoffer A Garin notes in his rollicking (2005) history of the cruise lines, *Devils on the Deep Blue Sea*, Fraser's family had been doing this for generations: back in the day they owned plantations in Jamaica and would export bananas and citrus fruit to the States on their own ships.

Fraser's wartime daring earned him the respect of the Dominican Republic dictator General Rafael Trujillo, who after the conflict rewarded him with a cheap charter deal on the *Nuevo Dominicano*, a passenger vessel actually owned by the Dominican government. It was as if a king had offered him a castle at a knock-down rent and invited him to turn it into a hotel. Frank Fraser didn't need asking twice, and suddenly he was in the cruise business.

Fraser had intuited that the context of the battle for the high seas had changed entirely. '[I]nstead of selling the prospect of less time at sea, he'd be selling a *better* time – more sunshine for the money, in other words.' In 1954, Fraser bought two 30-year-old steamships, had them refitted and equipped with air conditioning, and sent them out on cruises to Nassau, Haiti, Jamaica and South America. The ships departed port to 'band music, blasts of their whistle and confetti and streamers filling the air, just like any grand liner taking leave of New York'. Stranded onlookers no doubt promised themselves they would be aboard next time.

Fraser succumbed to a heart condition in 1962 – but in less than a decade, spurred by his success and that of his imitators, the city of Miami's authorities had come to understand that the nascent cruise industry would play an important role in its future. By 1966 they had established a sparkling new port infrastructure on an artificial island named Dodge Island (apparently named after some friends of the director of the City of Miami's planning board). The very fact that confidence remained high after a terrible tragedy only the previous year – in which an elderly cruise ship called the *Yarmouth Castle*, once owned by Frank Fraser, caught fire and sank, killing 91 passengers – was testament to the industry's growing power.

Carnival and Caribbean

Ted Arison, the founder of Carnival Cruise Lines, a man whose name is indelibly associated with the staggering transformation of the cruise business in the 1970s, almost didn't make it in the industry.

Arison was born in Tel Aviv in 1924, in what was then the British Mandate of Palestine. He cut his teeth in the cargo shipping business and moved to New York in the early 1950s as 'a manager for El Al's cargo operation', according to Garin. Later he co-founded an air freight enterprise, turning his first few million when his partner bought him out. Subject to a non-competition clause for four years, he began looking for new opportunities.

Inspiration came in the form of an Israeli cruise ship called the *Nili*, which he saw at port in Nassau while investigating another business entirely – refrigerated shipping. Through a connection, he was even able to take a tour of the ship. It seems to have been love at first sight. When Arison learned that *Nili* was coming onto the market, he chartered her, also taking on her sister vessel into the bargain. Then he set up shop in Miami and began selling tickets. But the deal went sour just as rapidly: it transpired that the *Nili*'s owner was close to bankruptcy and the ship was soon seized by the Israeli authorities. The second ship slipped out of Haifa anyway – only to collide with another vessel in the harbour of Naples, remaining afloat but severely damaged. Result: Arison had an embryonic cruise business – and no ships.

As you've surmised, he wasn't about to give up. His next gamble was to reach out to a Norwegian shipping heir named Knut Kloster, who had an intriguing problem. Kloster had diversified into the passenger business from the oil shipping sector. He had a brand new car ferry called the *Sunward*, on which he had hoped to transport British travellers from Southampton to Gibraltar, where they would begin motoring holidays across Spain. But in an outburst of political posturing in the summer of 1966, Spanish dictator General Francisco Franco closed the border between Gibraltar – which was, of course, a remnant of the British Empire – and the Spanish mainland. The *Sunward* was stuck in Southampton.

Arison's call to Knut Kloster went something like this: 'I've got passengers – and you've got a ship.'

The *Sunward* set sail, so to speak, for Miami – and what became Norwegian Caribbean Lines. Once again, however, the story didn't end happily: Kloster and Arison fell out, and Arison left the business amid a bitter legal wrangle over the company's finances. (The company they started together went on to become the highly successful Norwegian Cruise Line, which pioneered many innovations now familiar to the industry, such as an informal dress code that finally shrugged off the legacy of the liners.)

The last roll of the dice, however, proved to be the definitive one. Arison had acquired another ship, a former Canadian liner called *The Empress of Canada*, 'a dilapidated old tub he'd found in Greece,' as Garin's description would have it. Arison renamed her the *Mardi Gras*, made her the flagship of the new Carnival Cruise Lines, and sent her out from Miami in 1972 on a tide of optimism. Unfortunately the tide wasn't high enough – the *Mardi Gras* ran aground almost immediately, within shouting distance of Miami Beach.

Once again, Arison gritted his teeth and forged on. As tugboats worked to haul the ship off the sandbar, passengers worked on the open bar. In the spirit of the times, an enterprising barman improvised a compelling form of crisis management: he mixed a new cocktail called Mardi Gras on the Rocks. The tugboats remedied the situation, and having been assured his vessel was undamaged, Arison decided to continue the cruise to Puerto Rico, as advertised.

When the *Mardi Gras* finally returned to Miami, Arison set about slowly refurbishing and updating her. As his obituary in *The New York Times* reported years later (quoting the 1997 book *Selling the Sea*, by Bob Dickinson and Andy Vladimir), this cost him dear, because Carnival was not even close to profitable; in fact, 'the company lost millions of dollars as the *Mardi Gras* sailed on a sea of red ink'. ('Ted Arison, Carnival Founder, Dies At 75', 2 October 1999.)

By then, though, Arison had set upon the formula that would save him – and underpin the future of the cruise industry. As the article cited above summarized, he began to market 'the array of activities and entertainment available on board, rather than its destination. The strategy eventually caught on, so that by 1975 Carnival was making a profit'.

Carnival's big rival was Royal Caribbean, founded in 1969 and, on the face of it, another Norwegian affair; a joint venture between the shipping companies IM Skaugen, Anders Wilhelmsen and Gotaas Larsen. But in reality Royal Caribbean was born out of the vision of an old Miami hand, Edwin W Stephan, who had worked in the hotel trade before stints at the Yarmouth Steam Company – owner of the ill-starred *Yarmouth Castle* – and the Commodore Cruise Line.

An article that appeared at the time of his retirement summed up the story rather well. 'Stephan journeyed to Oslo, Norway, in 1968 with a dream that would become Royal Caribbean. He had an idea for a ship designed especially for pleasure cruises in the balmy Caribbean. In Oslo, he enlisted the support of three Norwegian ship owners, and Royal Caribbean Cruise Line A/S was born January 31, 1969.' ('Royal Caribbean founder Edwin W. Stephan retires from board after 35 years with company', *PR Newswire*, 12 May 2003.)

Ed Stephan's dream was of a ship that had nothing in common with the liners: it would be built *specifically* for cruising. Comparatively light and economical, it would also have a sleek hull that would enable it to dock directly at its island destinations, rather than lurking out to sea. Safety and accommodations would be top notch, although the cabins would be smaller than usual, allowing Stephan not only to carry more passengers, but also to get them out and about spending money in his bars and gift shops. 'He set up a two-room office in a stucco building at 853 Biscayne Boulevard as work began in Finland on the 724-passenger *Song of Norway*, the largest vessel ever built in Scandinavia.'

One of the peculiarities of Stephan's design was that he had envisaged a lounge bar attached to the soaring funnel, which he felt would give his ship as distinctive a profile as the Space Needle in Seattle. Marine architects were sceptical, but in the end 'the Viking Crown Lounge became a distinctive feature on all Royal Caribbean ships'. Shortly after *Song of Norway* arrived in Miami, Royal Caribbean ran its first print advertisement, featuring the saucer-shaped bar gripping the funnel. 'Sail a Skyscraper,' read the copy.

Royal Caribbean scored design firsts throughout Stephan's career. '*Sovereign of the Seas*, for example, in 1988, was the first ship with a soaring, five-deck atrium,' noted *PR Newswire*.

That came later – but for now, in the early 1970s, Royal Caribbean was setting standards that Ted Arison's Carnival couldn't hope to match. Typically, Arison wasn't going to let that stop him. *The Mardi Gras* may not have been a floating hi-tech entertainment factory like *Song of Norway*, but she was still bigger than any other cruise ship in Miami and had a robust, buccaneering charm about her. Arison took that character and played on it, turning her into a party ship for the man and woman on the street. As Garin puts it, Arison brought 'belly flop contests and beer pong to the high seas', selling cruises to customers 'who thought they would never be able to afford one'.

At that stage, neither Stephan nor Arison could afford to spend much on conventional advertising. Their billboards, by and large, were the ships themselves – which were usually absent from the harbour. Travel agents could wax lyrical about the cruise experience, but beyond word of mouth, first-time passengers who were expected to pay up front for a cruise could never be sure what they would get for their money.

Then, in 1977, along came a little TV show called *The Love Boat*. TV producers Douglas S Cramer and Aaron Spelling – the popular culture genius behind hit shows like *Charlie's Angels* and *Fantasy Island* – adapted the idea from a book by Jeraldine Saunders (the J is not a typo) called *The Love Boats*, which captured romantic entanglements and other shenanigans aboard cruise ships. The pair turned it into a romantic comedy, more or less, with a syrupy theme song, a regular cast of eccentric crew members and a weekly list of even loopier passengers, all embarking on honeymoons, affairs, breakups, reconciliations, second honeymoons or vaguely larcenous schemes.

It was sugar-injected bilge and the audience loved it. What's more, it sold them the idea of taking a cruise. The show featured a ship called the *Sun Princess*, part of the real-life Princess Cruises, founded in 1965 by Stanley B McDonald – an entrepreneur who'd got into the business by chartering a ship to take visitors to the 1962 World's Fair in Seattle. Now he'd been granted the ultimate product placement. ('Princess Cruises and "The Love Boat" Connection,' www.princess.com.)

But the series buoyed up the entire industry. Kristoffer A Garin writes: 'The more than US$100 million it earned for its producers paled next to the untold billions it indirectly generated for the entrepreneurs in Miami and elsewhere who, by the time the show went off the air ten years later, would be well on their way to becoming genuine robber barons of the high seas.'

Princess was part of P&O, the storied Peninsular & Oriental Steam Navigation Company, created in the 19th century to take mail, freight and passengers from London to the Iberian Peninsula (Spain and Portugal). Its history took many turns, and it diversified into a variety of sectors – long before the Channel Tunnel, P&O ferries transported millions of travellers between England and France – before spinning off its cruise business as P&O Princess Cruises in 2000.

By then, Carnival was a leviathan, its single plucky yet battered vessel long in the past. It had gone public on the New York Stock Exchange in 1987 and embarked on an acquisition spree, snapping up Holland America, Costa and – of course – Cunard, among others, earning it the nickname 'Carnivore'. Soon Carnival set its sights on P&O Princess. But there was a snag: P&O had already agreed to a merger with Carnival's old nemesis, Royal Caribbean. Carnival waded in with its own offer which, after a bidding war that dragged on for a year, P&O deemed 'financially superior'. ('Carnival on course for P&O victory', *The Daily Telegraph*, 22 October 2002.)

The battle for the high seas was as good as over. Carnival, now under the leadership of Ted Arison's son, Micky, controlled half the cruise sector – with Royal Caribbean a distant second. Today, that relationship persists and Norwegian Cruise Line is the third largest player. The original Miami buccaneers have become the navy.

Looking back, Ed Stephan and Ted Arison represented two of the elements required for outstanding business success: the ability to imagine the future and build it in the face of scepticism; and the determination to never, ever give up. A little luck helps too – but if you're no longer around when it comes along, well, you've missed *The Love Boat*.

Targeting today's cruise crowd

Carnival and Royal Caribbean embrace numerous brands covering the entire spectrum of the cruise market. As we've already established, cruises are by no means just for retirees: there are family cruises, party cruises, theme cruises and eco-cruises.

It can be difficult to justify taking a cruise if you're in any way politically correct, however. From the start the industry has been accused of unethical practices: dodging local laws and taxes, by registering ships under 'flags of convenience' at ports far from the United States; labour abuses, by underpaying and overworking staff; and pollution, by dumping oily bilge water at sea.

An article by Nicola Hill on the ethical travel website Tourism Concern expressed the opinion that 'the lucrative industry hides a host of human rights abuses alongside exploitative practices and an appalling environmental record'. It added that while international maritime law was 'robust', individual countries were responsible for holding cruise lines accountable. 'Unfortunately, it has proven near impossible for states to enforce domestic and international laws on cruise lines when they are in international waters.' ('Floating Abominations: Exposing the Cruise Ship Industry,' www.tourism-concern.com, 27 March 2015.)

The cruise giants may be headquartered in Miami, but they are incorporated elsewhere: Panama, Bermuda and even Liberia.

Still, the industry regularly maintains that it is making efforts to stick to and even improve on regulations – and the customers keep coming. One former cruise industry marketing executive told me that repeat business is high. 'Customers tend be extremely loyal,' she said. 'They'll book the same cabin on the same ship every year, and since they know the crew they feel part of a family. The number of cruises they've taken becomes a source of pride.'

Repeat customers are offered discounts and perks. Meanwhile, first-time passengers are seduced by extras like welcome cocktails or free shore excursions. The attractions of a cruise are obvious, she added. 'It's a really easy way to see the world. You sail at night, and when you wake up you're in a different location. All the stress of travelling is taken away from you. Plus it's a way of testing future destinations – you can go to Bali for a day and just get a flavour of it.'

Meanwhile there are the many diversions of a floating city: cinemas, theatres, casinos, restaurants – a cocooned fantasyland that's not so far removed from *The Love Boat*, only far bigger.

Finding an advertising budget is no problem for the cruise lines these days. One standout campaign was for Royal Caribbean, by the US agency

Mullen Lowe. Aimed at younger customers, its tagline was 'Come Seek', and it focused on the attributes of Caribbean destinations – the wildlife, the people, the beaches – in colour-saturated rapid-cut montages that resembled social media posts rather than conventional advertising. 'You are not a tourist,' the subtitles suggested. 'This is not the Caribbean. This is The Royal Caribbean.'

Carnival went a step further towards attracting ethical young travellers by creating a brand just for them: Fathom. The idea here was 'social impact travel': voyages to the Dominican Republic and – in an industry first – Cuba, where travellers could volunteer to work with locals on worthwhile projects such as tree planting, assisting in English classes and making ceramic water filters. On the way, they were given Spanish lessons and shown films about the local culture. Not that the passengers had to eschew the fun stuff like snorkelling and windsurfing; after all, they were paying upwards of US$1,500 per person. ('Take A Deep Dive Into Fathom, Carnival's New Cruise Line For Volunteers', *Fast Company*, 14 September 2015.)

Inevitably there were cries of opportunism and 'Greenwashing', but the launch of Fathom showed that the cruise industry, massive and consolidated though it was, could still innovate.

Tour highlights

- For over 100 years, the main selling proposition of the liners was that they could get from A to B as quickly as possible.
- Later liners competed on luxury and sophistication; ironically they made most of their profit from 'steerage' passengers.
- With the dawn of the jet age liners fell out of fashion, aside from a few holdouts like Cunard's *QE2*; like other liners, she was soon repurposed to 'cruise' to multiple destinations.
- A small group of entrepreneurs in Miami realized that they could sell the experience of cruising – the on-board activities, the bars, the restaurants – as a swinging 24-hour party.
- By the end of the 1990s the Miami pioneers – led by Carnival and Caribbean – had swollen into giant concerns.
- The somewhat sceptical attitude of younger consumers has led cruise lines to refocus their sales pitch on exploration – and even on the possibility of having a positive social impact.

The airline pioneers

07

'Flying was not just a way of reaching a destination.'

New Year's Day 1914, St Petersburg, Florida. A chilly morning with light, variable winds. Nevertheless, even before 9am, a crowd of 3,000 people had gathered on the town's waterfront. Many of them could not see the object of their excitement – although it would soon be soaring high above them. It was a Benoist XIV flying boat, currently sitting at the top of a greased ramp with its nose pointed at the water. In less than an hour's time, it would take to the skies to inaugurate the world's first scheduled commercial airline.

There was another attraction that morning too. It was certainly not Percival E Fansler, the businessman who had made the airline possible. Nor was it Abe Pheil, the town's former mayor, who had bid US$400 to be the airline's first passenger. After giving a short speech, Fansler introduced the true hero of the hour: the flying boat's pilot, Tony Jannus.

Having already made headlines with his aviation exploits – such as flying 250 miles along the Mississippi River from Paducah to St Louis, competing in 'aerial derbies' and surviving a crash in which his plane caught fire – Jannus cut a dashing figure. This morning he was smartly attired 'in white duck pants, a dark jacket and his usual bow tie', according to the (1997) book *Jannus: An American flier*, by Thomas Reilly. In fact, apart from his 'black leather gloves nearly to the elbow and a visored cap', he looked as though he was dressed 'for a night on the town, not a 21-mile flight in an open cockpit'.

Greeted tumultuously by the crowd, Jannus promised that he would do his utmost to make the airline a success, while always keeping 'the maxim "safety first" foremost in my mind'. Bright-eyed and smiling, Jannus did not look nervous. As Reilly points out, he had no reason to be. 'Other than the historical significance attached to the first flight, there was nothing to differentiate it from any other. Jannus had flown almost daily since his first flight… in November 1910.'

His passenger, Abe Pheil, might have had more reason for trepidation. The plane itself did not inspire confidence. Made of wood and muslin, it was 'powered by a noisy, 6-cylinder, 75-horsepower engine… with its pilot and one passenger sitting on a small wooden bench, exposed to the elements'. ('First Airline Offered No Frills, Many Thrills', *The Wall Street Journal*, 1 January 2014.)

Still, it was too late to turn back now. Jannus stepped up to the ramp and proceeded to hand crank the plane's engine. The events that followed were reported by Gay Blair White (cited in Robert Bluffield's 2009 book *Imperial Airways: The birth of the British airline industry, 1914–1940*). 'The old Roberts [engine] wheezed, coughed, fired once and died. Tony Jannus inserted the crank again. It was a cold New Year's morning, but he was warming up to the job. Once more he pulled down hard on the crank and this time the old two-cycle burst into life with a bellow of smoke from the stacks.'

When Jannus was in the cockpit and the engine had 'smoothed to a loud purr', Abe Pheil clambered aboard. 'Both waved to the excited crowd as the airboat slid into the water.'

For now the plane was little more than a motor launch, chugging toward the west of the harbour. Then Jannus 'turned the boat into the wind and opened up the throttle'. Throwing out fans of water, the lumbering apparatus 'picked up speed and skipped twice, floated into the air as she came to the mouth of the harbour'.

Cheers rang out. Percival Fansler checked his watch. 'It was exactly 10am; the world's first airline was on its way.'

Precisely 23 minutes later, Jannus had crossed Tampa Bay and landed his craft within sight of the Tampa Electric Company. The St Petersburg–Tampa Airboat Line (Fast Passenger and Express Service) was open for business.

Dashing pilots, daring passengers

Technically speaking, it was not the first commercial airline at all. The company established by Count Ferdinand von Zeppelin in Germany to exploit his airships had carried almost 20,000 passengers on 881 flights between March 1912 and November 1913 (although many of these, writes Bluffield, 'were pleasure trips and short joy rides'). Nevertheless, the Tampa Bay service was certainly the first to run scheduled flights in a fixed-wing, heavier-than-air craft.

The airline had come about when Percival Elliot Fansler, the Florida sales representative of a firm that made marine diesel engines, became intrigued by the exploits of Jannus and the possibilities of air travel in general. A frequent traveller, Fansler had noted that the 20-mile trip across Tampa Bay took a torpid two hours by steamship. A flight, he reckoned, would slash that time by at least half. Sensing an opportunity, Fansler wrote to Tom Benoist, the inventor of the 'floatplane' and the technical genius behind Jannus's airborne adventures. Benoist was enthusiastic – his new XIV aircraft was ideally suited to the task.

Officials in Tampa were less welcoming – expressing reservations about the safety of 'heavier-than-air' flying, they also worried that a fast service to St Petersburg would take tourists and trade away from their own city. Undaunted, Fansler took the idea to St Petersburg itself. Leading figures there quickly saw the potential of the project. It was embraced from the start by Mayor Lew Brown – who also happened to be the proprietor of the biggest local newspaper – and real estate developer Noel E Mitchell. Nicknamed 'The Sandman' for his ability to make dreams come true, Mitchell agreed to underwrite the new airline for US$1,000. Writes Reilly: 'Successful or not, the airboat line would generate publicity for St Petersburg, as well as his own real estate business.' Once Mitchell gave the project his blessing, the rest of the business community came on board.

The steamboat lines did not feel particularly threatened: at five dollars a trip, the airline would be a 'premium' service, aimed at the well-heeled traveller who was willing to pay more in order to save time. And presumably for the thrill, too – although communications around the project had a double discourse. While it played on the celebrity of the pilot, Jannus, it also reassured potential customers of the safety of the service. Cuttings from the *St Petersburg Daily Times*, cited by Reilly, described Jannus as 'one of the most careful aviators in the world', while the Benoist Airboat, among safety features such as 'three thicknesses of spruce', had an engine that was placed 'down in the hull of the boat, behind and below the operator', thus lowering the centre of gravity and making it 'in case of a tumble, much less dangerous'.

'Careful' or not, Jannus was clearly a draw. It's astonishing to note how little the pilot – that aristocrat of the air – features in airline communications today. Even the miracle of flight is largely taken for granted: we're more concerned about legroom. One exception was a commercial for Delta Airlines in 2015. Narrated by Donald Sutherland in a gravelly whisper, it showed only a tyre-scarred runway rushing beneath an aircraft on take-off. 'What is happening here is not normal,' it began, 'it's extraordinary. 291 people, 350 tons, 186 miles an hour… you are a test pilot, breaking through where others broke.' The ad reclaimed some of the drama of flying, but most travellers probably prefer to think of their plane as a very tall bus. Abe Pheil, that first passenger, showed real backbone. And Jannus was a genuine test pilot.

At first, the airline soared. It made 172 scheduled flights and a number of chartered trips. When the city's subsidy ran out, the service shut down – temporarily, hoped Benoist, who was drawing up plans for a flying boat that could carry up to 12 passengers. His ambitions were thwarted by the First World War.

The war also took the life of Tony Jannus – whose Curtiss plane plunged into the Black Sea in 1916 while he was training Russian pilots. Tom Benoist died in a freak accident a year later: he stepped off a moving trolley car directly into a telegraph pole.

But their project had an undeniable legacy, as *The Wall Street Journal* piece observes, giving rise to imitators 'including an airline flying between the Los Angeles area and Catalina Island, off the Pacific coast, and a company that flew between New York and Atlantic City, NJ, in 1919, using war-surplus flying boats. Soon, another airline linked Florida and the Caribbean…'.

One airline that was to have an indelible impact on commercial aviation – and our romanticized view of its past – took to the air in 1924: Imperial Airways, in Great Britain. Its mission was to connect the furthest corners of the British Empire.

Discussions about the potential of using aircraft to link the British Isles to the wider world were held at the highest levels even before the end of the First World War. In 1917, a panel of experts convened by the government included HG Wells, the science fiction writer, which provides some idea of how futuristic passenger flight still seemed.

Inevitably, the Royal Air Force ran a clutch of irregular mail and non-military – largely diplomatic – services from 1918. The government finally opened the way for private companies to provide 'civilian flying services' in 1919. One notable pioneer was Aircraft Transport and Travel (AT&T), created by newspaper proprietor and aviation fanatic George Holt Thomas in August that year. Using planes built by his own company, Airco, it ran regular mail and passenger flights to Paris. But the costs involved – petrol, oil, maintenance, the pilot's pay – meant that all of the aircraft's eight seats had to be filled on each flight if the company was to break even. That was rarely the case, and AT&T ceased operations in December 1922.

Other, more successful airlines followed: Handley Page Transport, founded by Sir Frederick Handley Page, whose aircraft company had expanded into a major concern during the war on the strength of its ability to build large planes – in other words, bombers. These were ideal for conversion into passenger use, and were soon serving Paris, Brussels and Amsterdam. Instone Air Line, established by the shipping magnate Sir Samuel Instone, ran services to Paris and Cologne. Daimler Airway, part of the BSA group (originally Birmingham Small Arms), bought the assets of the failed AT&T and began operating services to Amsterdam, Hanover and Berlin. And finally, British Marine Air Navigation, a flying boat service, was founded as a joint venture between Supermarine – which built the planes – and Southern Railway, which at that time owned Southampton docks.

All of these competed for the same tiny pool of potential customers, often on the same routes. It was obvious that not all of them could stay aloft. Finally, in 1923, the government announced a plan to merge them into a single – and hopefully profitable – state-supported airline. After a lengthy skirmish with the pilots, whose pay and conditions widely differed, Imperial Airways lurched into life on 26 April 1924, when Captain HS Robertson flew a DH34 from Croydon to Paris (Le Bourget).

By then, the former RAF airfield at Croydon had evolved into London's main aerodrome, as it offered easy access to the south coast – where the majority of flights were headed. Initially, writes Robert Bluffield, it had 'no control tower and wartime huts... had to be converted to use as makeshift offices and for the Customs shed'.

Fortunately, a hotel company with a sharp eye on the future, Trust House, 'spotted the potential of the old canteen on the site and quickly applied to convert this into a hotel... [Its] bar soon became a jovial and cosy meeting point for Europe's most flamboyant fliers'.

Marketing gets off the ground

Compared to today's sanitized flying experience, the rollicking heyday of Imperial Airways can take on the hue of a golden era. Its fleet included the C-Class Empire flying boats, built by Short Brothers, among the most charismatic aircraft ever to take to the skies. In just over a decade, its network extended to the Middle East, Africa, India and Australia. But, as you can no doubt imagine, air travel between the wars was far from comfortable.

Imperial's planes were so primitive that they were unable to fly at night, so they were forced to land at sundown. Occasionally they lost their way – more than one landed in the desert. As the aircraft could fly no higher than 3,000 feet, the cabins were not pressurized. Passengers were told they could wear normal clothes, but were advised to don an extra layer *if they opened the window*. Pilots flying over the African bush occasionally diverted so their passengers could watch wild animals stampeding below. The plane's racket scared the game almost as much as it rattled the eardrums of its passengers.

Few of these people would have been tourists in the modern sense. They were colonial officials, bureaucrats, engineers and entrepreneurs, geographers, journalists, geologists and archaeologists. Occasionally they were big game hunters, who recouped the cost of their trips by selling skins and tusks when they returned. But the sheer length of the journey and the number of stopovers turned all of them into what historian Gordon Pirie refers to as 'incidental tourists'. He writes: 'High fares deterred leisure travel by air, but air passengers flying long-distance errands incidentally became tourists by virtue of the slow, low-altitude daylight flights that stopped frequently for refuelling.' ('Incidental Tourism: British Imperial Air Travel in the 1930s', *Journal of Tourism History*, 19 March 2009.)

An overnight stop in, say, Cairo, automatically became a sightseeing opportunity. Pirie adds: 'Airline publicity, documentary films and passenger accounts and diaries, stressed this in-flight and en route experience: flying was a new way of seeing and experiencing foreign and historic places... Flying was not just a way of reaching a destination.'

Some early travellers were less than impressed. According to Robert Bluffield, one passenger – a racing driver named SF Edge – wrote to Imperial in 1925 pointing out that he had been the sole passenger on his flight to Paris, and one of three on the way back. He put this down to inadequate publicity, 'the level of smartness at Croydon' and the flying experience itself. His seat, fitted into metal slots in the floor, 'disengaged from its moorings' when he leaned back. No explanation was provided by the crew for the stomach-churning steep climb on take-off, the banking turns or the frankly alarming phenomenon of turbulence. 'Edge's diatribe added that all passengers should be issued with ear plugs to counter the terrible noise from the engines.'

Imperial was certainly aware of the problems of its ageing fleet and the gap between first-time passengers' expectations and reality. Plus, it had competitors. These included KLM (*Koninklijke Luchtvaart Maatschappij*, or Royal Dutch Airlines in English), today the oldest operational airline still bearing its original name. Headed by another dashing young aviator, Albert Plesman, with the backing of Queen Wilhelmina, KLM had begun flying from Croydon to Amsterdam in 1920. Rather like Imperial, it was destined to connect the Netherlands to its overseas territories – by 1924 it was running services to Java in the Dutch East Indies. Its network also covered Rotterdam, Brussels, Paris, Bremen, Copenhagen and Malmö, and later a transatlantic service to Curaçao, a Dutch colony in the Caribbean.

With KLM edging onto – or over – its turf, Imperial needed to buff up its image. In association with an advertising agency, Charles F Higham, the company embarked on an ambitious promotional campaign, which included placements in 'London daily and weekly newspapers... an English language

Parisian newspaper and some European publications'. In addition, the company's impressive stand at the 1925 Wembley Exhibition – which glorified the achievements of the British Empire – featured a Vickers Vulcan and a 10-seat Bristol Biplane aircraft 'alongside a model of a lighthouse and a replica of the Croydon Airport control tower'. Leaflets 'extolling the wonders of air travel' were handed out to some of the 300,000 visitors to the event.

In what feels like a very modern innovation – branded content *avant l'heure* – Imperial also commissioned a magazine called *Airways*. Although the publication wasn't entirely about the company, Imperial agreed to pay £100 per month for the first six months to help it through the launch period. In return, it got two advertising pages per issue, plus 4,000 copies to distribute to customers on its mailing list. More copies were handed out free of charge at Croydon Airport. Under the contract, negotiated by its ad agency, Imperial could veto competitive advertising and negative commentary and, to cap it all, would receive 15 per cent of the magazine's profits.

Its planes may have been somewhat primitive, but Imperial's public image was sophisticated. Bluffield writes: 'Much of the literature was tastefully designed, with excellent graphics in the Art Deco style of the period. The artist Theyre Lee-Elliott, who had also designed posters for London Transport, created many original designs for Imperial Airways, including the famous "Speedbird" logo in 1931.'

Destined initially for luggage labels, this became a company-wide branding device, appearing on aircraft themselves from 1939. It survived the transformation of Imperial into BOAC and finally British Airways, before being retired in 1984. But an echo of it lives on – in the form of the international radio call sign for British Airways.

Tour highlights

- The early airlines played on the heroic aura surrounding pilots, although they were at pains to stress the safety of their machines. The high cost of flying gave it a status appeal.

- Most passengers on the early airlines were 'incidental' tourists, flying on business or governmental missions, but forced stopovers encouraged them to visit the sights. Flying was thus marketed as enlightening and educational.

- Threatened by competitors, the UK's Imperial Airlines was one of the first to invest heavily in branding, advertising, promotional events and even its own customer magazine.

Pan Am: from seaplanes to the jet age

08

'Mass travel by air may prove to be more significant to world destiny than the atom bomb.'

Juan Trippe, the founder of Pan Am, had no Latin blood. He was a Yale-educated Irish–American named after his mother's half-sister, Juanita, daughter of the Venezuelan sugar baron Juan Terry. When he was a kid, Juan hated his first name. But as an airline entrepreneur, he would have had to admit that his exotic moniker – combined with the prophetic 'Trippe' – was wildly appropriate. In common with all great brand builders, he understood the importance of perception.

As his airline took shape, Trippe could often be seen smoking his pipe before the 5-foot tall globe in his office on the 58th floor of the Chrysler Building, plotting his next move. According to the (2013) book *Pan Am: Aviation legend*, by Barnaby Conrad III, 'he saw oceans and continents not as barriers but as playing fields. His goal was complete domination of the air.'

Trippe's ambition propelled Pan Am to lofty heights – and when he was gone, it began its slow decline. In the meantime, though, he had transformed air travel and launched the jet age.

In his younger days, his background set him firmly on course for a place in the world of finance – after all, his father was a prominent investment banker. But an incident in Juan's childhood planted a seed in his mind, perhaps akin to those twin-bladed sycamore seeds that twirl through the autumn air. A keen observer of the early flying machines – he once built a balsawood model powered by a rubber band – he was thrilled when his father took him to watch aviators Wilbur Wright and Glenn Curtis race their planes around the Statue of Liberty in September 1909. From that moment on, there was only one thing he wanted to do.

While still studying at Yale, he enlisted in the Marine Corps as a flying cadet. His poor eyesight should have disqualified him, but the legend goes that he got hold of a copy of the test and memorized the bottom line. He completed his first solo flight in a Curtiss 'Jenny' in Long Island in 1918. Now part of the US Naval Reserve, he was almost sent to fight in France – but Armistice was declared before he could step aboard the ship.

After Yale, as Barnaby Conrad III reports, Juan 'dutifully went to Wall Street as a bond salesman'. Not surprisingly, the job didn't take. Since his father had recently passed away, he perhaps felt less obliged to follow a conventional path. Instead, he bought a handful of ex-navy training aircraft and launched an air taxi service called Long Island Airways.

At some point during this period, the barnstorming stunt featured in the introduction took place. As I suggested before, it may well have been a PR exercise. But while it got Trippe noticed, it didn't enable his first company to survive for very long. Trippe's other pilots were also barnstormers and stuntmen, unreliable characters who 'didn't show up on time or, after a night on the town, didn't show up at all'.

But Juan was not ready to let go of his boyhood dream just yet. Pulling together his network of contacts from Yale and Wall Street (including William Rockefeller, Sherman Fairchild and William Vanderbilt), he convinced them to invest in what became the Aviation Corporation of America (AVCO).

So where was AVCO going to fly? Trippe had heard that the US Postal Service wanted to establish a new route between Key West and Havana – a 90-mile flight – and that the contract was up for grabs. The two other contenders were Florida Airways and Pan American Airways, smallish outfits established by veteran wartime pilots. Slyly, Trippe slipped behind their backs to negotiate an exclusive contract with the Cuban dictator, Gerald Machado, which effectively barred any other airline from landing on Cuban soil. It was an example not only of his ruthlessness, but his force of personality.

Florida and Pan American metaphorically threw up their hands in defeat. Trippe took them over and the new Pan American – *his* Pan American – was born. One of the elements that set the seal on the nascent airline's success was Trippe's choice of what these days would be referred to as a brand ambassador: Charles Lindbergh.

Fresh from his pioneering nonstop solo flight from Long Island, New York to Le Bourget, just outside Paris, 26-year-old 'Lucky Lindy' was a true aviation hero. Although Lindbergh was besieged by offers from potential employers and sponsors, Trippe characteristically barged them aside by inviting the passionate aviator not only to inspect his Caribbean outfit, but to actually fly one of his brand-new Pan American Fokker aircraft. In the words of Barnaby Cohen III 'these two practical dreamers clicked'.

The props on the Fokker had barely stopped turning when Trippe offered his new friend 'a retainer of US$10,000 a year and an option to purchase one-tenth of Pan American Airways' shares at half the present value'. On paper hired as a 'technical adviser', Trippe knew that Lindbergh's 'real value would be in terms of public relations'. Cohen also points out that Lindbergh's new bride, Anne Morrow, was the daughter of the US Ambassador to Mexico.

With Lindbergh at his side, Trippe negotiated with 16 different governments to set up a network that soon connected the US with the Caribbean and South America. Of the latter, Cohen writes: '[Trippe] believed it was the United States' right – and its duty – to bring progress to the continent through a "peaceful conquest". He found a fellow believer in US Postmaster General Walter Folger Brown, serving in Herbert Hoover's administration.'

The US Postal Service – backed by the government – and Pan Am effectively formed a public–private partnership that would create a merchant marine of the air whose routes criss-crossed the globe. Ironically, the airline's eventual dominance of the skies sowed the seeds of its later destruction. But let's not get ahead of ourselves. First, in order to take ownership of the air, Trippe took advantage of the sea.

'The Caribbean basin had one thing going for it: water everywhere,' writes Cohen. 'Why build airstrips when planes could land on water?' Flying boats were a crucial part of the airline's strategy and soon became central to its image.

Trippe's seaplanes were made by Sikorsky Aero Engineering Corporation, founded by the brilliant Russian émigré and aeronautics engineer Count Igor Sikorsky. The planes both confirmed and enhanced Pan Am's merchant marine positioning. With an eye on perception, as usual, Trippe ensured that the company:

> … incorporated maritime custom and lore into every aspect of service. The pilot was a Captain assisted by a First Officer. The speed of a plane was calculated in knots, or nautical miles; time was given in bells; and a crew's tour of duty was referred to as a watch. The kitchen was called the galley and the bathroom the head. The highest rank an early Pan Am pilot could achieve included a rather magnificent title, Master of Ocean Flying Boats.

When clippers ruled the skies

Writing a book like this one often involves sitting in hushed libraries or waiting for parcels containing long out-of-print titles to show up. One particular morning an Amazon parcel arrived in the mail. When I picked it up I heard the distinctive rattle of a DVD.

The movie inside was *China Clipper*. Made in 1936, it stars Pat O'Brien and Humphrey Bogart. The film is named after a massive Pan Am flying boat and was made with the tacit encouragement of Juan Trippe himself. His PR man, William Van Dusen, handled the negotiations with Warner Brothers. Although the names are changed, the film essentially tells the story of Pan American Airways ('Trans-Ocean Airways'), starring Pat O'Brien as the Juan Trippe character ('Dave Logan') and Humphrey Bogart as his best pilot. O'Brien gives a performance of solid teak – Bogart's is rather better. To his credit, Trippe allowed himself to be portrayed on the screen as driven and autocratic. At one point, half of Logan's staff threaten to walk out on him over low wages and high pressure.

But at the end of the film, his biggest financial backer tells him: 'Because of your vision and determination, we have achieved the greatest advance in transportation that the world has ever known.'

That advance – and the fulcrum of the film's story – was the first commercial flight across the Pacific.

It actually began on 22 November 1935. A crowd of 25,000 gathered on the shore at Alameda, California – across the bay from San Francisco – to watch the huge flying boat that Trippe had christened 'China Clipper' set off on what he had been assured was an impossible journey. Crossing the Pacific entailed a treacherous 2,400-mile nonstop flight from San Francisco to Honolulu, before island-hopping down to Manila for another 8,000 miles. The route would later be extended to Hong Kong.

The plane was a Martin M-130, weighing 25.5 tons and driven by four 800-horsepower engines which delivered a cruising speed of 130 miles per hour. It was piloted that day by Ed Musick, although empty of passengers. The crowds, the press corps and the brass band were not just window dressing – this was a momentous occasion, the equivalent of a moon landing.

It also had a political subtext. As Cohen notes: '[N]o other airline could advance America's presence in the Pacific as ably as Pan Am… The Japanese were steadily building up a military presence in Micronesia and other island chains, making it imperative that America improve contact with other Asian nations, particularly China and the Philippines, which were increasingly threatened by the Japanese juggernaut.'

US Postmaster James A Farley was present at the launch of the China Clipper; with its maiden voyage, Juan Trippe was to cement his position as one of the most powerful and influential men in the United States.

In the end, the take-off was far more dramatic than its cinematic counterpart. As the great plane lumbered across the bay, Musick realized that he wouldn't be able to get enough lift to clear the Bay Bridge. Skimming the water, with ice-cold expertise he flew the giant aircraft *under* the bridge, before lofting it into the air to no doubt rapturous applause.

On 29 November Musick landed the China Clipper in Manila Bay, having flown 8,210 miles in 59 hours and 48 minutes, not including stopovers for fuel and refreshments.

Years later, another airman, Captain Dick Vinal, reminisced about co-piloting the China Clipper with Musick. '[The plane] cured me of the smoking habit. With the fuel tanks in the hull, we could never keep the cabin free of gas fumes.' And since pilots could be in the air for 25 hours at a stretch, it was important to resist the urge to light up. Vinal also recalled the time they flew through a typhoon on the way to Manila. 'Cruising at 105 knots in a 160-knot wind, you can go backwards and sideways. We did. The M-130 may not have been fast, but we proved she was really rugged.' (Audio recording on www.panam.org, 'Dick Vinal's China Clipper'.)

By 1939, Trippe had all the planes he needed to service the Pacific and Atlantic routes: he'd paid US$3 million to Boeing for six Model 314 aircraft, hefty beasts with 106-foot fuselages which could comfortably carry 70 passengers. Their dining lounges alone could seat 14 passengers at a time, served by stewards in immaculately starched white jackets and black trousers.

Inevitably, all this aerial flamboyance was curtailed by the Second World War.

The heights before the depths

Pan Am pilots made a number of daring supply runs at the beginning of the war, notably delivering anti-tank shells to the British Eighth Army in Egypt in 1942, during the Battle of El Alamein. But in December that year the army effectively took control of Pan Am: 'The age of elegance ended for the Clippers as they were drafted into various branches of the armed services... Pan Am crews had military status and now wore khaki while under army command and green when flying for the navy.'

Although the term 'clipper' recurred throughout Pan Am's history, the flying boats never regained their pre-war status: Cohen reports that by 1945 the iconic China Clipper was plying a 'backwater' route between Miami and Léopoldville in the Belgian Congo.

But Trippe hadn't finished innovating – not in any sense – and bounced back quickly once the war was over. After first replacing the clippers with more prosaic twin-engine DC-3 aircraft (which used conventional runways), in 1947 Pan Am unveiled its first Lockheed Constellation, which thanks to its pressurized cabin could fly at 20,000 feet and cross the Atlantic in 10 hours. By then, Cohen notes, Pan Am had grown in just 20 years 'from two planes and twenty-four employees to a global network of 19,000 employees stationed in sixty-two countries'.

The airline followed up the Constellation in 1949 with the Stratocruiser, a spacious redesign of a B-29 bomber. Now it delivered a different kind of payload, particularly if you made your way down the spiral staircase to the on-board cocktail lounge. In common with more traditional luxury brands, Pan Am played on its heritage in order to reassure customers and set itself above rivals: its new slogan in 1950 positioned it as 'The World's Most Experienced Airline'.

Flying was still accessible only to a minority. As Keira Desbiens points out on the Passion Marketing site (www.passion-marketing.com): 'In the 50s, the US economy boomed. While the upwardly mobile couldn't afford Pan Am's luxurious "President" service, they still wanted to fly. To expand its market, Pan Am invented the tourist class in 1952.' However, adds Desbiens, 'the limitations of propeller planes kept prices high and the market small', with a return ticket costing the equivalent of almost US$4,000 today. ('Pan Am, How to create and market a myth', 17 October 2011.)

Air stewardesses – controversially from today's perspective – became the living embodiments of refinement and smooth service. Originally, they were a product of necessity: with most young men drafted for the war effort, Pan Am needed flight attendants. But these women were not merely decorative: the majority were college-educated and were required to speak at least one foreign language. They were expected to be sociable, cool-headed in an emergency and – not surprisingly – strong swimmers.

'It was one of the best jobs a woman could get back then,' former Pan Am stewardess Christel Vane, who worked for the airline from 1959 until 1984, told a British journalist. 'I spoke languages and I wanted to travel; it was a very exclusive job and difficult to get. There was nothing else open for women, unless you wanted to be a secretary.' ('Being a Pan Am stewardess was the best job for a woman', *The Daily Telegraph*, 5 March 2013.)

There was certainly no question of a woman becoming a commercial pilot in the 1960s. Over 500 women applied for the job Christel eventually got, and she took full advantage of it, revelling in the status her position afforded while travelling the world. She admits there was sexism – mostly from arrogant or condescending passengers – but rose above it with humour and self-confidence. 'I was never the aggressive type; it was up to me to take control of the situation.'

Although the feminist movement of the 1970s might have prompted her to question her career choice, it was not a suggestion of inequality that spoiled the job for Christel, but the flying experience itself. Planes grew bigger, faster and more crowded; in-flight entertainment systems cut passengers off from crew. 'Suddenly things became a little less glamorous; the human aspect of being able to communicate with people got lost.'

Nevertheless, the cliché of the glamorous yet level-headed stewardess persists, an all-too-frequent image in ads for airlines ranging from Singapore Airlines to Qatar Airways (at the time of writing, a print ad for Qatar shows a little girl bestowing an admiring gaze on a stewardess). While 'The Singapore Girl' has been smiling from posters since the 1970s, Pan Am was arguably the first to represent the flight attendant as an icon.

But if stewardesses appeared to represent an aspirational, elitist approach to flying, Trippe was actually interested in changing the world via mass travel. 'By 1957... the number of air travellers had quadrupled to a million' since the late 1940s, notes Cohen, 'a trend for which Pan Am could take considerable credit.'

Addressing the 1955 meeting of the International Air Transport Association, Trippe said: 'Mass travel by air may prove to be more significant to world destiny than the atom bomb. For there can be no atom bomb potentially more powerful than the air tourist, charged with curiosity, enthusiasm and goodwill, who can roam the four corners of the world, meeting in friendship and understanding the people of other nations and races.'

We'll return to that theory later in the book. Meanwhile, in 1958, Pan Am literally left its rivals standing by taking delivery of 48 jets and launching the first jet-powered flight from New York to Paris. While the trip had taken 25 hours by flying boat, it now took just 7. Trippe's dream of accessible air travel was about to become a reality. Writes Cohen: 'During the first three months of 1959 the Pan Am 707s carried 33,400 passengers, racking up a 90.8 per cent seat occupancy'. To handle the huge volume of reservations, in 1962 Pan Am created PANAMAC, one of the first global airline reservation management systems (see Chapter 13, Lastminute and other dot-coms).

Launching the jet age required an entirely new marketing approach, as Desbiens reports. 'Pan Am's image had to embody what it was: the world's airline, an ambassador for the jet age and American achievement.' It also needed to embody the aspirations of its new clients, 'a younger clientèle that saw itself as rich, but weren't yet'. The vaguely 'country club' trappings of the flying boat era were outmoded. Pan Am set out to make itself 'more dynamic by closely associating its corporate identity to its audacious planes'.

Enter the airline's new consultant designer, architect Edward Larabee Barnes, and his partner Charles Foburg, along with their colleague Ivan Chermayeff. The trio worked together to redesign the airline's logotype and symbol. 'They replaced the existing symbol, a stylized wing and globe motif, with a simplified blue globe overlaid with parabolic lines: a symbol of the drive and ambition that continued to define Pan American's pioneering spirit.' ('From Pan Am to the Pompidou', *Creative Review*, 5 May 2011.)

Chermayeff returned in 1970, now as one half of the agency Chermayeff & Geismar, to continue his work. The first step was to officially change the airline's name from 'Pan American World Airways' to its short form version: Pan Am. This resulted in a sleek, minimalistic approach that suggested up-to-the-minute sophistication. 'A refreshed globe and a new logotype set in Helvetica Medium promoted a cleaner, more modern tone, with the airline's signature colour palette of royal blue still firmly in place,' adds the article cited above. 'Pan Am retained the iconic blue globe until its demise in 1991.'

Its *demise*. Now we get to the crux of the matter. How did this highly successful company, a brand that remains iconic even today, vanish from existence?

The answer is simple – yet complex.

The simple part lay with Juan Trippe himself, who stepped down as CEO in 1968. Far earlier in Pan Am's history, back in the cash-starved late 1930s, the airline's board had tried to edge Trippe out of daily operations and into a more backseat role, forcing him to relinquish the title of CEO while remaining president. It didn't work. After the company's largest shareholder, Sonny Vanderbilt Whitney, largely failed as CEO, the board voted Trippe back into the post. 'The board [had] learned that the secrets to making Pan Am a success were filed deep in Juan Trippe's complicated mind...'.

More than 30 years later, this was apparently still the case. Just before he retired, Trippe had achieved one last miracle: he was the driving force behind the creation of the Boeing 747, the 'jumbo jet', the jet age equivalent of the majestic clipper ships. As 'long as a football field' and 'as high as a three-storey building', with 350 seats and, once again, a cocktail lounge. The investment could have crippled Pan Am; instead, it was a soaring success.

Trippe left a solid, seemingly impregnable company, symbolized by the iconic Pan Am building (now the Met Life building) at 200 Park Avenue and East 45th Street, completed in 1963. All around the world, when passengers stepped from hot and chaotic airports into the air-conditioned calm of their Pan Am jet, they were greeted by a crisply attired stewardess and the words: 'Welcome to Pan Am. You're halfway home already.'

Secretly, however, Trippe was already aware of Pan Am's great weakness, which lay in domestic US routes. Cohen writes: 'For decades, US presidents and their advisers had denied Pan Am domestic routes for fear of creating a monopoly.'

Trippe chose as his successor Najeeb Halaby, a former head of the Federal Aviation Administration – and incidentally an ex-test pilot – who supposedly had links with Washington. These were not strong enough, however, and the block on domestic routes persisted. As the recession of the early 1970s roiled the economy, Pan Am's fortunes began to flag. The board asked for Halaby's resignation.

He was replaced by a 'steely eyed' former US Air Force Brigadier General named William T Seawell, who proceeded to rein in the company by slashing staff (from 42,000 to 27,000) and cutting routes. Pan Am staggered from near bankruptcy back into profit, but the government insisted on limiting its supposed dominance by awarding domestic routes to other airlines – some of them from overseas. Worse, it allowed domestic airlines (such as Delta and National) to operate foreign routes, giving Pan Am further competition.

The visionaries who had built the aviation industry were disappearing. In 1974, Charles Lindbergh slipped away, dying at his home in Maui.

Juan Trippe himself suffered a stroke in September 1980. He died at his home in Manhattan on 3 April 1981. There were enough people at the great man's funeral to fill a jumbo jet.

Pan Am's last flight

Pan Am ceased operations on 4 December 1991. That morning, Captain Mark Pyle was the pilot of the Pan Am 747 known as Clipper Goodwill. For the time being, he was unaware of the bad news.

'The approach along the western coast of Barbados is surreal,' wrote Pyle, in the June 1992 issue of *Air Line Pilot*:

> The island is truly a multi-coloured jewel set in a background of turquoise sea. We landed to the east, as the trade winds nearly always dictate, touching down 4 hours 30 minutes after our departure from New York. We taxied to the gate and shut down our engines as we had done hundreds of times before. This time there would be a difference, a notable difference! In the four and a half hours of our flight, tragic history had been made.

Pyle was still in the cockpit when the station manager opened the door and handed him a sheet of teletype paper. Pyle, who had worked at the company for 18 years, quickly read it. Then he walked back through the cabin to tell the crew. 'None of our flight attendants could restrain their emotions, or their tears. All were at least 20-year veterans with Pan American or National Airlines.'

The station manager asked Pyle if he wanted to complete the final leg of the flight, to Miami. Pyle said he did: 'Many passengers were stranded, and some Pan Am employees were packing to leave their stations and their jobs.' The pilot and his crew waited for almost two hours 'in mostly silent thought' while the remaining passengers checked in and employees gathered their belongings.

Slowly, the last passengers filed aboard. At 2pm EST, Pyle reports, 'the wheels came up on Clipper 436 hailing from Bridgetown, Barbados, and bound for the city of Pan Am's birth'.

Not far from their destination, Pyle was surprised when his engineer – 20-year Pan Am veteran Chuck Foreman – told him that air traffic control wanted them to make a low pass over the field. After initially expressing disbelief, Pyle grasped the symbolism. 'With the passengers briefed carefully as to our intentions, I called for flaps 15… We now executed the requested low pass – my first since I left the navy many years ago.'

As Pyle's aircraft roared low down the centreline of Runway 12, the tower issued a final statement: 'Outstanding, Clipper!' Pyle pulled up and turned downwind for final approach and landing.

When his 747 touched down, Pyle saw that the fringes of the taxiway were lined with cop cars, fire trucks, outside broadcast vans and TV crews. As he rolled the plane to a halt at the gate, the Pan Am ground crew stood to attention. 'We approached the gate and set the brakes… We shut down systems for the last time and secured the faithful engines. Sadly gathering our belongings, we shook hands. Our final flight was over. No eyes in the cockpit were dry.'

The last of the Pan Am clippers had landed.

Juan Trippe had built Pan Am with a mixture of vision, guile, arrogance and political manipulation. Once he had gone, the company seemed to lack purpose; it was a kingdom without a king. Can it really be a coincidence that the brand vanished from the radar just over 10 years after his death?

Strategic errors, changing times and bad luck all played their parts. In 1980, Seawell decided to solve the domestic route problem by buying National Airlines for US$374 million. But there were huge clashes of culture and service, and Pan Am was forced to plough cash into advertising to convince passengers that it could still provide the smooth, comfortable flights they were used to. Now Pan Am was losing a million dollars a day, according to Cohen.

Seawell sold the Pan Am building to Met Life for US$400 million. Then he sold off the airline's hotel chain, InterContinental, to the British group Grand Metropolitan for a further US$500 million. Scenting panic, the board ousted him.

C Edward Acker was next in the pilot's seat, a 'smooth-talking' Texan who had run the airlines Braniff and Air Florida. Forcing employees to take pay cuts, he was faced with a strike in 1985. Then he took a huge bite out of Trippe's legacy by selling 18 planes and all of its routes to Asia and Australia for US$750 million. It was far more than they were worth, but the move was symbolic: 'Acker had sold out Pan Am's fabled heritage as the pioneer of the Pacific'.

Pan Am was left to compete with its ambitious rivals on the domestic and Atlantic routes. But far worse than that, the age of airline terrorism had begun.

The airline's image was only dented by the 1986 ground hijacking of a Pan Am 747 in Karachi. But on 23 December 1988, at 7.03pm, a Libyan terrorist's bomb ripped apart Pan Am Flight 103, the 747 clipper Maiden of the Skies, above Lockerbie, Scotland. The 243 passengers and 16 crew on board died instantly; 11 more people on the ground were killed by the rain of wreckage.

As Cohen puts it: 'The bombing stunned the world and panicked American travellers. Americans began flying "neutral" airlines such as Air France and Swiss Air.'

By now, Acker had gone the way of his predecessors and the board had replaced him with Pan Am's latest and last boss: Tom Plaskett, a laptop-toting Harvard MBA. But even if Plaskett applied modern thinking and an acute grasp of the numbers game to Pan Am, it was already too late. When his attempt to buy Northwest Airlines and strengthen domestic routes failed, he saw the writing on the wall. Pan Am routes were quickly sold off to United Airlines and Lufthansa. On 12 August 1991, its remaining assets were sold to Delta Airlines for US$416 million. On that fateful 4 December, the offices of Pan Am opened for business 'and then quickly closed'. Delta had decided not to keep the brand on life support.

Oddly enough, though, the Pan Am brand has proved unexpectedly resilient. In fact, the airline has become a modern myth, inspiring fantasies of the early jet age – like the ABC TV series *Pan Am* (2011–12), which focused on the lives of stewardesses in the high-flying 60s.

The power of the Pan Am logo lives on in the form of Pan Am Brands, a company based in Dover, New Hampshire, which acquired the brand in 1998. The firm sells vintage memorabilia acquired from the airline, as well as replica branded bags, key rings, cufflinks and other accessories, through its website http://panambrands.com and selected stores.

For those interested in the history of the airline, the Pan Am Historical Foundation has a richly detailed website (www.panam.org, cited earlier) full of images, anecdotes, taped interviews and videos.

Pan Am is the Orient Express of airlines – a name evoking a more civilized and sophisticated era. The next time you step aboard a 747, spare a thought for Juan Trippe, the king of the clippers.

Tour highlights

- Juan Trippe used emerging air mail routes and a tacit public–private partnership with the US government to create an unrivalled global network of passenger services.

- An instinctive manipulator of image, Trippe hired aviation hero Charles Lindbergh as his brand ambassador.

- Trippe called his flying boats 'clippers' after the old trade ships and adopted nautical language – crew, captain, knots, galley – to make the innovative planes seem both reassuring and adventurous.

- Pan Am turned the dearth of available young men during the war years to its advantage, recruiting female flight attendants and remoulding them into the iconic figure of the 'air stewardess'.

- As the inaugurator of the jet age, Pan Am marketed itself as being at the nexus of technology, design and culture.

- With determination and personal magnetism, Trippe forced through the innovations that made the brand great. But he failed to pass this pioneering spirit on to his successors.

- Pan Am's logo and mythology are so evocative that the brand lives on in the form of accessories, books and pop cultural products.

Business or pleasure?

'The trick in packing a box is to pack a full box.'

There's a story about Conrad Hilton, possibly apocryphal, that everybody loves. Hilton is on *The Tonight Show*, being interviewed by Johnny Carson. In true journalistic style, Carson is pushing his guest for a great exit line. So he asks Hilton if he has a message for the American people. Hilton glowers into the camera and says: 'Please, put the shower curtain *inside* the bathtub.'

Having read Hilton's (1957) autobiography, *Be My Guest*, I'm not entirely sure he was joking. 'Connie' was capable of having fun – he professes a lifelong love of dancing, and he had an eye for the ladies – but he took his business seriously. His impact on the hospitality industry certainly can't be treated lightly. We've talked about grand hotels – those flamboyant palaces for the rich and aspirant – but at the heart of the travel trade are chains of comfortable, well-managed, rather uniform hotels serving frequent-flying business people and middle-class travellers.

Although it's one of the best-known brands in the business, Hilton is not the largest hotel chain. That honour goes to Marriott, which after its merger with Starwood in early 2016 could boast 1.1 million rooms, 5,500 hotel properties and 30 distinct brands. The deal bumped Hilton down to second place in the global room number ranking, with 735,788 rooms, followed by the InterContinental Hotels Group (701,146), Wyndham Worldwide (667,095) and Choice Hotels (506,062). (STR Global figures quoted in 'Marriott makes a return trip for Starwood', *Financial Times*, 16 November 2015.)

In terms of their approach to serving customers, Conrad Hilton and J Willard Marriott Sr had a lot in common.

Hilton was born in San Antonio, New Mexico (not to be confused with its more famous Texan counterpart). His sonorous first name gives him a certain gravitas, but according to his autobiography he was known as 'Connie from the start'. His father was a colourful character: Augustus Halvorsen Hilton, known to one and all as 'Gus', a Norwegian immigrant who'd come to the Wild West to be a 'trafficker and trader'. This was the real deal, with stage-coaches and lawlessness. Gus was once caught up in an Apache raid; another time, he faced off an armed drunk in a saloon. Gus was a hearty, optimistic, back-slapping fellow with a surfeit of determination.

'[A] backbone of the frontier,' his son wrote, many years later. 'Gus had courage and initiative… he sought out opportunities. Instead of waiting for business to come to his store he went out into the wilderness country, along the Gila and Mimbres rivers, in the wilds of the Black Range; bought or traded for beaver pelts and deerskins… then turned them into money when he shipped them to St Louis.'

This trade evolved into a thriving general store, the Hilton Mercantile Company, but it's clear that Gus preferred being on the move to serving behind the counter. Is it any wonder that his son became a lynchpin of the escape industry?

His mother was a very different character, but equally influential. Mary Genevieve was a staunch Catholic. 'Probably the most exciting regular event in our lives was Sunday church,' Hilton wrote. She insisted on the power of prayer, a lesson he integrated and never forgot.

In his early 20s, Conrad flirted with politics, becoming a Republican representative in the New Mexico Legislature. Meanwhile, the fortunes of the Hiltons fluctuated. Briefly rich, they later sank so low that they were forced to turn the family home into an inn; an early iteration of a Hilton hotel. Disheartened by the corruption and self-interest at the heart of the political world, Connie decided that he preferred working at the general store. At the same time, he yearned to get out from under his father's shadow. His solution was to start a bank – quite an innovation in a place where, as he put it, 'a teapot or a buried chest or an old-fashioned safe had proven a reliable repository for years'.

He got on his horse and literally went door-to-door seeking stockholders: rich local widows, ranchers, trappers. Finally, in September 1913, The New Mexico State Bank of San Antonio opened for business. Connie's first customers were so unused to the idea of a bank that he had to explain the concept of borrowing to them. The upside was that, 'once they got the idea they were scrupulous about their payments'.

When the US entered the First World War, he sold the bank for a tidy sum and enlisted in the American Expeditionary Force, where he seems to have passed an unremarkable time, shifted from Paris to the Vosges mountains and back again. The most significant incident of that period was the death of his father in an automobile accident. A pioneer to the end, Gus had been one of the first people in the area to own a car.

Back from the war, Conrad Hilton decided to cut his ties with the past and 'seek his own frontier'. He focused on Texas: 'Where there's oil there's activity... banking.'

Casting about for a suitable spot, he happened upon Cisco: a 'cowtown gone crazy' with oil wealth, it possessed no fewer than four banks. One of them was for sale, for US$75,000. Hilton wired the owner in Kansas City 'that I was prepared to buy at his price'. The owner wired back: 'Price up to $80,000 and quit the haggling.' Infuriated, Hilton sent off another wire: the owner could keep his bank.

Now he was stuck in Cisco and badly needed a place to sleep. Which is how he happened on the Mobley Hotel, where the owner none too politely informed him that all of its 40 rooms were full. 'Come back in eight hours when we turn this lot loose,' the man added, referring to the current guests. These words snapped Conrad Hilton alert. Here was a boom town with a hotel so popular that it was getting a full turnover of guests three times within 24 hours. 'They'd pay to sleep on the tables in the restaurant if I let 'em,' the owner added.

Following the thread of the conversation, Hilton learned that the hotel's owner – Mr Mobley himself – was both greedy and bitter. He'd sunk 'every nickel' into what he described as a 'glorified boarding house', while he dreamed of going into the oil business and getting rich quick. Hilton asked if he could take a look at the books. 'Three hours later... I thought a man would be crazy to want oil. If [the books] told the story, this had banking beat all hollow.'

He went back to the owner and made an offer. Although he did not run it under his name, the Mobley became the first Hilton hotel, acquired after a little haggling for US$40,000.

Hilton's folly

Hilton now dreamed of a chain of hotels across Texas – and he pursued that dream assiduously, either leasing 'dowager' hotels and refurbishing them, or building from scratch on leased land. Each potential hotel was a love affair, he wrote: 'Romance blossomed the minute I could see through a frowsy façade to potential glamour – the ability to make money.' The first hotel he built from the ground up – and the first to carry the Hilton brand name – was the Dallas Hilton, an innovative 14-storey high-rise establishment.

Anybody walking into the lobby of the hotel would experience something of a retail assault: it contained a drugstore, a men's outfitters, a beauty store, a barber, a café, a news-stand and a telegraph office. These spaces had been rented out to bring additional income to the hotel, while also providing the extra services Hilton believed his guests deserved.

Maximizing space was one of the two key lessons he learned at his very first hotel, the Mobley.

He wrote that the idea came to him in a dream. First he heard an echo of 'old man Mobley', saying: 'They'd pay to sleep on the tables if I let 'em.' Next he saw the ghost of his father, Gus, teaching him how to pack freight as tight as possible. The next morning, he rose with a crackle of energy and a radical new plan for the hotel.

He closed the dining room and transformed it into extra bedrooms. He cut the desk in the lobby in half and removed a dusty potted palm. This left him with enough space for a news- and tobacco stand, as well as a novelty shop 'which we rented immediately'. Within weeks, the hotel's accounts showed that he was on to a good thing.

'The trick in packing a box is to pack a full box,' he wrote. 'This had nothing to do with crushing or crowding, only the intelligent use of what is available.'

The second lesson, not unexpectedly, was about service. Or rather, how to encourage staff to provide it. Hilton decided that the key was *esprit de corps*: 'Wages won't do the whole job,' he insisted, remembering something he'd observed in the Army. You had to convince your men that they were part of the best outfit in the entire military, and that 'they were the ones who made it that way'.

Summoning his staff, Hilton told them that the future of the hotel was in their hands. 'You're the only ones who can give smiling service. Clean rooms, spotless halls, plenty of fresh soap and linen. Ninety per cent of the Mobley's reputation is in your hands. You get steady jobs, good money, pay rises, if Cisco means the Mobley to travellers.'

Conrad Hilton married three times – including a short-lived and costly marriage to the actress Zsa Zsa Gábor – and charmed many others; but the love of his business life was the Waldorf Astoria Hotel. In the depths of the Great Depression, with his company fading and bankers taking control of his affairs, he clipped a picture of the new hotel out of the newspaper to reassure himself that he could still dream.

He bought a controlling stake in the hotel in 1949. In the meantime, he'd fought his way back from near bankruptcy. The Depression had almost crushed him: 'People weren't travelling. Salesmen weren't selling.' Occupancy fell off a cliff. To keep his hotels going he was forced to borrow from a wealthy Galveston-based family, the Moodys. They owned – among other things – a bank, an insurance company and a newspaper. Pretty soon they owned Conrad Hilton too. Fortunately, they also owned a struggling hotel company. Instead of taking control of Hilton's chain entirely, they proposed a merger. He would be one-third owner and acting general manager of the new entity. From this base, slowly but surely, Hilton regained control of his business.

The economy started moving again – and so did people. Hilton now had eight hotels and he wanted more. He bought the Stevens Hotel in Chicago – all 2,673 rooms of it. Then he set his sights on the Waldorf Astoria. He realized that this was an impractical ambition: opened just before the Depression, the hotel was still struggling to fill its rooms. But the new hotel and its older namesake – demolished to make way for the Empire State Building – had the allure of myth.

Hilton wrote: 'It was the All-American dream of the Waldorf's first manager, George Boldt, to make his hotel a social centre as well as a superior lodging – a luxury clubhouse, an integral part of his city's life and history.' Even so, he admitted, the original hotel had been known as 'Boldt's folly'. The newer establishment also bore the fingerprints of history. Its guests had already included Winston Churchill, Pandit Nehru and Pope Pius XII. 'This, then, was the hotel I wanted... It made history. It made news. It made everything but money.'

Hilton struggled to convince his investors that the hotel was a good bet – and in the end they failed to resist its charisma. Conrad Hilton's company finally acquired 249,024 shares of stock in the Waldorf Corporation at US$12 a share, which gave him control. On 12 October 1949 he became, in his own words, 'The Man Who Bought the Waldorf'.

Even at the Waldorf Astoria, Hilton made maximum use of space: having discovered that the towering columns in the hotel's lobby were 'phonies, decorator's items, completely hollow and contributing nothing to the support of the building', he had glass display cases installed in them; pretty soon 'discriminating perfumers and jewellers fought for the privilege of displaying their wares there'. His investors had been right to trust him.

The Hilton Hotels Corporation gained full ownership of the Waldorf Astoria in 1972. Conrad Hilton died seven years later, at the highly respectable age of 91. As the brand's website states, his name had come to be 'synonymous with hotels across the globe'. So much so that travellers can still jump in a taxi and utter the slogan that he coined: 'Take me to the Hilton.'

JW Marriott – a people person

A devout Mormon, John Willard Marriott Sr also believed in the power of prayer. And he was a stickler for service who was well aware of the need to implicate his employees in his mission. When his son JW 'Bill' Marriott Jnr wrote a book about the company in 2012 – *Without Reservations* – he stated: 'Dad felt very strongly that the concerns and the problems of the people who worked for him were always worth listening to. In his eyes, a successful company puts its employees first.'

The company still refers to its employees as 'associates' as a mark of respect.

Like Hilton, JW Marriott came from a rural background: he grew up on the family farm in Utah. But the seed of the hotel chain was planted in Washington DC, many miles away. In 1921, Marriott was passing through the city on his way back from a mission for the Mormon Church in New England. He noticed how hot and sticky Washington was, and how hard it was to find a cooling drink.

Later, back in Salt Lake City, he noted cars lining up around the block for the A&W Root Beer stand. All this he filed neatly in his memory until 1927, when he'd left university. Through a family connection, he convinced A&W to let him set up a franchise – in Washington. He headed to the city with his new wife, Alice Sheets Marriott, who would also be his bookkeeper. His son takes up the tale:

> On their wedding day in early 1927, they jumped into a Model T Ford and headed to Washington DC… With only a bit of cash lent to them by my grandmother from her cookie jar, they bounced along the nation's rough dirt roads for 11 days to reach their destination… When the couple finally reached Washington, they moved into an apartment with some friends and got busy on the root beer franchise.

But of course, Washington was not always sweltering. In winter, it became icy cold. So Alice 'cooked up the idea of adding hot foods like tamales and chilli to the menu. They called their restaurant the Hot Shoppes. A year later, they opened the first drive-in east of the Mississippi River. From there the business grew like crazy, even during the Great Depression'.

Their first hotel, opened in 1957, was The Twin Bridges Motor Hotel in Arlington, Virginia – far from coincidentally, it was within sight of the then Washington Airport (now Reagan National Airport). Within a few years the lowly two-storey hotel had sprouted a five-storey tower with meeting rooms, restaurants and a rooftop lounge. Marriott later claimed, with some justification, that he had pioneered the concept of the upmarket airport hotel for business travellers.

This, then, was the basis for the operation that grew into the world's biggest hotel company. Marriott's son Bill was groomed to take over from the start, officially joining the company in 1956 – after learning every aspect of the business, he became CEO in 1972. In his book, Bill Marriott emphasizes that if the company flourished under his guidance, it was because he stuck closely to his father's credo: 'Take care of your employees, and they'll take care of your customers.'

He sums up the company's 'five core values' as the following: 'Put people first. Pursue excellence. Embrace change. Act with integrity. Serve our world.'

In 1995 Marriott International acquired 49 per cent of the Ritz-Carlton Hotel Company, followed by majority ownership three years later. As you may remember from an earlier chapter, Ritz-Carlton has also benefited from a focus on delivering exceptional service (see Chapter 4, From rags to Ritz).

They may have been pioneers, but Hilton and Marriott could hardly have expected to keep the entire sector to themselves. The world of premium hotels became a crowded one: in 1957 two young entrepreneurs named Hyatt Robert von Dehn and Jack Dyer Crouch had also acquired their own airport hotel, at Los Angeles International Airport. Hyatt himself left the business shortly afterwards, but it grew into an international brand. Other names to reckon with include the InterContinental Group, which also embraces the upscale Crowne Plaza and the far more accessible Holiday Inn brands, among others; and France's Accor, with its posh Sofitel and not-so-posh Mercure and Ibis offerings. In fact, all these groups have swarms of spin-off and boutique brands to suit almost every taste and price point.

And then there was Starwood.

Compared to Hilton and Marriott, Starwood Hotels & Resorts Worldwide is a tricky brand to get a handle on, history-wise. It was set up in 1991 by a Chicago real estate acquisition company, Starwood Capital Partners, backed by 'high net worth families' (starwoodhotels.com). In 1998 it acquired Westin and Sheraton and opened the first W Hotel. It named its luxury brand, St Regis, after the former Sheraton hotel of the same name in New York. Always in tune with trends, in 2007 Starwood launched two youthful new brands: Aloft Hotels and Element Hotels. Aloft offers 'urban-inspired, loft-like guest rooms' with 'enhanced technology services' for the millennial traveller; Element has an environmentally-friendly positioning.

Merger talks with Marriott began in 2015. It turned into quite a dance, as at one point Starwood looked as if it would accept an alternative offer from a consortium led by the Chinese Angbang Insurance Corporation. Marriott raised its bid to US$13 billion and clinched the deal in April 2016.

The merger may have created the world's largest hotel group – but its guests were mainly interested in one thing: what would happen to their loyalty points?

A question of loyalty

Herding hotel guests – reserving rooms, checking parties in and out, noting special requests – was a laborious process for a surprisingly long time, even after the advent of the desktop computer. Property management systems (PMS) provided a solution. The pioneer in this field was the Fidelio Property Management System, which appeared in 1987. Its name derived from the fact that its co-founder, Keith Gruen, originally began designing software for opera houses:

> I certainly was an outsider when I entered this industry. In fact, it all happened by accident. You see, my initial intention was to write software for opera companies. But my partner in the business, Dietmar Mueller-Elmau... convinced a luxury resort in the Black Forest of Germany to buy our software... When we officially founded the company a few months later, we named the company Fidelio, after the opera, thinking that we would continue to sell opera software. We sold that opera software a total of one time. The hotel software.... well it was somewhat more successful.

'PMS Yesterday, Today and Tomorrow', www.hospitalitynet.org, 5 March 2007

After 'watching over the shoulders' of the hotel staff who were using his service, Gruen revised and expanded the system. 'We didn't copy anyone's features or screens. But we did develop features early on that no one else had ever heard of.' This included a customizable guest profile screen, which became the key to hotel CRM (customer relationship management):

> I am quite sure... that we made the first guest-centric PMS. Those original resort hotel customers of ours were fanatic about their guest profiles and guest history. They stored everything about every visit of every guest. Not only such basic data as the names and birthdates of the kids, but each room the family stayed in and which wines they ordered in the restaurant. Guest history was not optional, it was mandatory.

Stoking guest loyalty has evolved into something close to an art form. Every hotel group – and of course every airline – has a loyalty scheme: Hilton

HHonors (that double H is a proofreader's nightmare), Marriott Rewards, Hyatt Gold Passport and so on. They offer similar clutches of benefits: discounts, upgrades, free internet, late checkout – all adding up to an extra layer of cosseting. (By the way, after the Marriott–Starwood merger, the two loyalty schemes ran in parallel, with 'bridges' between them so guests could benefit from the offers of both brands.)

There's even an annual prize-giving ceremony for the best frequent traveller schemes: the Freddie Awards were created in 1988 by Randy Petersen, founder of *InsideFlyer* magazine, a monthly publication devoted to frequent flyers. Petersen named the awards after low-cost airline pioneer Sir Freddie Laker (see Chapter 12, 'Flying for less').

What makes the Freddies so intriguing is that they're based on customer votes, rather than simply comparing which loyalty schemes deliver the most value in terms of perks, points and so on. As *Forbes* magazine put it: 'As a result, consumer sentiment can also play a role in the results, for example pushing airlines and hotels with a negative brand presence further down the charts.' ('The best hotel and airline loyalty programs', 5 May 2015.) This reaffirms the fact that building a great brand is not just about what you *give* your customers, but how you make them *feel*. It's barely tangible, this extra touch, but it has a lot to do with the interaction between the human beings on both sides. (To find out who won the latest awards, by all means pay a visit to freddieawards.com.)

Entire films have been made about frequent travellers who obsessively collect loyalty points (well, at least one – *Up in the Air*, from 2009, directed by Jason Reitman and starring George Clooney as a travel-addicted executive). And indeed there's a whole parallel world of travel that revolves entirely around the business community.

When I was a child, my father was something of a frequent traveller himself – although as the area manager of a chain of electrical stores he racked up road miles rather than air miles. He did, however, possess an American Express card, which to my innocent gaze bestowed a worldly glamour upon him.

American Express had its roots in the 19th century as an express mail service. Its links with the word of travel date back to a European tour undertaken by JC Fargo (brother of co-founder William G Fargo), who took with him traditional letters of credit – which he found painfully difficult to cash. His experience prompted the creation of the American Express Travellers' Cheque. The company's mission to ease travel led in turn to the founding in 1915 of a chain of travel agencies. Today, American Express Global Business Travel is a standalone company, still smoothing the way around the world for corporate road warriors.

One of its major competitors is Carlson Wagonlit Travel, another mega travel management company taking care of business trip itineraries for corporate clients. It has links right back to the age of steam: as mentioned earlier, the 'Wagonlit' part of its name derives from the travel agency that acted as a portal for the Orient Express.

But these big travel management companies have a problem, because the image of the suited, Amex-toting frequent flyer is beginning to look as outmoded as the steam train. There's another kind of business travel- ler – working in technology, or in a creative profession, or winging it as a freelance consultant – who's more likely to be wearing sneakers and toting a Mac. These travellers prefer to book via their phones and pick quirk- ier hotels – or even Airbnb apartments – outside the corporate travel net. Virtual travel assistants in the form of apps based on artificial intelligence – which allow users to 'chat' in real time about flights and hotel reserva- tions – are also stealing them away. The travel management companies have tried to stem this 'leakage' with their own mobile apps and 'gamified' points systems, but the landscape of business travel is changing fast.

Smart suppliers have been tracking this evolution – and one of them has come up with a very interesting hotel concept indeed.

Disrupting the business hotel

Hans Meyer has been a hotelier from the start – he was educated at the Hotelschool in The Hague and at the Cornell School of Hotel Administration. After that he worked internationally for a number of big chains, a period that came to an end in 2003 with the Spanish NH Hotel Group, where he was responsible for development for northern Europe.

'At that point I realized two things,' he says. 'One, I wanted to innovate in the hotel business. Two, it's quite difficult to do so within a big company.'

Hans left his job, initiating and co-founding what became the CitizenM hotel concept, based on the idea of affordable luxury for young (or young-minded) travellers. To quote its YouTube video: 'Living room-style lobbies, the latest technology, excellent cocktails and food available 24/7, and all the things that we think should be free in the 21st century, like Wi-Fi and movies on demand.'

Cheers to that. Having disrupted the leisure hotel model earlier, Hans now set his sights on the business sector. And he began to think pretty big:

> Over the last 15 years, the internet coupled with faster broadband speed and
> better infrastructure have enabled the ability to work independently of time and
> place. During my career I've had periods where I travelled roughly 25 days per

month, and over the years I noticed the limitations to this lifestyle becoming less noticeable. So my question was: what happens when you want to explore the world not from a backpacking point of view, but from a working point of view?'

While CitizenM had turned around the concept of luxury hotels for casual travellers, the extended stay and serviced apartment sectors were still horribly traditional. Ripe for the hacking, thought Hans. 'There had been a lot of innovation in the traditional hotel sector, but in the extended stay sector you were pretty much limited to a double-sized hotel room with a microwave, and that was about it.'

In the intersection between agile young business travellers boosted by technology and bland serviced apartments there was – almost nothing. Perhaps Airbnb, but then who's going to come and pick up your laundry? Hans spotted an opportunity.

'How would it be if I could create an entire new product category? A hybrid between a home and an office, with hotel services and the buzz of a thriving neighbourhood, so it would also be a very social place.'

To test his theory that it was now possible to run a company from anywhere, Hans worked for two months at a time in Buenos Aires, Washington and Bali. The results were entirely satisfactory, so he began questioning other nomadic business travellers – 150 in total – to confirm his ideas. He asked the Future Laboratory in London to conduct further research into this emerging segment. All the indicators were positive.

'Together with my business partner and co-founder Marc Jongerius, we decided to go ahead and create what we've called an "offline social network", a series of places where people who live this kind of lifestyle can meet others.'

The first Zoku hotel – the Japanese word can mean 'family', 'tribe' or 'clan' – opened in Amsterdam in June 2016. It comprises 133 loft-style spaces containing everything you need to live independently, with the added benefit of hotel-style services like dry-cleaning and housekeeping, as well as business-oriented options like office supplies and projectors, standard and 3D printing, and staff who can help you build your local social and business network. Alongside the bar, living room, kitchen and communal work areas, there are meeting rooms and event spaces.

'The hotel is actually designed for long-stay living,' says Hans. 'The longer you stay, the more value you'll get. If you stay for two days, it's going to be roughly the price of a four-star hotel. But if you stay for two weeks, it's more like a three-star – with far more advantages.'

In other words, he's not targeting business people who fly in to the city for a couple of days, but those who might be there for weeks – with time to get bored or lonely:

That's why we have members of staff we call 'sidekicks', who are your go-to people for help. They know their way around the city and can help you build up your social network, or business network. The hotel trade has tended to be very process-driven: you meet the person who books you in and you have contact with them for about 15 minutes. But we wanted to look beyond that. Our staff are more like personal assistants.

When guests check in, a sidekick will offer to have a coffee with them, to chat about their interests and needs. 'It may be that they know other people within the hotel, or within the city, with similar interests or backgrounds to your own. And if you feel like it, they can set up a meeting.'

Regular events within the hotel will bring guests into contact with inspiring individuals and companies. 'We want people to leave feeling more educated about the city than they were when they arrived.'

Marketing was done via PR and digital media, based on the slogan: 'The end of the hotel room as we know it.'

Hans explains: 'In 99.9 per cent of hotel rooms the focus is on the bed, which sort of prevents you inviting people to your room for a meeting or a drink. In our rooms, the focus is on the kitchen table.'

In Zoku rooms the bed, up on a mezzanine accessed by a retractable staircase, can be discreetly tucked away behind attractive shutters. Below, the room is organized around a four-person table that can be used for everything from working to dining. The concept was demonstrated by a short online video, which went viral when it was picked up by the news site Reddit – and attracted attention from mainstream media brands.

For Hans, though, design is only half the story: he's clearly passionate about creating a sort of parallel world populated by sociable, techno-literate business travellers.

Or as he puts it: 'Our hotel is very different, but at the end of the day, it's only brought to life by the people who stay there.'

Tour highlights

- Conrad Hilton quickly realized that the key to running a profitable hotel was to maximize use of space.

- Hilton turned the hotel lobby into a source of income by renting out spaces for news-stands, clothing retailers and coffee shops.

- Both Hilton and his rival JW Marriott understood that creating a sense of pride, responsibility and 'esprit de corps' among hotel staff resulted in better service for guests.

- Generating customer loyalty in a crowded market has become an obsession of hotel groups. All have loyalty schemes and technology designed to keep track of guest preferences.

- Many large companies have outsourced the organization of corporate travel to specialists like American Express and Carlson Wagonlit Travel.

- But a new generation of tech-savvy 'global nomads' are looking beyond conventional business hotels.

How boutique became chic

'I don't sell sleep – I sell magic.'

The next time you're staying at a boutique hotel and your room seems a little small, it may be worth remembering that the term was coined by an ex-convict. Steve Rubell was also a former nightclub proprietor. With his best friend Ian Schrager he ran the legendary discotheque Studio 54 in New York. To say that their business practices were unorthodox is an understatement; even Rubell admitted that their accounts were kept in three columns: 'cash in, cash out and skim'. ('New Yorkers & Co', *The New York Times*, 11 July 1988.)

Convicted of tax evasion in 1979, the pair shared a cell together at a Federal prison in Montgomery, Alabama. They tossed for the top bunk. Schrager won, but he let his old pal have it anyway. The pair had already been through a lot together: according to the *New York Times*, they met when they were dating the same girl at Syracuse University. Then there was Studio 54 itself, which still feels as if it ought to be the place to be, even though it trailed out of the back door of history in the 1990s, long after its founders had moved on. For a brief period at the end of the Seventies, when they were at its helm, it was the world's most desirable nightspot. It was partly a matter of design: nightclubs had previously been gloomy and intimate; Studio 54 was all about lighting and theatricality, with 'sets' that could be shifted and reconfigured. It was a place to be seen, not a place to hide.

Rubell and Schrager still had this theatrical design aesthetic in their pockets when they got out of jail after 13 months. They had little else. In the words of *The New York Times*: 'They owed nearly $400,000 to Uncle Sam, Citibank would not even open a checking account for them, and credit cards were an impossible dream. Their felony conviction meant that they could not get a liquor license, effectively barring them from running clubs.'

They were not proud of their recent past: interviews from the time find them chastened, yet determined to bounce back.

Naturally, they decided to open a hotel.

Everybody comes to Morgans

The move was driven partly by necessity, but also because they had an instinctive feel for the vibe of the city. And at that point they could tell the nightlife scene was waning. There was a lot of talk about AIDS. People were into cocooning rather than partying. 'This is not a club time,' Rubell told the *Times*. (Tragically, Rubell himself was to die of AIDS in 1989.) The solution was to provide the perfect cocoon.

The pair found a 'dowager' hotel called the Executive on Madison Avenue, between 37th and 38th streets, not far from the former home of the pugnacious financier JP Morgan (1837–1914). This was not a posh place: some rooms were rented several times a night. They put down all they had – US$60,000 – to secure the contract for the shabby US$6.3 million edifice, then convinced a major New York property developer to back them. It helped that the contract came with something called a subordination clause, which effectively meant that they could use a building they did not own as collateral on loans. But even with this in their favour, they knew they'd have to cut corners.

Fortunately, their nightclub days had taught them how to do glamour on the cheap. There was a lot of black-painted plywood at Studio 54. Years later, Schrager told a *New York Times* journalist: 'Since we're doing highly stylized things... we've been able to jettison traditional ideas of opulence.' Instead of a free pen in your hotel room, you'll get a black pencil. And since it looks cool, you'll be fine with it. Similarly, you probably won't care that the bathroom floor is tiled with Vermont slate instead of pricey imported marble. ('The Cool War', 27 May 2001.)

Morgans had 154 smallish rooms. By the time Rubell and Schrager had finished with them, they didn't feel so small. The entrepreneurs tapped a chic Parisian interior designer, Andrée Putman, to help them give the place a makeover. Putman recalled that the first time she saw the Executive, she was genuinely dismayed. 'I thought it was a joke. You know, I am French, and I have certain ideas. I could not believe it was going to be a place to go. It was shocking. The most depressing kind of people. Probably the ugliest furniture I've seen in my life.' ('The Comeback Kids', *New York Magazine*, 22 July 1985.)

A test room at the hotel showed what could be achieved with little. The walls were sprayed with Zolatone, a texturized grey paint that lent an inexpensive sophistication. The glass in the shower was normally used for bus shelters. With this as her template, Putman set to work. 'The idea was to be unpretentious and discreet and to look like anything except a commercial hotel room,' she said. This translated as a lot of black and grey, with 'a touch of pale melon and dusty turquoise here and there'.

A raft of small details contributed to what Rubell referred to as a 'boutique' feel, making each room feel like a tiny fashion store, or an arty New York home. There were black-and-white Robert Mapplethorpe photos on the walls, 'wall niches to keep phones out of sight and close at hand, blackout shades on the windows, small snack-filled refrigerators, black ice buckets… silver television sets and black toothbrushes'.

One thing everyone seemed to notice were the beds, which had duvets rather than traditional bedspreads, covered in Brooks Brothers shirting material. But the design of the 'miniscule bathrooms' was true genius, with their perception-scrambling black-and-white checkerboard tiles, airline-sized stainless steel sinks and oval mirrors. ('Design Ideas in two New Small Hotels', *The New York Times*, 20 September 1984.)

Morgans officially opened on 1 October 1984 with a painstakingly cast front-of-house team who resembled (and often were) budding actors and models. Initially its guests were mostly businessmen, but Rubell and Schrager still knew enough A-listers to pull in a few names. Bianca Jagger was a friend; Calvin Klein had pledged his support. The first-time hoteliers couldn't afford to advertise, so media coverage and notoriety were crucial. This would be the strategy going ahead. As Schrager later put it: 'You can get a million dollars of free publicity by underwriting a party for $10,000.'

The famous came calling – and the press wrote about them. By December, *The New York Times* was already suggesting that the Rolling Stones had thrown a party at the hotel and that Bianca Jagger had been regularly spotted in the elevator. At the same time, it ran a sympathetic article about how the hotel's oldest resident – 'sprightly 96-year-old' Beulah Baer, who had moved into the Executive in 1927 – had been allowed to stay in her room, benefiting from 'the fancy little soaps and the luxurious towels' just like the trendier guests. ('A voice from the past in the stylish present', 15 December 1984.)

As its founders had intuited, nobody who stayed at Morgans cared about the size of the rooms. Most of them were up too late partying to notice. 'I don't sell sleep,' Schrager once commented. 'I sell magic.'

With Morgans firmly established as home-from-home for the fast set, the business partners turned their attention to the Royalton, a rather grander affair. The 205-room neo-Georgian building on 44th Street stood diagonally across from the storied Algonquin Hotel. Schrager, Rubell and their associates planned to make the Royalton as fashionable among the creative crowd of the late 1980s as the Algonquin had been in the 1920s with the wisecracking writer Dorothy Parker and her hard-drinking literary circle.

This time their chosen designer was Philippe Starck, who became almost as closely associated with the boutique movement as its instigators. A sense of minimalist luxury was conveyed with 'dark green marble, grey-green slate, gleaming mahogany and moulded aluminium'. The lobby, 'a spectacular columned space of 10,000 square feet' would become a social hub, with 'an intimate, stand-up bar modelled after the bar of the Ritz in Paris' and a 100-seat restaurant. ('At 90, a Dowager of a Hotel Turns into a Witty Sylph', *The New York Times*, 29 September 1988.)

And so it continued. Starck returned for another project, the Paramount, on West 46th Street. Rubell sadly left the party, but Schrager continued building the business. The list of hotels lengthened, initially with the Morgans Hotel Group (the Delano in Miami Beach, the Mondrian in Los Angeles and St Martin's Lane in London, to name a few), and then under his eponymously named company (by all means drop in for a drink at the 'haute bohemian' Gramercy Park Hotel in New York). A Schrager hotel is synonymous with eye-popping design, aspirational guests and a certain sense of excitement. All of them display his signature blend of fantasy and practicality.

The template has been widely copied, just as over the years the term 'boutique' has been used and abused. For a while, any hotel with a trendy vibe and mildly idiosyncratic décor felt obliged to describe itself as such.

One group, however, pushed the notion to extremes.

W Hotels and the boutique boom

The concept pioneered by Rubell and Schrager was bound to attract imitators – and it did, in their thousands. But Starwood Hotels & Resorts took the idea and industrialized it. The buzzing bar scene, the destination restaurants, the 'auditions' for front-of-house staff: all would be familiar to anyone who'd stayed at a Morgans group hotel. Starwood called its new brand W and positioned it as a design-driven lifestyle experience.

The first iteration was the W New York, which opened in 1998 on the site of the former Doral Inn Hotel at 41 Lexington Avenue. The group's website describes it as 'an instant phenomenon'. It adds: 'Its success drove the development of more than a dozen new properties in colourful destinations – including Los Angeles, Chicago, Seattle and Seoul – in an unprecedented two-year span. Each hotel offers signature restaurant and bar areas that attract not only hotel guests, but local tastemakers as well.' ('About W Hotels', Starwoodhotels.com.)

Over the next decade, Starwood rapidly opened a series of similar properties. When the W brand arrived in Boston's Theatre District in 2008, general manager William Bunce described it as 'the world of wow'. The 34th W establishment, the 235-room Boston hotel incorporated 'a restaurant by renowned chef Jean-Georges Vongerichten... a spa and an underground lounge'. ('W Hotel ready to enter, stage left, to spotlight', *The Boston Globe*, 18 October 2008.)

The article noted that, at the Times Square W hotel in New York, the rug in the elevator was changed three times a day to say 'good morning', 'good afternoon' and 'good evening'. The lighting in the lobby, known as the 'living room', was bright in the morning but softened throughout the day, until by night-time it was intimately sombre. Bunce described the W concept as 'an urban oasis'.

Another name associated with the boutique movement is Kimpton Hotels & Restaurants, founded by Bill Kimpton in 1981. Kimpton believed that the key to the perfect hotel was 'individuality', both in terms of the style of his establishments and his staff's approach to guests. 'The best way to care for guests... is to relate to them as one unique person to another unique person.' ('How Kimpton Hotels Scaled Its Culture', *Inc.* magazine, March 2014.) The brand's strategy was to focus on delivering quality in every area, from interiors to service to dining. For that reason, the brand evolved cautiously. Although it became the biggest boutique hotel group in the United States, for a long while it did not expand abroad. 'The need to sustain culture affects the rate of hotel openings. Kimpton refuses to franchise and has been cautious about expanding overseas, wary of how the "Kimpton magic" will translate to other markets.'

However, all that looked set to change with the acquisition of Kimpton by the InterContinental Hotel Group in 2014, followed by the opening of the first Kimpton outlet overseas, in Amsterdam.

InterContinental is by no means the only group to have invested in the boutique sector. As the big hoteliers began chasing Airbnb for a slice of the millennial demographic, a raft of spin-off brands appeared, including Cordis from Langham, Hotel Jen from Shangri-La (cleverly positing 'Jen' as a fictional hotelier who integrates design ideas from her global travels) and Marriott's EDITION brand, which was created in association with – wait for it – Ian Schrager. All of them offer a slightly different take on the idea of hotel as social magnet and design emporium.

It would be remiss of me not to mention another flamboyant hotelier in the Schrager mould: André Balazs, whose career followed a similar trajectory, although it started rather differently. Having made his fortune from a biotech company, Biomatrix, which he developed with his father, in 1990 he acquired the legendary yet somewhat faded Chateau Marmont hotel on Sunset Boulevard, Los Angeles. Balazs managed to update it while conserving its 1920s Old Hollywood soul. His next hotel was something new: the

Mercer, in SoHo, acquired in 1989 but beset with 'delays and snags and more snags' until it finally opened almost a decade later, to compete with the district's existing boutiques ('Up in the Old New Mercer Hotel', *New York Observer*, 9 March 1998.)

The Balazs hotel empire now embraces the Sunset Beach in Long Island, four hotels under the Standard brand (in downtown LA, Hollywood, the High Line and the East Village in New York) and the much-hyped Chiltern Firehouse in London. In interviews, it becomes clear that his approach echoes that of Schrager and Rubell: these are not hotels, they are 'experiences'. He has even spoken of each property having a 'narrative', a story that seduces guests.

'I see my role and my company's role as kind of like an old-school Hollywood studio,' he told design website Dezeen. 'We kind of put together who's the best writer, director, who are the actors we can bring in, who's the best production designer, the best composer and we'll assemble a team. We have people designing uniforms, people designing various aspects of it.' ('We don't go to architects who have a signature style, says André Balazs', 10 September 2015.)

He has also drawn a comparison between the role of bars and restaurants at his hotels with that of perfume and sunglasses in the luxury fashion business: they are the accessible part of the dream, while pricey guest rooms are the equivalent of haute couture. ('André Balazs, l'hotelier star', *Les Echos*, 15 July 2016.)

Talking of which, the conflation of hotels and 'lifestyle' has driven a number of fashion brands to launch their own boutique-style offerings: among the more successful are the 'Casa Camper' hotels in Barcelona and Berlin – run by the Spanish footwear brand – and a handful of Armani- and Bulgari-branded establishments. Renzo Rosso, founder of the denim brand Diesel, bought the Pelican Hotel at South Beach in Miami 'on impulse' after visiting the area in 1990. While the word 'Diesel' is nowhere in sight at the Pelican, its retro-futuristic décor reflects the brand's offbeat style. Rosso, like Camper, owns his hotel, but most retail-branded operations are joint ventures with conventional operators (such as Bulgari with Marriott and Armani with Dubai-based Emaar Hospitality). The brands have effectively licensed out their names.

For consumers, the landscape of boutique hotels is a confusing one. Since every establishment boasts its own quirks, how can you be sure of choosing the one that best suits your style? Business hotels, in comparison, have a reassuring uniformity to them. The chains mentioned earlier may offer a promise of consistency, but what if you want to stay in a truly independent hotel?

Some of them are members of associations along the lines of Leading Hotels of the World. Take Design Hotels, for example (www.designhotels. com), which embraces 260 hotels in 50 countries. Member hotels get access to shared sales and distribution channels, while consumers can browse the sumptuous images on its website (or in its 500-page annual catalogue) and make reservations with a minimum of research.

But the boutique boom also created an ecosystem of curators: bloggers and travel advisers who've made it their business to review and recommend the world's best hotel experiences. One of the most amusing is the British website Mr & Mrs Smith. The name, of course, comes from the pseudo-nym unmarried couples hypothetically use while checking in to a hotel for an illicit tryst (and not from the film starring Angelina Jolie and Brad Pitt, which actually came later). The brand was founded in 2003 by James Lohan and Tamara Heber-Percy, who are now married but were dating at the time.

The trigger, they told the *London Evening Standard*, was a 'particularly miserable weekend in the Lake District', alongside a general feeling that they'd been steered wrong by a number of guide books. So they decided to create a guidebook of their own, taking a month off work (Lohan ran a London members' club and Heber-Percy a dating agency) to tour no fewer than 200 hotels. They were uninterested in how many stars an establishment had – they judged purely by the quality of the experience. Lohan said: 'Does it do an amazing breakfast? Can you fit two in the bath? Can the barman mix you a brilliant cocktail or pour the perfect pint? That's what we look for.' ('Mr & Mrs who work for our comfort', 7 April 2014.)

Unable to find a publisher for their upmarket and cheekily-titled guide, the couple went ahead and published it themselves. It was a success, partly down to their launch stunt: 'We put a live naked couple in a bed in Foyles bookshop window and built a boudoir of books around them. Anything to get the word out there.'

The guide sold so well that one hotel told the couple that 'Mrs & Mrs Smith' was generating half its weekend business. That's when they decided to get into the hotel booking game, launching the site in 2008 after raising £2.5 million in private investment. Each hotel on the site would be visited by a member of the Smith team before being anonymously reviewed by a couple. By the time the article cited above appeared, the site embraced 900 hotels and more than 900,000 members.

In 2013, when they were married and had become parents, the couple launched a family-oriented spin-off, Smith & Family. A recent father my-self, I interviewed Lohan shortly afterwards for the trend-tracking website www.stylus.com.

'It's definitely a generational thing,' he told me. 'Like our customers, we grew up loving unique and beautiful boutique hotels. When we got married and had kids, we wanted the same thing, with a family atmosphere. We're willing to make certain sacrifices, but we don't see why we shouldn't have a stylish holiday.'

As any parent knows, kids can be embarrassing – even mortifying – and you definitely don't want to choose a place where the staff 'look down their noses at you when you arrive with children,' in Lohan's words. Once again, the couple seemed to have hit on a marketing niche, as an increasing number of hotels began catering to families from the 'boutique generation'. There was a sudden plethora of kite-making workshops on the beach, cooking classes in the hotel kitchen and art lessons with local painters.

Lohan said: 'It starts with the details, like a welcome gift for kids at check-in, proper children's menus and swimming times for families. Some big hotels think parents just want to dump their children at a kids' club – but it's more subtle than that.'

My own search for the perfect family hotel led to Greece, and a particularly talented hotelier.

How to be small but cool

'If it wasn't for kids, this would be just another good hotel,' says Nikos Tsepetis, proprietor of the Ammos Hotel, not far from the harbour town of Chania in Crete. 'As it is, I'd say we are one of the best family-friendly hotels in Europe.'

He's not wrong: my wife discovered the Ammos through word of mouth and at the time of writing we've stayed there twice. 'Most of our guests are repeaters,' Nikos confirms. 'The rest are friends of repeaters.'

The Ammos resembles a modernist villa, pristine white and garlanded with trails of purple bougainvillea. It's perched atop a shallow slope above a crescent-shaped bay, whose sandy beach shelves so gradually that even the clumsiest toddler can wade out for yards without risk of mishap. This alone may be why Nikos found himself with a family hotel on his hands, when he started out creating a destination for couples, filled with his own eclectic design and art finds.

'Perhaps it was destiny,' he ponders. 'My father was a gynaecologist–obstetrician and my mother was a midwife. We literally lived in a clinic, so I grew up surrounded by babies. But as I'm not married and don't have any children of my own, that was not my intention at first.'

The hotel started out as the family's vacation home. It was, in fact, 'a little wooden house', which was knocked down to make way for the hotel when the family realized they could take advantage of the island's tourist influx. 'But it was never finished, so it stood there for about 10 years until I finished my studies and took over the property.'

Nikos studied political science – and he's still quite happy to share his views on Greece's current problems – but found he had a talent for décor and hospitality. 'I've always had rather odd tastes,' he jokes, 'so the design inevitably reflected my personality.'

The hotel was renovated in 2006 by architect and designer Elisa Manolas, who contrasted the sparkling white exterior with colourful mosaics, walls painted in vibrant colours, and teak custom-made furniture from Bali. All the other design objects and whimsical touches are down to Nikos, who has a particular penchant for lovely chairs. There's a broad shady terrace and a pool – complete with monitored children's area – surrounded by soft green lawns.

'I was surprised when I first began seeing people with babies, but I adapted,' Nikos says. He created a playroom, overseen by a nanny in the afternoon, so couples with young children could relax. It's probably fair to say that the hotel is more 'parent-friendly' than family-friendly. Everything is calibrated so that newish parents with a modicum of taste can pass an unhurried, stress-free vacation. Delicious local dishes (and pasta for the kids) are available night and day. The service is faultless; the staff are loyal. Nikos admits that he is a fairly exacting boss.

'Everything goes through me, and I like to do things in a certain way. So I tend to hire staff who haven't been in this business before, and then mould them into my way of thinking. The main thing is that guests should feel as if nothing is too much trouble. If their baby is sick on the terrace, nobody makes a fuss. We just smile and clean it up.'

The result is that the hotel tends to attract a specific demographic: 30s to 40s, vaguely arty but mostly unpretentious. Holiday friendships are born while the kids splash in the pool. At night, everyone sips the local rosé on the terrace while tribes of children scamper among the cats. When one of the sprogs throws a tantrum, fellow parents smile indulgently.

'These days I discourage people from coming if they don't have kids,' says Nikos. 'I am the gatekeeper. I handle every single booking by e-mail or on the phone, personally. So I can gently let people know if I don't think they'll be happy here.'

He's not keen on teenagers – there's nothing very adventurous to do for the over-10s – or groups, who tend to 'take the place over and keep to themselves'. 'My typical guests would be a couple with one young child,' he says.

Exceptional word of mouth means that he has 'never had to spend a penny' on marketing. He has an Instagram account, 'but it's just for fun', although he doesn't underestimate the importance of TripAdvisor. 'Ten years ago it was very influential, and we still keep an eye on it. But it's become too big. I've even had people asking for discounts because they're TripAdvisor reviewers.'

In fact, Nikos inspires loyalty through the human touch. When we returned for our second stay, we were welcomed like old friends, by staff who genuinely remembered us. The secret of the ultimate family hotel is that it makes you feel part of the family.

Tour highlights

- The term 'boutique hotel' is said to have been coined by nightclub supremo Steve Rubell, who with his business partner Ian Schrager launched Morgans Hotel in New York in 1984.

- With only small rooms – and a small budget – to play with, the pair hyped up the design and the detail.

- Unable to afford advertising, they counted on the media pull of celebrity guests and a subsequent aura of trendiness.

- The 'boutique generation', couples who grew up staying in stylish, idiosyncratic establishments, did not want to downshift to cookie-cutter chain resorts when they had children. This led to the rise of 'parent-friendly' boutique hotels.

- Parents are loyal repeat guests who can be won over by the human touch and staff who go the extra mile to ensure that both they and their kids have a trouble-free vacation.

'More beds, more places, more often.'

There was a moment in the 1980s when, as the cliché had it, the advertising in Britain really was better than the TV shows. Specifically, that moment was May 1983, when Saatchi & Saatchi debuted its 'Manhattan' spot for British Airways.

Clearly influenced by Spielberg, it showed air traffic controllers guiding what looked like a giant spacecraft in to land. As our jaws dropped – mirroring those of the onlookers on the screen – we realized that the spectacular UFO was in fact the island of Manhattan. Then came the payoff: 'Every year, we bring more people across the Atlantic than the entire population of Manhattan.'

The ad was as epic as the stakes: at that time, the near-bankrupt airline was losing £300 million a year and had been forced to cut 26,000 jobs. Margaret Thatcher's government had decreed that Britain's national airline should be privatized and appointed Sir John King (later Lord King) – a self-made businessman who had made a fortune from ball-bearings – as chairman, with the task of navigating British Airways back to health.

As *Campaign* magazine put it, Sir John 'needed advertising that would not only restore City confidence and fire up staff but put bums on seats. With Manhattan he got it'. (www.campaignlive.co.uk, online archive.) Bill Muirhead, who handled the British Airways account at Saatchi & Saatchi at the time, said: 'BA's situation was so bad that we couldn't show planes or staff. When I saw the rushes, the hairs on the back of my neck stood up.'

It was by no means the last time British Airways would make advertising history. In 1989, Saatchi & Saatchi graced screens with an even more ambitious spot. Filmed in Utah, it showed a vast crowd of people, clad in different colours, assembling on a vast salt flat to form the shape of a giant face, shot from above. 'Every year,' said the narrator, 'the world's favourite airline brings 24 million people together.' The face 'winked'. These days, of course, the effect would be achieved with CGI – but the thousands of extras in 'The Face' were real. The music, an adaptation of the Flower Duet from the Léo Delibes opera *Lakmé*, was used in many subsequent commercials and can still be heard when you board BA flights today – an example of sonic branding.

The founders of Saatchi & Saatchi – Maurice and Charles – continued their relationship with BA for 23 years, even after they'd broken away from their first agency and formed another, M&C Saatchi. One of the M&C creatives who worked on the account at the turn of the millennium was Matt Eastwood, now worldwide chief creative officer at J Walter Thompson. 'The first work I did on the account was in 2000, when British Airways had launched the first lie-flat seat in business class. BA led that market for a least 18 months or two years before anyone woke up and got a new seat into their cabins. Our campaign at the time was based around the idea of "More beds, more places, more often".'

By now, economy travellers have become resigned to the fact that they come far lower down the list of priorities than high-spending first- and business-class customers. Economy seems to have grown ever more cramped and inhumane, while business-class passengers have access to the latest seat technology, a wider choice of entertainment, better quality meals and more cabin staff per head. On certain airlines, first-class passengers benefit from enclosed mini-suites. Few things provoke a sharper sting of envy than shuffling through business class with your kids on your way to a knee-destroying spot in economy.

At the time of Eastwood's campaign, BA's reputation was pretty solid – partly thanks to the work put in by Saatchi – but it had made the occasional marketing blunder. The most notorious of these was when the airline repainted its tailfins in 1997 with the flags of different nations, or 'world images', replacing the stylized Union Jack. It was difficult to find anyone who didn't hate the £60 million rebranding – including then Prime Minister Margaret Thatcher, who pointedly draped her handkerchief over the tail of a model 747 when the new designs were displayed at that year's Conservative Party conference. Finally, in 2001, the British flag returned to the tailfins. ('British Airways restores Union flag design to all tailfins', *The Daily Telegraph*, 11 May 2001.)

Eastwood recalls: 'When they made the decision to move back there was still a residual bit of ill-feeling from British customers, but I don't think it was shared by the rest of the world. Financially they were strong, and they were still flying the Concorde, so everything was pretty hunky dory. The real challenge came later that year – September 11.'

The agency and its client had just held a meeting about how to adjust the airline's marketing strategy for the evolving digital world, but the terrorist attacks of 9/11 shut those plans down overnight:

> Their business just dropped off a cliff. They told us, 'We'd love you to remain our agency, but we won't be advertising for a while. We're not even sure we'll

be able to pay you for 18 months. We'll understand if you don't want to hang around.' Of course we did. And in fact the hammer fell again because an American Airlines plane crashed in Rockaway, New York, that November. We were wondering how we were ever going to convince people to fly again.

These incidents had an even longer-term impact than might have been expected, as the business community began using Skype and other technology to hold virtual meetings. In short, people realized that they didn't need to fly. 'So we had to reassure customers, while also convincing them that face-to-face meetings were better,' says Eastwood. 'The focus of the marketing became "getting people together".'

This approach is summarized by the 'It's better to be there' spot from 2002. An American businessman reacts coldly to deals pitched to him by letter and phone – and warmly greets a team that strolls into his office in person. A later ad showed passengers travelling to the airport and boarding the plane, shadowed at each stage of the journey by members of an orchestra playing the Flower Duet. 'The idea was that, when you book a British Airways flight, you feel a sense of calm and comfort even before you reach the airport.'

I asked Eastwood – who has worked for a number of carriers apart from British Airways – if it's easy to convince airline clients to move beyond the advertising clichés of comfortable cabins and smiling stewardesses?

'It's difficult because every airline is proud of its cabins and its staff, and they'll all tell you hand on heart that theirs are the best. In terms of staff, it only works if you genuinely own the concept, as Singapore Airlines does with "The Singapore Girl". What she really represents, of course, is Asian hospitality.'

The Singapore Girl has barely evolved since her first appearance in 1972, when French fashion designer Pierre Balmain designed her uniform, a chic twist on the traditional 'sarong kebaya'. By now, accusations of sexism seem almost redundant – the Singapore Airlines stewardess has become a living logo.

Eastwood suggests that airline advertising works best when the chatter about service and comfort is linked to a grander ideal. 'When I worked for Qantas its positioning was "The Spirit of Australia", which summed up a whole attitude and way of life for the passengers, and also gave the crew a sense of purpose.'

One of Eastwood's favourite campaigns during his period working for British Airways focused on the Club World 'sleeper' service. The TV spots showed a businessman climbing into a bed in the middle of New York City and then waking up, refreshed, in the same bed in the centre of London:

We actually set that up for real – today you'd probably do it in post-production. The print campaign showed the bed in various iconic locations around the world. That campaign told you everything you needed to know in terms of the benefits, but it didn't actually show the product. British Airways were very smart in that they understood the value of visual iconography.

The ad man says that, at least on his watch, British Airways consistently got its marketing right. 'They never sought to do work that was dumbed down or unintelligent, they always respected their audience. I've seen other airlines who've tried for the lowest common denominator, but BA never did that.'

Apart from the tailfins fiasco, there was one thing that made the airline seriously lose its British stiff upper lip. It was called Virgin Atlantic.

Virgin and 'dirty tricks'

Before Richard Branson transformed it, Virgin Atlantic started out as British Atlantic Airways. It had its roots in what seems, in retrospect, to be a rather eccentric scheme by a US lawyer and a former Laker Airways pilot (see Chapter 12, Flying for less), to set up a low-cost air service between London and the Falkland Islands in 1982, just after the Falklands War had ended.

The lawyer, Randolph Fields – who was also a well-known poker player – originated the idea and approached the pilot, Alan Hellary, who had been thinking along similar lines. But they were quickly forced to drop their Falklands proposal because the runway at Port Stanley was too short. Next they turned their attention to a potential service between Gatwick and JFK in New York, but British Airways and Caledonian blocked their bid to obtain a licence. Finally, they were awarded a route to Newark, New Jersey. Given the transatlantic competition, this would be a far pricier venture, so they needed funds. Enter Richard Branson – who agreed to finance, and soon acquired, the whole show. ('Virgin Atlantic History', www.airreview.com.)

Branson is, after all, like so many of the pioneers you've met in these pages, a showman. Entrepreneur, yachtsman, balloonist, philanthropist – he is the very definition of 'larger than life'. According to Virgin's website, it was almost inevitable that he would get into the airline business, given his passion for aviation: his mother was a stewardess and his uncle flew Spitfires ('Why did Richard Branson start an airline?', Virgin.com). When Virgin Atlantic celebrated its 30th birthday, in 2014, Branson himself told his side of the story. It all started, he wrote in *The Telegraph*, when he was trying to join 'a beautiful woman' who was waiting for him in the British Virgin Islands (naturally):

American Airlines decided to bump all of the passengers on an evening flight from Puerto Rico to the BVI – yours truly included. So I went to the back of the airport, hired a plane, borrowed a blackboard and wrote 'Virgin Air, $39 single flight'. I walked around all the stranded people and filled up the plane. As we landed, a passenger said to me: 'Virgin Airways isn't too bad – smarten up the service and you could be in business.' While I laughed, he had a point.

'30 years of fun, flying and competition', *The Daily Telegraph*, 21 June 2014

Branson, who flew a great deal while running Virgin Records, felt that service in the airline industry was 'horrendous', characterized by 'uncomfortable seats, lack of entertainment, rude staff and poor food... I thought if Virgin had an airline we could put the fun back into flying and bring glamour back to the skies. So I called up Boeing and said I wanted to buy a second-hand 747.'

This, presumably, was the leased 747-200, re-christened *Maiden Voyager*, that set forth on Virgin Atlantic's inaugural voyage on 22 June 1984. Branson describes the flight as 'such an incredible party that most people who were on board can't remember it'.

With its cheeky image and cabin crew outfitted in vivid scarlet, Virgin did feel fresh. Branson wrote:

We took our skills from the entertainment industry and translated them to work in airlines. This meant stand-up bars in Upper Class, limo transfers and that inimitable Virgin attitude. We started planning for the future, too, developing seat-back video long before the rest of the industry. A constant desire to innovate and do things differently has always been at the heart of Virgin Atlantic.

Branson's own swashbuckling image helped – he admits that he deliberately put himself 'front and centre of marketing, creating a public personality'.

British Airways took note. And in 1991, when Virgin secured a slot at Heathrow and became a direct competitor, it took action. This was the start of the so-called 'dirty tricks' campaign against Virgin. Branson's airline claimed that BA was poaching passengers, hacking into its computers and leaking anti-Virgin stories to the press. When officially approached by Branson, BA denied the accusations.

Then it made a mistake. British Airways' weekly staff newspaper, *BA News*, ran a story suggesting that Virgin had invented the claims as a publicity stunt. Branson sued Lord King and British Airways for libel. *The Guardian* takes up the story: 'BA countersued but, faced with the increasing likelihood that it would not succeed, it was then forced to concede that there was some foundation to the allegations.' ('Row over dirty tricks led to a decade of hostility', 2 August 2007.)

British Airways admitted in the High Court that staff had engaged in 'disreputable business practices' such as shredding documents, passenger poaching and trying to plant 'hostile and discreditable' stories about Virgin in the press. BA apologized 'unreservedly' and settled by paying Branson £500,000, which he divided among his staff and called the 'BA bonus'. Another £110,000 was given to Virgin Atlantic. But relations between the two airlines remained acrimonious until 2000, when Branson met Rod Eddington, the new CEO of British Airways 'to discuss a truce over tea'.

If anything, the 'dirty tricks' episode solidified Virgin's image as the plucky underdog fighting the establishment.

For Matt Eastwood, who began working for British Airways long after the incident was closed, Virgin was always 'the challenger brand':

> They pitched themselves as 'we're the cool, groovy alternative to stuffy old British Airways'. And that was fine, because it's the same kind of argument as W hotels versus Westin. I had the feeling that business travellers felt comfortable with the kind of sophistication British Airways offered – they didn't want the glitzy stuff, the equivalent of walking into a boutique hotel lobby with flashing lights and loud music. To my mind, Virgin appealed more to leisure travellers. In fact it's toned itself down and become more elegant since then.

Beyond the association of Virgin's image with that of Richard Branson himself, the airline has done some smart marketing. In 2013 it took a close look at its customers and decided, not surprisingly, that they were 'mavericks – adventurous and pioneering'. In an ad campaign featuring cabin crew with near superhuman skills, it positioned itself as 'Flying in the face of ordinary'. Then it took to social media and found everyday examples, like an Instagram photo of a construction worker at an airport carrying a stewardess across a snow bank, so she could deliver cupcakes to passengers stranded by a blizzard. Everything the airline does is calibrated to reinforce its image as an exciting outsider. ('How Virgin Atlantic's Marketing Nails It', www.inc.com, 12 April 2013.)

Virgin has experienced plenty of turbulence over the years, with profits climbing one year, only to lose altitude the next. In 1999 Virgin Group sold a 49 per cent stake to Singapore Airlines. Nine years later, Singapore was looking to offload Virgin – the buyer turned out to be Delta Airlines, in a deal that finally went through in June 2013.

In 2015, despite the partnership with the more conservative Delta, Virgin was still refusing to shrug off its anti-establishment image. Interviewed by Skift.com, Virgin Atlantic CEO Craig Kreeger happily admitted that the brand 'hasn't really changed over the last 30 years'. ('Virgin Atlantic CEO on Building a Lasting Airline', 4 August 2015.)

He added: 'We want to be the airline most loved by our customers and we will achieve this by putting the customer at the heart of everything we do.'

The airport factor

Whatever your personal experience of Virgin Atlantic may be, it deserves kudos for introducing a cool, disruptive brand into an industry that had vanishingly few of them. In late 2015, the design company Teague began teasing airline bosses with news of an innovative new carrier named Poppi, which would do for air travel what Uber had done for ground transportation. They were perhaps relieved to discover that Poppi was entirely fictional.

However, Teague's concept included ideas that felt as if they were just around the corner. At the core of Poppi is a mobile app from which you can smoothly book tickets or change seats. Naturally, it also provides real-time alerts about gates, boarding and delays. On board, overhead bins are replaced by slim compartments with room only for coats and laptops; luggage has been whisked away before you even leave home, but fitted with an RFID tag that enables you to track it via your app. Those despised middle seats are now sponsored by brands, offering gifts and perks to passengers who sit in them, while vending machines take the place of beverage carts. Movie buffs have an entire 'cinema class' just for themselves, with a bigger screen and blacked-out lighting.

All very laudable and attractive. In general, airlines have raised their digital game – certainly many of them have embraced social media as a valuable way of keeping in touch with passengers and responding swiftly to complaints.

Of course, one of the factors that makes air travel seem less glamorous is the airport itself. The state-of-the-art shopping and often exceptional restaurants seem unable to efface the misery of vast, alienating spaces and long lines at check-in and security.

An article in the *International New York Times* waxed nostalgic about the 1970s, 'when you could smoke anywhere, stroll leisurely through security and hug your loved one at the gate before boarding the plane'. The writer, Chris Holbrook, looked in vain for an airport that did not feature 'lighting... brighter than a World Series night game' and 'ambient noise – the endless gate changes, the last calls for boarding, the CNN late-breaking news – [that] makes it almost impossible to relax'. He admitted, however, the architects faced 'an almost impossible juggling act' as they tried to 'create art and, at the same time, make room for sightlines, security checkpoints and control rooms'. ('Airports: for everyone but the passenger', 9 April 2016.)

That same year, Aéroports de Paris, the organization that ran the two major Paris airports – Roissy Charles de Gaulle and Orly – undertook a €12 million rebranding exercise that featured a modernized logo and a new(ish) name: Paris Aéroport. Tied in with this was a customer service drive that included new shuttle buses with on-board Wi-Fi and a promise to reduce time at security to 10 minutes per passenger.

One amusing aspect of the project was an online video that portrayed the airport as a space where stories, often romantic ones, are played out. As a couple embrace at the end, the screen shows the slogan: *Paris vous aime* – Paris loves you. As well as linking the airport to the many positive values that swirl around the brand of Paris itself – food, culture, chic! – the clip attempted to do something far more ambitious: give an airport a soul.

Tour highlights

- In the 1980s, a troubled British Airways polished its brand identity with spectacular advertising that portrayed the airline as both patriotic and unifying.

- After 9/11, it reassured customers by reminding them of the comfort and security a big, experienced carrier can provide.

- Richard Branson's Virgin Atlantic positioned itself as the anti-British Airways. Hot, happening and resolutely pop, it was the boutique hotel of the airline world.

- Airline advertising works best when messages about comfort and service are linked to a grander ideal.

Flying for less   12

'Buying a ticket would be as simple as for a train.'

Of all the low-cost pioneers, the late Sir Freddie Laker is my personal favourite. A cheerfully robust fellow, with a wispy crown of thinning yet tenaciously curly hair, often concealed in the early days by a battered panama hat, he had the perpetual light tan of a man who liked to spend weekends on his yacht. But Freddie was no ordinary airline millionaire.

Laker had a feel for planes the way some people have a feel for horses; he was an aircraft whisperer. As the (1980) biography by Roger Eglin and Berry Ritchie, *Fly Me, I'm Freddie*, points out, Laker was 'one of the few airline bosses who [could] do any job in their business, from figuring the complexities of a multi-million dollar aircraft deal to repairing their own planes'.

Until Laker's Skytrain finally got off the ground in 1977, it was surprisingly hard to lay your hands on a cheap flight, especially if you wanted to cross the Atlantic. Most budget travellers flew charter as part of cut-price package holiday deals. So they'd find themselves on airlines like Court Line, which had a symbiotic relationship with the UK tour operator Clarksons Holidays, for whom it flew British vacationers to Mediterranean sunspots.

In some ways Court Line was an archetypal low-cost carrier, with its cabin staff outfitted by fashion designer Mary Quant and its planes painted in cheerful pastel tones. The catering, particularly, offered a foretaste of the extreme – if innovative – cost-cutting measures that would make the budget concept really fly. Court Line pioneered 'seat-back catering', which meant meals – cold salads or sandwiches on lidded trays – stored in little cubbyholes in the backs of seats. The airline could thus do away with galleys in the rear of its aircraft and squeeze in a few extra seats. ('Travel: Pioneering airlines set standards that today's carriers could only exceed', *The Independent*, 1 May 1999.)

Another budget airline was Iceland's Loftleidir, which is still going strong. It secured its place in the history books by launching the first low-cost flight across the Atlantic, from New York to Luxembourg (which it called 'the heart of Europe'), in 1955. In the late sixties, due to its popularity with students, it became known as 'the hippie airline'. ('Our history', www. loftleidir.com.)

In those days, as now, air travel standards were overseen by IATA, the International Air Transport Association, which represented the world's major airlines. One of its main tasks – if you asked people like Freddie Laker – was to protect its most powerful members, the state-run 'flag carriers' like British Airways, by setting officially agreed minimum fares. So it was naturally opposed to price competition and disruptive practices by plucky independents like Laker Airways.

One of IATA's more absurd rulings was that flights across the Atlantic could only be chartered at low cost by 'affinity groups' – chess clubs, horticultural societies and the like. Needless to say, fake affinity groups emerged and briefly flourished until IATA scrapped the rule in the early 1970s in favour of the Advanced Booking Charter (ABC), which allowed passengers to buy cheaper tickets if they booked four weeks in advance.

It was a start – but it wasn't enough for Freddie Laker. 'All most affinity travellers wanted, he reasoned, was cheap point-to-point transport. They did not want the frills: reservations, hotel bookings or even meals. Buying a ticket would be as simple as for a train. If it was full, people would simply have to wait for the next one.'

Laker came up with the formula for his no-frills airline in 1971. His rivals did everything they could to prevent it from becoming a reality.

The rise and fall of Skytrain

At the start of the Second World War, 19-year-old engineer Freddie Laker joined the Air Transport Auxiliary, a colourful outfit nicknamed the Ancient and Tattered Aviators, because it provided a refuge for pilots the RAF had deemed otherwise unfit to fly. 'It boasted three one-armed pilots and a number of women,' write Eglin and Ritchie. Its mission was to deliver planes and supplies to the RAF. It was here that Freddie learned to fly, eventually becoming a flight engineer.

But it was an event after the war, the Berlin Airlift, that really made Freddie Laker. He'd done brief stints as an engineer at British European Airways and London Aero Motor Services, but had more fun buying and selling war surplus gear on the side. He sold trucks with painted-over camouflage to whoever would have them, and offloaded aircraft radios to British South American Airways. In 1947 he transformed this activity into a business called Aviation Traders, based at Southend Airport.

Freddie had his eye on 12 Halton planes – the civil version of the wartime Halifax bomber – that were being auctioned off by BOAC. He estimated that they'd cost about £42,000. Laker's capital at that point was around £4,000. Over drinks with a wealthy friend, Bobby Sanderson, he casually mentioned this dramatic shortfall. Sanderson, who thought Laker had a bright future ahead of him, wrote him a cheque right there and then in the pub. Freddie would have his planes.

Then the Russians blockaded Berlin. As regular readers of espionage novels know, post-war Berlin – which was in effect an island stranded 100 miles inside Soviet-controlled East Germany – was divided into occupation zones, with the United States, the United Kingdom and France sharing the west and the Soviet Union controlling the east. In June 1948, in a bid to force the allies out, the Soviets surrounded Berlin and cut off access to the western sectors by rail, road and river. Food and water supplies were blocked.

The decision was made to ship in supplies using cargo planes – the theory being that the Soviets wouldn't dare to shoot down non-military aircraft on a humanitarian mission. Happily, that turned out to be correct. With the RAF only able to provide a certain number of planes, back-up was needed from charter airlines. The government agreed to foot the bill for flying hours and freight fees. One of the first private companies involved in the airlift was Bond Air Services (I'm not making this up), but it needed additional planes – Freddie Laker's planes. At the height of the year-long operation, 'Freddie was overhauling 12 planes for Bond Air Services and acting as spares supplier and servicer to many of the other 90-odd planes on the civil airlift'.

Freddie instinctively developed an approach to business that worked for him in the future. He surrounded himself with 'quiet, unflappable men, foils to Freddie's own ebullience' and then piled his energy into motivating them. 'He inspired them with his enthusiasm and convinced them with his own practical ability, so they undertook projects with breath-taking implications.'

The success of the Berlin enterprise set the scene for many other adventures in the world of aviation, including a tenure as managing director of British United Airlines. But it was inevitable that, sooner or later, Freddie would want his name on the side of an aircraft.

He launched Laker Airways in 1966, as a 'contract carrier to the package holiday trade'. Eglin and Ritchie report that his signature charm imbued the flying crews and cabin staff with enthusiasm. It worked on passengers, too. 'In the first season he flew on many of the flights himself, mingling with the passengers and flattering them with his attention to detail.' A few years later, in 1973, he ran the world's first ABC flight, between Manchester and Toronto. But he was still itching to put his Skytrain plan into action.

The bureaucracy and plotting that delayed the launch of the service could fill an entire book – and indeed it has. The saga began in 1971 when the Air

Transport Licensing Board (ATLB) rejected Laker's application to run a low-fare service between London and New York. He appealed – and won. Then, in late 1972, the ATLB was replaced by the new Civil Aviation Authority. Laker was told that he would have to apply all over again. He did – and won.

But before he could get organized, Britain's Labour government, under pressure from the major airlines who were suffering from inflated fuel prices during the global energy crisis, turned around and revoked his licence on 9 July 1975. Undeterred, Freddie took the government to the UK High Court – and won.

After another few twists and turns, including a positive intervention by the US President Jimmy Carter, the inaugural Skytrain flight took off from Gatwick on 26 September 1977. For the moment Laker had beaten what he called the 'Infamous Six' airlines operating the London to New York route – TWA, Pan Am, British Airways, Air India, Iran Air and El Al – and their loyal watchdog IATA. Not only that, but passengers were literally lining up to support him. Laker had stated many times, in court and in the press, that he was fighting to make flights available for 'the forgotten man' – an ordinary working man with a low income and a family.

'Laker's five year battle to get Skytrain flying had earned millions-of-dollars-worth of free advertising,' Eglin and Ritchie observe. Naturally, the big IATA players weren't going to let him get away with it, and quickly agreed to offer cut-price seats themselves, in a concerted attempt to throttle Skytrain at birth. By 'plotting together to counter-attack Skytrain,' write Eglin and Ritchie, they played right into Freddie's hands, convincing 'many ordinary people that IATA really was a wicked cartel and that Laker was a mortal St Christopher'.

Skytrain kept costs low by selling tickets on the spot, packing wide-bodied DC-10 aircraft, charging for meals and, according to Elin and Ritchie, seriously underpaying staff; although apparently many of them accepted this as part of Laker's mission to democratize air travel.

It worked like a dream at first, as Skytrain added routes and pressed on to Los Angeles. But then came the fall: on 5 February 1982, Laker Airlines went bankrupt.

There were many reasons for the collapse. Laker had borrowed heavily – at an inflated interest rate – to buy his fleet of wide-bodied aircraft, a miscalculation that was to turn around and bite him later. When an identical American Airlines DC-10 crashed at Chicago O'Hare in 1979, Freddie's entire fleet was temporarily grounded while an investigation into the planes' airworthiness was conducted. And as the effects of the early 1980s recession began to take hold, Laker's 'forgotten men' felt the strain on their income.

But perhaps most significantly of all, the major airlines continued their aggressive policy of slashing ticket prices to match those of Skytrain, even if it negatively impacted their own profits. They reasoned, correctly, that their pockets were deeper than Laker's. It was simply a matter of waiting until Skytrain bit the dust.

The airline's legacy was considerable, however. Its influence can be seen on Virgin Airlines, easyJet and Ryanair, to name but three. Skytrain 'alerted the public – and politicians – all around the world' to the fact that barriers to competition and price-fixing by members of IATA had kept fares artificially high. Freddie Laker proved that there was a need for low-cost airlines.

American ingenuity

In 2013 a photo appeared in *Fortune* magazine of a man in a cowboy hat, pouring himself a slug of bourbon in his Dallas office. The man was Herb Kelleher, and the accompanying article identified him as 'the Wild Turkey 101-drinking, chain-smoking founder of Southwest Airlines', which he'd started 40 years earlier. ('Southwest's Herb Kelleher: Still crazy after all these years', 14 January 2013.)

Behind the sharp-shooting image lay a man who, like Freddie Laker, understood that the keys to developing a strong corporate culture were hiring the right people, and then inspiring them. He told *Fortune*'s Jennifer Reingold:

> Some people will say, 'Well, this is not a strategy,' because they like the word
> 'strategy.' You know, it sounds important, like the Strategic Air Command…
> I think it was Tolstoy, if I remember correctly, who said, 'How does Napoleon
> march onto a balcony in France and get a whole bunch of French troops to
> march into Russia to their death?' And I said, 'Well, the strategy involved was
> his imperial ambitions, right? But what made the troops march? The culture.'
> And I said, 'It's the troops marching that defines the culture.'

But Kelleher was not the first US budget airline entrepreneur to replace frills with a strong culture. When he was planning his new service back in the late 1960s, he took note of its near-namesake, the now-defunct Pacific Southwest Airlines, or PSA.

Pacific Southwest Airlines was started in 1949 by a former World War Two flying instructor named Ken Friedkin. Originally the operation was designed to augment the income from his new flying school in San Diego.

An early attempt to set up a service from San Diego to El Centro in Southern California was a flop – but a travel agent advised Friedkin to try out a weekly run to San Francisco.

'The whole operation was very cooperative,' recounts PSA's semi-official nostalgia site. 'Pilots loaded baggage, flight attendants cleaned aircraft, and when winter weather struck, everyone helped put on the de-icing boots.' Since many of its passengers were sailors and marines from nearby bases, it was nicknamed the 'Poor Sailors' Airline' (PSA-history.org). Passengers were pampered out of necessity and lost luggage dealt with promptly; the airline couldn't afford disgruntled customers, or settlement fees.

PSA battled on into the jet age, although Friedkin passed away in 1962. His colleague (and fellow flying instructor) J Floyd 'Andy' Andrews seized the torch and enthusiastically fanned its flame. Under Andy's leadership, the airline adopted a flamboyant style that recalled Friedkin's signature Hawaiian shirts. The late sixties were PSA's golden era, when the smiles painted on the noses of its aircraft – initially for an advertising shoot – reflected its slogan 'The World's Friendliest Airline'. Rather like Virgin later on, it had an identifiable character and attitude, a 'fun' positioning that engendered passenger loyalty. The Airline Deregulation Act of 1978 – which swept away a raft of restrictions on which airlines could serve specific routes – enabled it to expand beyond its California patch to further destinations across the US. The quirky PSA brand only vanished in 1988, when the airline merged with rival USAir.

But its spirit lives on in the form of its semi-namesake Southwest Airlines. From the start, Herb Kelleher adopted PSA's upbeat attitude and photogenic cabin crews. In the end, Southwest not only outlived its distant relative, but outstripped its reputation. These days its cabin crew are known for their humour – YouTube is studded with their jokey in-flight announcements and even a song or two – and the airline regularly features on *Fortune* magazine's list of the world's most admired companies. It is famous for having never laid off staff, even temporarily, because of its insistent focus on its people.

Compared to the venerable Southwest, jetBlue is a young whippersnapper, having been founded in 1999 by David Neeleman. JetBlue's strategy was to make the entire low-cost experience more comfortable, and even somewhat premium, with leather seats, more legroom, free snacks and – an industry first – 24 channels of live satellite television at every seat, at no extra charge. ('Our company – history', www.jetblue.com.)

The airline's determination to provide low-cost flights while delivering an advanced level of customer service has allowed it to compete with standard airlines as well as its budget rivals. It has certainly taught its UK equivalents a thing or two.

British grit

The elements of the low-cost model are more or less visible to passengers. They include a single-class service, the use of 'secondary' airports that charge lower landing fees (ah, the glamour of the Luton to Beauvais run!), deploying staff in multiple roles – the crew member who scans your ticket at the gate shows up later to sell you a sandwich – seats that don't recline, and additional charges for checked bags, on-board snacks... and just about anything else they can get away with. Low-cost airlines also 'hedge' on fuel costs by buying in bulk while prices are low, and push for modifications in aircraft design that allow for more seats inside and reduced drag outside.

The internet, of course, changed everything. Once passengers could buy tickets, register luggage and even check in online, the entire process of filling an aircraft and getting it aloft could be streamlined – while direct booking did away with the costs associated with travel agents.

One of the main beneficiaries of this revolution was Ryanair, notoriously the low-cost carrier with the fewest frills of all. It was started in 1984 by a group of Irish businessmen, including Tony Ryan, founder of aircraft leasing company Guinness Peat Aviation. Ryanair began flying between Waterford and Gatwick Airport to compete with British Airways and Aer Lingus, adding the Dublin–Luton route in 1986.

The true mastermind of Ryanair's pared-to-the-bone service was its chief executive officer Michael O'Leary, who had absorbed the lessons of Southwest. In 1990, 'copying the Southwest Airlines low-fares model the airline [was] re-launched... as Europe's first low-fares airline'. Its innovations included 'high frequency flights, moving to a single aircraft fleet type [and] scrapping free drinks and expensive meals on board'. ('History of Ryanair', www.ryanair.com.)

In 1992 the European Union deregulated the airline industry, allowing European carriers to greatly increase their scheduled services across the region – an opportunity Ryanair seized.

Ryanair's website came online in 2000. Nine years later, it was able to dispense with check-in desks: passengers did everything online, apart from dropping off their bags. Ryanair's ultra-low-cost model was occasionally satirized – but the airline itself was happy to make outrageous statements as a way of stirring publicity. Around the time that it was poised to remove check-in desks, O'Leary mentioned in a BBC interview that the airline was thinking of charging passengers £1 to use the on-board toilets. He later admitted that the idea was unfeasible and went against EU regulations. ('Spend a penny, pay a pound with Ryanair', *The Guardian*, 27 February 2009.)

Ryanair took a similar no-frills approach to promotions, with internally-produced black-and-white print ads that courted controversy: a 2012 campaign featuring lingerie-clad flight attendants under the line 'Red hot fares & crew' was one of many to attract the ire of the Advertising Standards Authority.

But the airline's skeletal service also equated to a lousy customer experience – exacerbated by tetchy and impatient staff – and passengers began to drift away. Chastened, the airline launched a campaign of improvements, such as allocated seating, permitting a second carry-on bag and 'giving more flexibility for frontline staff to tolerate minor infringements' of its rules on baggage size, for example. Profits began to rise, although a drop in fuel costs also contributed. ('Fewer rules, less hassle, more profit – how being nice paid off at Ryanair', *The Guardian*, 30 May 2015.)

In truth the airline was playing catch-up with another British low-cost pioneer. No-frills airlines have come and gone, but Ryanair's natural rival has always been easyJet. Its founder, Stelios Haji-Ioannou, was a big-picture entrepreneur in the Laker and Branson mould. His father was a Greek–Cypriot shipping magnate who helped him get a start in business. He launched easyJet in 1995, at the age of just 28, running a couple of leased Boeing 737-200 planes from London Luton to Glasgow and Edinburgh. Within a couple of years he had expanded to Amsterdam, Barcelona and Nice.

He told *The Telegraph*: 'With the money from my dad, I had the vision and the tenacity to go to Luton to make it happen. I was in the right place at the right time. Europe only opened up its skies once... if you tried to start an airline today, you wouldn't make any money and it would fail.' ('Stelios: "I ditched my Porsche when I started easyJet. I've had a Smart Car ever since"', 29 July 2009.)

Once again, easyJet adopted the Southwest pattern, although there were additional touches of genius, notably its vivid orange branding. The jets themselves played the role of billboards, with the airline's telephone number (later its website address) boldly displayed on their sides. Then in 1999 came *Airline*, a TV documentary featuring easyJet, which secured the carrier's place in British popular culture. EasyJet floated on the London Stock Exchange in 2000 and two years later bought another low-cost airline, Go, originally launched by British Airways.

EasyJet has reneged over the years on some of the traditional cost-cutting measures. Like Ryanair, at first it did not provide allocated seating – resulting in a jostling free-for-all at the gate – but it reversed that decision in 2012, enabling passengers to pay an additional fee for seats with more legroom or those at the front of the aircraft. It also flies from primary airports like

London Gatwick and Charles de Gaulle in Paris. Under the transformative leadership of CEO Carolyn McCall, who joined in 2010, it has attracted valuable business fliers by delivering improved punctuality and introducing flexible premium fares, which enable rebooking. McCall has also focused on staff training, with an in-house academy that exhorts crews to be smart, efficient and above all friendly: '[R]aising the customer satisfaction bar has been placed at the heart of what easyJet does,' noted the *Financial Times* ('EasyJet blazes trail on customer service', 23 December 2013).

Not that Ryanair or easyJet ever had a choice – that luxury now lies in the hands of the passenger. FlyBe, Wizz, Vueling, jet2.com, Air Europa… the website Flylc.com (www.flylc.com) lists no fewer than 32 budget airlines serving Europe alone. Shortly before I completed this chapter, a *Telegraph* journalist was able to fly *around the world* on 10 low-cost airlines, from easyJet to Norwegian. The entire round trip cost him less than the equivalent of US$2,000. ('Around the world by budget airline: 10 flights, £1,653 – here's how to do it', 8 April 2016.)

The sky-scape has changed utterly since the 1970s. Freddie Laker would be delighted to see that flying, while not always very comfortable, has definitely become accessible. We're all part of the jet set now.

Tour highlights

- Southwest Airlines in the US and Skytrain in the UK proved in the 1970s that there was a demand for 'no-frills' air travel.

- Southwest Airlines, PSA and Laker Airways demonstrated that a strong culture, a fun – somewhat anti-establishment – image and friendly service engendered customer loyalty.

- In the UK, Ryanair and easyJet emerged in the 1990s to take advantage of deregulation and – shortly afterwards – the internet revolution.

- The ICAO (International Civil Aviation Organization) now lists over 200 carriers worldwide that could be defined as 'low cost'.

Lastminute and other dot-coms 13

'The place to which you travel will be you.'

In common with many people of my generation, Lastminute.com was my first experience of online travel booking. I was certainly aware that there were other means of booking a holiday than just popping in to your local travel agent – a number of friends had snagged cheap breaks via Teletext, the text-based information service that could be accessed through your TV screen – but when Lastminute appeared on the scene, it immediately relegated them to history. The new dot-com seemed cooler and naughtier than other getaway plans; more dirty weekend than honeymoon.

Launched by fresh-faced entrepreneurs Brent Hoberman and Martha Lane Fox in 1998, Lastminute was part of the heady but doomed 'dot-com boom' at the tail end of the 1990s, which saw a number of dubious internet-driven enterprises burn through millions of dollars of investment cash, then pop like soap bubbles when confidence in tech stocks evaporated.

Lastminute was one of the few survivors. Perhaps its founders were smarter – or less rash – than many of their contemporaries. Both Oxford-educated, they were imbued with a useful blend of self-confidence and naïvety: Hoberman was 29 at the time, Lane Fox just 25. 'If we had known then what we know now, maybe we wouldn't have done it,' Hoberman has commented. 'But there's a great power to start-ups. You always think that it's the giant companies that will do what you are doing, but they find it harder to move on a dime, as Bill Gates said. They don't take risks.' (www.startups.co.uk, 15 August 2007.)

The idea behind Lastminute.com was simple: it offloaded soon-to-be remaindered stock. In the words of *The Guardian* – where writer Victor Keegan astutely picked Lastminute as one of the likely success stories of the boom – it sold:

> … a wide range of goods and services like hotels and holidays for last-minute
> purchasers… Whereas most web start-ups sell other companies' products,
> Lastminute specializes in selling distressed or vanishing inventory – like hotel

room vacancies which won't exist a day later if unused. It is creating genuine new demand for products that would otherwise be consigned to oblivion.

'We've only just begun', *The Guardian*, 27 January 2000

Its founders met when they were management consultants at Spectrum Strategy. Hoberman had the idea for Lastminute because, he said, 'I really am one of those people that books a hotel at the last minute on Friday night'. ('Lastminute wonders', *Marketing*, 3 March 2000.) By then Lane Fox had moved on to another job, but Hoberman persuaded her to quit and join his start-up. She had always loved travelling; in fact, in her youth she'd dreamed of becoming a hotel proprietor. 'I spent hours playing "hotel" games and made my mother and father check in to their "room" (our living room)', she told *The Independent*. ('My Secret Life: Martha Lane Fox', 5 July 2008.)

Lastminute took the inherent escapist, self-indulgent nature of travel and amplified it. One of its stunts was a 'boss is watching' button, which instantly transformed the Lastminute homepage into a mass of business-like statistics and graphs. Lane Fox would also mail witty, engaging newsletters to regular users. The pair knew their audience – in many ways, they *were* their audience.

'By using the power of the internet to match buyers and sellers, we were able to add value to both,' Hoberman comments in the Startups.co.uk article. 'I think we did bring a sense that you could just "do it" to business, and that it could be enjoyable… We showed that you could launch a consumer brand from scratch, and that the internet enables you to do it much faster.'

The pair raised £600,000 of venture capital to get going, then worked their socks off: '14-hour days and bucket-loads of persistence. Lane Fox is said to have once called Alitalia 150 times before being granted a meeting', according to *Marketing*. The media clapped eyes on them – Hoberman's dark good looks, Lane Fox's blonde locks – and lapped them up, pushing more custom their way in the process. By 2000 their concern was still far from profitable, but they had captivated the media and the City. The next step was a stock market flotation; appropriately, it came at the last minute, just before the bubble burst.

Lastminute.com made its debut on the London Stock Exchange on 14 March 2000, valued at over half a billion pounds. Shares began trading at 380 pence, closing at 487.5. Tech stocks would start to fall in a matter of weeks, but Lastminute had effectively secured the means to weather the storm.

There followed a rapid period of expansion as Lastminute acquired 14 companies in three years. This may seem reckless, but as Hoberman has explained, it allowed Lastminute to gain the heft it needed to defend itself against rivals like Expedia. Even when its share price dived to well under £1, its future looked bright enough for investors to stand by it. 'I was surprised at how many people thought the business was performing terribly, yet we were ahead of plan and still had £50 million in cash,' Hoberman told Startups. co.uk. 'I suppose that's the hard thing about running a public company.'

In July 2005, Lastminute was sold to Sabre Holdings, owner of the online travel agent Travelocity, for £577 million. It still enjoyed strong brand recognition and was not dependent on low-margin flights – its acquisitions had also given it hotel and car rental businesses. Sabre delisted Lastminute and pushed ahead with a plan to dominate consumer online travel through Travelocity in the United States and Lastminute in Europe. However, it was eventually foiled by the emergence of Expedia and Booking.com – of which you'll hear more later.

In March 2015, Sabre finally sold Lastminute to the Bravofly Rumbo Group – a Swiss-based concern that owns a variety of travel search and booking services – for US$120 million. The group's chairman, Fabio Cannavale, described Lastminute as an 'iconic brand'. But it has lost its rarity value in the cut-throat world of online travel. Meanwhile, Hoberman and Lane Fox have thrived, spreading their talents to a variety of entrepreneurial and altruistic projects. It's hard to deny that they were visionaries.

Back in 2000, as quoted by *Marketing* magazine, Hoberman described his vision of the near future: 'It's seven o'clock, your mobile phone rings and we offer you 25 per cent off at your local Italian restaurant, followed by an opera, because we know you've just come back from Italy and are feeling nostalgic.'

When data met mobile, everything would change.

The origins of digital travel

But let's go back a bit, if you'll bear with me, because technology and travel were bed-mates long before the internet era. You heard the name 'Sabre' earlier – and it's highly significant.

Around the time Pan Am was launching its pioneering PANAMAC electronic reservations system (see Chapter 8), others were doing the same. In fact, the very first was something called Reservec (Reservations Electronically Controlled), developed in the late 1950s by Trans Canada Airlines along with the University of Toronto and Ferranti Systems.

Hot on its heels came American Airlines' Semi-Automated Business-Related Environment (SABRE – see what I mean?) conceived with IBM and implemented in 1961. Delta followed with its Deltamatic flight reservation system in 1964, and United with Apollo in 1971. Ironically, given Juan Trippe's claim that mass tourism would have a greater impact on the world than the invention of the atom bomb, they had their roots in US military technology designed to calculate the real-time flight paths of missiles. Soon, travel agents around the world were equipped with terminals that would link to central computing centres and allow them to book flights instantly. A European competitor, Amadeus, founded by a coalition of European airlines, emerged in 1987. Other coalitions of airlines created Galileo and Worldspan in the early 90s.

So how did hotels get in on the act? The key brand name to remember here is Pegasus, founded in 1989 by John Davis. At the time, Davis was the CEO of a consortium of 15 hotel chains. He devised a technology that linked the chains' inventory with the airlines' reservation systems. Inevitably, he soon began selling the technology to chains beyond the consortium.

Before long, these global distribution systems were handling not only airlines and hotel chains, but car hire services, tours and cruises too. They remain a cornerstone of the travel industry's architecture.

When it became clear that the internet was going to revolutionize the way consumers found and purchased goods and services, travel was an obvious sector to target. Sabre Holdings – owner of the airline reservation system – launched Travelocity.com in 1996. This put a new spin on the phrase 'armchair traveller' by giving consumers direct access to Sabre's airfares and schedules, as well as the ability to pay for tickets, book hotel rooms, rent cars and purchase entire packaged holidays.

That same year, Microsoft launched Expedia, which brought together several global distribution systems and put them in the hands of consumers. Few people remember now that Microsoft created the brand, which it spun off in 2000. Expedia has since acquired a host of online travel sites – including Travelocity in January 2015.

Expedia also acquired another online booking site in 2015: Orbitz, which was originally launched in 2001 by a group of US airlines (Continental, Delta, Northwest, United and later American) to compete with Expedia and Travelocity. At the planning stage it was code-named T2, which supposedly stood for 'Travelocity Terminator'. ('The definitive oral history of online travel', www.medium.com, 4 June 2015.)

One of Expedia's advertising campaigns is illuminating when it comes to the psychology of leisure travel. The slogan is 'Travel yourself interesting', and the idea is that when you return from your vacation, with fascinating pictures and anecdotes, you somehow become more popular and desirable among your peers. Stereotypical underdogs – the chubby girl at the gym, the caterer on the movie set, the office drone – are transformed into attention magnets when they show off their holiday snaps, attracting crowds of admirers and stealing the thunder of their more charismatic rivals. In other words, we don't just travel for the experience – we also travel for the bragging rights.

Expedia's most resistant competitor in the world of online travel turned out to be Priceline.com, founded in 1997 by Jay Scott Walker, who is described as 'an inventor'. The term seems anachronistic, but for Walker it appears to be entirely appropriate. The founder of research and development lab Walker Digital in Stamford, Connecticut, he has his name on more than 450 issued and pending US and international patents ('Meet Jay', www.walkerdigital.com).

Born in Queens, New York, Walker is the son of a real estate developer and a champion bridge player – not a bad combination if you're looking for entrepreneurial competitiveness. 'Both his parents encouraged him to take risks,' reveals a profile in *Forbes* magazine. 'He did. At age 9, he started a newspaper. At 10, he travelled to Europe on his own. At summer camp, at 13, he would buy candy in bulk and sell it at prices below what the camp charged. "I was a black marketer," he grins. "I was serving customers. I simply bypassed the monopoly."' ('An Edison for a new age?', 17 May 1999.)

Something of this thinking lay behind Priceline, which allows users to 'name their price' for an airline ticket. You put in a low bid for a flight to your chosen destination, and if an airline has a seat that may go unfilled otherwise, they'll accept it. The downside is that the conditions – the time of the flight, possible layovers – are not revealed until you've paid for the ticket, which you cannot cancel. Plenty of travellers were willing to take that bet. With former *Star Trek* actor William Shatner as its brand spokesman – after all, who's travelled further than Captain Kirk? – Priceline became a phenomenon.

Today the Priceline Group embraces a number of travel concerns. In 2005 it acquired another major player in the digital travel field: Booking.com. This had its roots in Holland, where it started out as a local internet start-up called Bookings.nl. By 2015 Booking.com was so successful that the European Union targeted it as one of the internet companies which exercised 'undue power over their market sector'. ('EU warns of "point of no return" if internet firms are not regulated soon', *The Guardian*, 24 April 2015.)

Its advertising focused on the difficulty of finding the perfect vacation. Various TV spots showed travellers arriving at a destination, realizing that it's their idea of paradise on Earth, and responding with the exclamation 'Booking dot YEAH!' (The double entendre attracted a little criticism, but to any normal adult the commercials were reasonably hilarious.) Priceline also owns the powerful travel search engine Kayak, which it acquired in 2013.

It was perhaps inevitable that Google, the monster of all search engines, would enter the travel sector. That happened in September 2011 with the launch of Google Flights, a few months after it had paid US$700 million for airfare and price search specialist ITA Software. One of the advantages of Google Flights is that users aren't required to enter a specific destination when they search – they can simply find out what's available to suit their budget and timing.

All of which points the way to a more subtle and intuitive form of travel searching.

Fighting for online customers

These days the online travel market is divided into three segments: 'meta' search engines like Kayak or Skyscanner; online travel agents (OTAs in industry jargon) like Expedia; and of course direct booking with hotels or airlines. So which are the most popular with consumers?

Kevin May, co-founder of the travel industry news site Tnooz, says:

> Generally, in Europe and the US, about 40 per cent of leisure travel is now booked online. The flipside of that is that 60 per cent of travel is still booked through traditional travel agents or call centres. Digitization is huge – it's transformed the industry – but not to the extent that most people think. Travel agents still shift millions of passengers a year – and in particular they fly millions of people every summer from northern European countries down to the Med.

Online travel booking is not a generational phenomenon, he adds. 'Booking via mobile may skew younger for the time being, but really it depends on what any given consumer feels comfortable with. Booking online has been around for 20 years, so the familiarity issues that people used to have don't exist any more.'

Online travel agents, with their ability to bundle flights and hotels to create package holidays, had things pretty much their own way until the emergence of broadband in the mid-2000s. Then, speedier access to the web favoured the rise of price comparison engines. 'They did a really good job of marketing themselves as unbiased: "We just tell you the prices." This was reassuring for cost-conscious consumers who were going through a recession.'

Since then, however, Booking.com has become the name to reckon with. Consumers find it quick and convenient – but hoteliers have a love–hate relationship with the site. One obvious disadvantage of online booking sites for hoteliers is that they have limited interaction with their guests – and no contact whatsoever before arrival. 'This is not just about building a relationship with the guest – it also has a direct economic impact,' says May. 'Hotels like to "upsell" various extras to guests when they book – dinner at the restaurant on arrival, spa treatments, excursions and so on. They're starting to make a lot more money out of the ancillaries they sell on top of the room.'

As you'll have realized by now, the major upshot of the digital revolution was that hotels and airlines were reduced to the role of suppliers; although they had the content, they'd lost touch with the audience. Today they're feverishly trying to rebuild that relationship. In 2016 Hilton launched a global ad campaign encouraging customers to book directly with them. Its endline: 'Stop clicking around'. At the same time, the group upgraded its loyalty scheme to ensure members got more benefits by booking directly through the brand.

Hotels also baulk at relying on sites like Booking.com because of the commission they're required to pay – as much as 20 per cent depending on the size and location of their property. But some smaller establishments admit that they can't live without the business the site brings them.

May says:

> One hotelier told me he'd been reluctant to go on Booking.com for years, because he felt he couldn't afford the commission, and he didn't want to lose control of his relationship with guests. But during the low season occupancy was down to about 30 per cent, which is roughly the point where you consider closing for the entire period. After testing Booking.com, his occupancy rose to 85 per cent even in the low season. You may not want to be beholden to Booking.com, but they fill your hotel.

Another problem facing hotels is the way they're ranked in search results. Where a hotel pops up on a consumer's home screen – at the top or towards the bottom (which is basically nowhere) – depends on a variety of factors, including the amount of commission the supplier brings the site, customer reviews and even the quality of their photo. Appearing near the top has become even more crucial as booking on mobiles – with their smaller screens – becomes more prevalent. ('How Booking Sites Influence Which Hotels You Pick', *The Wall Street Journal*, 17 January 2016.)

The question of distribution – getting hotel rooms and airline seats in front of customers – is central to the travel industry. 'The distribution strategy drives the marketing; they're intrinsically linked,' says May. 'If you're a hotelier, your distribution strategy is based on what percentage of your inventory you're going to sell through Booking.com, how much you're going to put through a global distribution system, how much you're going to sell direct and so on.'

He also mentions 'bed banks', a distinctly horrible term referring to wholesale sites that provide consumers or the trade with access to a database of cheap hotel rooms, having negotiated special rates with the accommodation providers. The bed bank is yet another channel that a distribution expert can consider.

'The distribution strategists will then turn to the marketing people and say: "We plan to do X amount direct this year, which means you should probably devote 30 per cent of your marketing budget to pay-per-click advertising on Google."'

For hotels struggling to rebuild brands and attract direct bookings after years of relinquishing control to online vendors, marketing investment is likely to prove heavy and complex.

There are a number of ways hoteliers can regain control of their destinies. A multi-channel distribution approach would seem advisable, rather than relying on a single platform. Having said that, small or independent hotels might find that a niche platform, such as Mr & Mrs Smith or DesignHotels, delivers the right customer profile.

Once the guests have arrived, it's up to the hoteliers to develop a relationship with them, from personalized service to simply asking the guests for their e-mail address (which online booking services typically withhold) before they leave. That way, the hotel may be able to persuade the customer not only to return, but also to book directly. An attractive and mobile-optimized website then becomes a necessity, with discounts and benefits offered to direct bookers. One approach we've mentioned elsewhere is the lifestyle strategy – turning a hotel concept into a brand that customers aspire to or identify with. For hotels who don't have access to a large advertising budget, a well-managed presence on social networks can help here. More of that in the next chapter.

For now we'll turn our attention back to the customers, whom we find scratching their heads, faced with so much choice that they're not entirely sure where to turn when booking their next trip.

Inspirational searching

For a long while, travel sites were surprisingly bad at providing inspiration. They were great at delivering cut-price hotels and flights, but they tended to be based on the assumption that users knew where they wanted to go, and when. The 'daydreaming' aspect that's so important to travel was almost entirely absent from the chilly digital world.

Slowly, that began to change. In May 2010, Kayak launched its Kayak Explore tool, a map-based service that allows users to search for cheap flights without naming a specific date, airport or even country. And in 2013, Spanish airline Iberia launched its 'inspirational search engine' to help customers match their preferences to potential destinations. It comes with a snappy slogan: 'The place to which you travel will be you'. Users can drag icons representing activities, food and even clothing styles (shirt versus swimming trunks) into a search bar, before clicking to see a map of places that might appeal to them. A brief experiment was rather disappointing: apparently there were no destinations at that moment for a fish-eating shirt wearer who likes 'learning' and the sea. Luckily, I'd heard about San Francisco in advance.

Talking of San Francisco, in 2015 a travel site based in the city, Hipmunk, announced that its 'Discover' tool, available initially as a mobile app, would enable travellers to search by theme: beach, ski, romantic, adventure and so on. ('Hipmunk Redesigns Mobile App and Adds Inspirational Travel Search Feature', Reuters, 5 November 2015.)

The research company Phocuswright predicted back in 2012 that 'inspirational searching' would be the future of online travel. This was due to the length of time people spent making a decision about their next trip: 'Travellers spend weeks contemplating their holiday options and typically book months in advance... For example, in the US, the average discretionary traveller spends 21 days selecting a destination and this selection is made 87 days before departure.' The same customer will then spend as long as 17 days researching flights and accommodation (presumably in between other mundane quotidian tasks) before booking. (*Empowering Inspiration: The future of travel search*, researched and written by Carroll Rheem.)

The holy grail for online travel, as in other consumer sectors, is the ability to match options to consumers on a one-to-one basis, based on their habits. 'Eventually... programs will be able to "learn" from an individual's behaviour over time,' says Phocuswright's report. 'When someone executes a search for the fifth time, the results should be more relevant than the first time. Perhaps it will never be truly 1:1, but micro-segmentation will at the very least help companies analyse behaviour and deliver increasingly intelligent results.'

However, this simple theory is surprisingly hard to put into practice, as Phocuswright admits, 'mainly because people tend to be extremely inconsistent'. The report adds: 'An endless array of situational aspects, such as trip companions, the reasons for taking the trip and volatility in personal finance, can materially impact what an individual is looking for. On top of this natural variation, travel is often connected to the desire to do/see something entirely new.'

At the end of the day, human beings – and the romance of travel – actually win. 'For the vast majority of travellers, vacations are simply too novel to have a ritual formula.'

Tour highlights

- The creation of electronic reservation systems by the airlines was the first step in a process which eventually separated suppliers from their customers.
- These evolved into huge global distribution systems that enabled travel agents to book a variety of trips at the touch of a button.
- The internet put this technology in the hands of the consumer, resulting in myriad online travel agents and 'meta' search engines focused on delivering cut-price travel.
- A confusing online marketplace drove some consumers back to traditional travel agents; other travellers had refused to relinquish the human touch.
- Meanwhile, suppliers began a battle to reduce the power of the middlemen and regain direct contact with the consumer.

Mobile and social 14 explorers

'Empty hotel rooms are a hotelier's worst nightmare.'

The benefits of being able to book a hotel room with your mobile phone become quickly evident if you're ever caught up in a French rail strike. A couple of years ago I was on my way from Paris to Cannes, with a connection in Marseille. But Marseille was as far as I got. With a mixture of relish and defensiveness, a railway worker informed me that there would be no trains to Cannes until the following day.

I shrugged (living in France for 15 years will teach you how to do that). I'd known industrial action was planned for that day; I felt lucky to have made it out of Paris. The only problem was that it was past 5pm and I had nowhere to stay.

Actually, not such a problem. Not in the 21st century. I retired to a nearby café and fired up my phone. A few weeks earlier I'd downloaded an app called HotelTonight, which does pretty much what it says: the app releases an updated list of cheap room deals at noon every day. Within a few seconds I'd identified five hotels near the old port – the most picturesque quarter of Marseille – with cut-price rooms available. I booked one, slipped my phone back into my pocket and headed for a taxi. A couple of hours later, I was eating *rascasse* with *riz à la provençale* on a restaurant terrace while looking out at the twinkling lights of the harbour.

HotelTonight was arguably the first start-up to make the connection between mobile apps, travellers and hotels with spare beds. 'Empty hotel rooms are an hotelier's worst nightmare,' *The Economist* pointed out, describing HotelTonight as a 'pioneer' in the mobile travel market. At the time of the article, the habit of simply showing up in a place and booking a hotel on the spot had yet to catch on – 'global nomads' were still in a minority. Those who had recourse to the app were often in difficult straits, the piece argued. 'Two-thirds of HotelTonight users… are either too tired, too drunk, or are unable to make it home due to transport problems. About

60 per cent say they woke up that morning not needing a hotel room.' ('Touch here for a bed', 3 February 2013.)

The app was launched in 2010 by Sam Shank, Jared Simon and Chris Bailey. Shank had previous in the travel sector. After a colourful early career in which he attempted to break into the Hollywood horror movie scene – but found himself mostly 'going to the post office, getting laundry and making coffee' – he was attracted to the emerging dot-com industry in Silicon Valley. His first solo venture was TravelPost, a social site that enabled people to share their travel experiences. 'But we realized this wasn't a good business because there was no advertising around travel stories... We quickly moved to a hotel review model, and that proved more successful.' ('Sam Shank: From horror films to hotels', BBC News, 8 December 2014.)

Having sold TravelPost for 'some millions', Shank began looking at the discount travel sector. His eureka moment came one evening while he was watching TV. 'I realized I was looking at my phone the whole time... So I went to the app store to see what they had in the travel category, and there wasn't anything very interesting there. This was odd given that hotel booking is the most profitable category of e-commerce, and apps are the future computing platform of the world, I thought.'

Shank and his colleagues assumed that the likes of Expedia and Lastminute would come out with apps almost before they'd had a chance to launch their own – but that wasn't the case. 'With our app you could book a hotel 50 times faster than with the other guys... It only takes 10 seconds.' As BBC News reporter Matthew Wall pointed out, hotels were delighted at being given the chance to sell off their empty rooms in the nick of time, even at a heavy discount. 'It was the Lastminute.com business model but in the age of the connected smartphone.'

Empowered travellers

Once people began casually using apps for everything from hopping across town in an Uber car to identifying great restaurants within walking distance, the romance between the travel industry and smartphones began to heat up. In 2015, Expedia – which by then had an app, of course – released a survey called 'The Mobilized Travel Consumer'. It pointed out that 'consumers in the United Kingdom and the US spend more time (30 per cent and 22 per cent more, respectively) on mobile devices from one year to the next, with desktop time declining'. Although 'the majority' of consumers in those two countries still researched and booked travel via PC, the survey suggested that 21 per cent now did so via phone or tablet.

Not surprisingly, the study pointed out that consumers 'toggled' between devices during the day, using a PC for planning travel during daylight hours – often at work – but turning to their mobile or tablet device in the evening. 'Travel research and transactions that originate from mobile devices tend to peak during the evening – between 6pm and midnight in both the US and UK... This means marketers may want to shift their messaging as the day progresses, making a compelling call to action or incentivizing bookings in the evening.'

In other words, hotel and travel suppliers needed to ensure that their marketing messages were 'responsive', adapting to the environment in which they appeared. 'Of all travel-related ads served each month for the PC, some 500 million are viewed on screens that are less than 75 per cent of a PC's screen size.' ('The Mobilized Travel Consumer,' white paper, Expedia Media Solutions, 2015.)

Mobile is a crucial battleground, but so is social. Any platform on which travellers can share their stories and images has marketing potential. The elephant in the room here, of course, is TripAdvisor, which has evolved from a user-generated review site into, in its own words, 'the world's largest travel site'.

Founded by software engineer Steve Kaufer in 2000, the site was originally intended to aggregate reviews from 'official' sources such as guidebooks or travel magazines. But when Kaufer and his team gave users the possibility of adding their own reviews, the floodgates opened.

At its best, TripAdvisor provided an effective counterbalance to the glossy images that hotels and resorts pasted in their brochures or on their websites. For every exaggerated claim there was a TripAdvisor commentator with a smartphone and an opinion. It was a new media brand, fuelled by a world-wide network of citizen travel journalists.

As it grew, hoteliers developed an ambiguous relationship with the site, feeling that it had the power to make or break their businesses, despite the fact that they had little control over reviews. There were claims of fake reviews, of hoteliers planting favourable reviews of their own establishments, or negative reviews of rival establishments.

On its website TripAdvisor retorts that it has a 'content integrity team' of 300 people over seven countries, as well as a 'proprietary fraud detection process'. However, with 315 million monthly users, it admits that some fake reviews slip under the radar: 'We invest massive amounts of time, effort and money into identifying and blocking fraudulent activity on our site. Despite this, with over 80 new contributions a minute, 24 hours a day, we're aware that a handful of fake reviews can slip onto the site for a period of time.' (www.tripadvisor.com, 'Content Integrity Policy'.)

Indeed, in 2011 the Advertising Standards Authority in the UK ruled that the UK version of the site could no longer 'claim or imply that all the reviews that appeared on the website were from real travellers, or were honest, real or trusted'. TripAdvisor removed the claims, while issuing a statement saying that the ASA had taken a 'highly technical view' of its marketing copy. It added, with some justification: 'We know that our users approach TripAdvisor with common sense, and make an educated decision based on the opinions of many. If people did not feel the insight they gained from our site was an accurate reflection of their experience they wouldn't keep coming back.' ('TripAdvisor banned from claiming its reviews are real', www.telegraph.co.uk, 1 February 2012.)

TripAdvisor effectively handed hoteliers an additional task – that of damage limitation, or at the very least message control. Some of them used the site to effectively address guest concerns and improve their service. Others were bitter. In an interview in 2013, founder Steve Kaufer said: '[W]hat you see in the press tends to be the hotelier who is upset by the bad review. That's not new – hotels have always had complaints – but now the complaint is aired very publicly. It's all in the name of transparency and we think we've done a very good service to the hospitality industry by letting value and customer service level the playing field.'

It was the familiar internet-era tale of empowering the consumer. Kaufer added: 'If you're bad you'll be at the bottom of our ranked list. [Hoteliers] should read the reviews, hear what's being said about them, fix the problems and strive to do better. If they earn better reviews they'll rise in the rankings and turn around their own fortunes. The system works.' ('Interview: TripAdvisor founder Steve Kaufer, www.telegraph.co.uk, 2 April 2013.)

After being acquired by the Expedia empire in 2005, TripAdvisor was spun off as a separate business in 2011. By the time of the interview cited above, its stock market value had doubled to US$7.5 billion.

TripAdvisor has continued to grow, but to an extent its very size has blunted the edge of its influence. As hotelier Nikos Tsepetis noted in Chapter 10, it now has the heft of a mainstream medium, with so many reviews that – in the end – you don't know whose opinion to believe. In fact, a more intimate form of 'word-of-mouth' might be preferable.

How to shine on social media

A few months before starting work on this book, I was invited to give a talk in Georgia (in the Caucasus, not in the United States). So one evening in early December I found myself checking in to a new and rather lovely boutique hotel called Rooms in Tbilisi. Glancing around the lobby, I noted the glittering Christmas tree in the corner and the bookshelves lined with real, authentically battered paperbacks, which I was invited to browse. When I reached my room, I immediately took a picture of the antique claw-foot bath and 1950s writing desk with rotary phone. Wandering down to dinner, I noted the eclectic mixture of mid-century Scandinavian and American furniture. Local artworks decorated the walls. After taking my phone out of my pocket for the fifth time in half an hour, I thought: 'This hotel was designed for Instagram.'

Social channels like Instagram and its many relatives – Facebook, Twitter, Pinterest and Snapchat, plus all those who've come along since I wrote this sentence – have given brands an opportunity to engage with mobile consumers, and the travel industry has not been slow to take advantage of them. Instagram, which offers the possibility of posting the kind of lush imagery that inspires travellers, is used with particular efficiency. Marriott (#travelbrilliantly), Hyatt ('Welcome to your daily dose of travel inspiration' #Hyatt), InterContinental (#InterContinentalLife) and Thomas Cook ('tag your best holiday shots with #ThomasCook') are among those who seem to 'get' the platform. Many smaller hotels and tour operators have also grasped its potential. The secret, of course, is not only to share your own pictures, but to encourage customers to share theirs, via your hashtag. It makes them feel part of a club – a timeless marketing tactic.

Charlie Scott, co-founder of the custom tour operator Trufflepig (see Chapter 15), believes Instagram locks in to both traditional and contemporary travel marketing. 'The way that travel is "sold", especially custom and experiential travel, is often visual, and we're increasingly seeing that approach online,' he says. But he warns that a picture is not just a picture – the style of the image (saturated, black and white, filtered or not) should reflect your brand identity. 'The way you take a photo of, say, Hong Kong, says a lot about how you'd approach that destination as a trip planner.'

Clearly, a social media strategy is focused more on brand-building than rapidly filling rooms. But social media also offers an unprecedented means of generating and influencing virtual word-of-mouth. The most popular

'Instagrammers' have thousands of followers, so even a small hotel may find that pictures of its amazing bathrooms or pretty gardens reach a global audience of potential guests.

Meanwhile, hotels or organizations that have a lot to say – or more often, *show* – on social media are building loyalty, because their fans will follow them. It's easy to feel a certain affection for even the largest travel company if they're delivering terrific content to your phone every day. A glimpse of a beautiful infinity pool in Penang tends to lighten your day. More to the point, you may even start wondering how you can get yourself there as soon as possible.

A vast group like Hyatt takes its social media strategy very seriously – and it can afford to. Indeed, in 2013 it launched the 'Control Room', a social services team tasked with engaging guests 'at a deeper level'. In practice this meant, among other things, monitoring positive tweets about Hyatt and reacting to them: anything from a bottle of champagne delivered to a guest's room to an upgrade. ('Inside Hyatt's revamped social media strategy', www.digiday.com, 11 July 2014.) The team could pick its way through the complex ecosystem of social media, from posting videos on YouTube to keeping Facebook updated with images, events and special offers.

Similarly, in 2016 Marriott was described as a 'genius' in a survey by US brand consultancy firm L2 for its variety of mobile and social offerings, including the Travel Brilliantly microsite – on which guests can post their own content – its mobile app and responsive website, as well as the online Marriott Traveler magazine. Marriott even has its own Content Studio which, among other things, produces extremely high-quality videos for YouTube, such as interviews with celebrity travellers and its own chefs ('Digital IQ Index: Luxury Hotels 2016', www.L2inc.com).

While they may not have the budget for a content platform, boutique hotels are in a surprisingly advantageous position in the digital era. Quirky properties like Rooms in Tbilisi are crammed with Instagram-friendly details, and they're also easy to get around. A manager, marketing director or owner could be simultaneously touring the hotel, greeting guests and snapping social-friendly images. Updating Facebook or Pinterest via mobile takes only a few moments, after all. In this world, a small property with a social-savvy manager can rack up 'likes' with the efficiency of a corporate giant.

The next level of interaction is to be found among mobile messaging services like WhatsApp, Facebook Messenger and even good old SMS, which for many of us are replacing e-mail as our means of staying in touch with the world. A travel brand that enables a relationship with its customers through these services can answer queries, defuse complaints, offer guidance and delight individuals in a way that makes call centres seem positively redundant.

Anything that brings the supplier closer to the customer will be welcomed. Travel, after all, is made possible by companies providing a service – tour operators, airlines, hotels – and the most satisfying service is delivered by warm, intelligent and knowledgeable human beings.

Tour highlights

- It did not take travel companies long to make the connection between smartphones and 'mobilized' consumers.

- HotelTonight was the first app that enabled travellers to book a discounted room on the spot when they arrived at a destination.

- As in so many sectors, digital put more power in the hands of the consumer. The most dramatic example was TripAdvisor, which turned hotel (and restaurant) guests into the 'citizen journalists' of the hospitality world.

- The travel business has hit back by forming closer relationships with consumers through social platforms and messaging apps.

- Social may not fill rooms quickly, but it builds brands, reaches influencers and engenders customer loyalty.

Special agents   15

'Connecting people to what they love.'

When I was 16 or so, I was finally allowed to leave my parents at home and go abroad with my best friend Tim. We were broke, obviously, but a travel agent found us a cheap week at the Italian seaside resort of Lido di Jesolo. Despite the fact that we had to travel by coach, it felt like the most sophisticated thing we had ever done. We spent our time drinking cappuccinos, getting sunburns and trying, mostly failing, to interest Italian girls. To get a little culture we signed up for a day trip to Venice, which we found staggering – not so much foreign as entirely alien.

On the last day we learned that the coach company had gone bust. Nobody seemed entirely sure how we were going to get home, or with whom. Mobile phones and the internet were still some way in the future. Having been turfed out of our hotel rooms, the whole coachload of us camped out on the terrace, drinking yet more cappuccinos. The hotel manager told us he had called the travel agent back in the UK, but for the time being he had no news. Surely they wouldn't abandon us?

Finally, as night began to fall, a replacement coach showed up. I can't remember all the details today, or even who the company was, but I was made dimly aware of the disadvantages of placing all your travel arrangements in the hands of a middleman. Since then, I've mostly made my own plans.

Travel agents and tour operators have suffered during the digital era. The latter perhaps less so, as they have always provided a curatorial, service-based experience, with a presence on the ground. But the travel agents – retailers and intermediaries, broadly speaking – have struggled to retain their dominance in a world where you can book a flight and a hotel with a few clicks of a mouse (or taps on your phone).

However, they are fighting back. Some have closed their storefronts but ramped up their virtual presence, using social media and apps to build relationships with customers. Access to data delivered by social tools also provides insights into travel habits and desires. Others, as we heard from Thomas Cook, have focused on brand familiarity and improved customer service to attract or retain clients.

'Smart travel agents are evolving to better meet the rising needs of today's traveller,' read an article on Skift.com in early 2016. 'Wary of being commoditized as just another sales channel, they are becoming increasingly focused on end-to-end customer experience, acting in part as concierge, advisor and confidant. More emphasis is being placed on building long-term relationships.' ('Smart travel agents adopt the concierge mindset', www.skift.com, 26 January 2016.)

The article suggested that travel agents should become 'trusted advisors', constantly available through digital channels. 'Travellers can easily text or call their advisor to fix a problem mid-trip. They can even Snapchat, WhatsApp and Facebook message many of them as they become more integrated in the daily lives of their customers.'

At the same time, the social chatter of individual customers can improve their overall experience. 'When a travelling couple shares a photo on Instagram at an obscure locale in Rotterdam or Seville, the top comment might be from their advisor recommending the best underrated restaurants or off-the-beaten path attractions down the road.'

Agents are using data, explains Skift, in a different manner to other industry sectors. 'Focused travel sectors like hotels, airlines, and cruises collect "vertical" data based on singular interactions between brand and traveller. Agents need to take a wider approach, collecting "horizontal" data to map out all travel habits from flights, accommodations and travel within a destination.'

But conversations, both virtual and face-to-face, are the real treasure trove for travel agents. 'In-depth conversations and post-trip debriefs will give advisors an advantage that online booking sites can't replicate,' Skift observes.

In part for this reason, many travel agents are resisting the pressure to close stores and go virtual. In the United States, Liberty Travel continues to open new stores. Dean Smith, president of Flight Centre USA – which owns the brand – told Skift:

> While there is obviously a very big trend in the market to go home and to cut your costs by being virtual, it undermines the industry to a degree because the customers just don't know that the brands exist, although the service exists. We want a billboard for our brand. Most of our enquiries still come either by e-mail or over the phone... [But] the fact that we have the billboard means that people see, recognize and acknowledge the brand.

> 'Bricks and mortar travel agents are still important, says Flight Centre's president', www.skift.com, 8 January 2016

Advice from expert human beings is still desirable, particularly for family holidays or once-in-a-lifetime trips like honeymoons. Travel is surprisingly hard to get right – and modern travellers are demanding. That's why they occasionally turn to very specialist operators indeed.

The world on two wheels

Some tour operators inspire an almost familial loyalty among their customers. I suspect Butterfield & Robinson is one of them. Since 1966, the company has been 'slowing down to see the world'. It specializes in organizing upmarket cycling and walking tours, of both the pre-packaged and bespoke variety. Based in Toronto, Canada, it has been voted the world's best tour operator by the readers of *Travel & Leisure* magazine. When it launched, it practically created the luxury active vacation category.

I caught up with its co-founder, George Butterfield, as the brand celebrated its 50th anniversary. 'This all started when I was a young lawyer,' he says. 'With my best friend Sidney Robinson and his sister Martha, who later became my wife, we had this idea of organizing grand tours of Europe for students over the summer. The idea was to have an adventure and also to contribute something. For some reason the professors accepted that they wouldn't be as good as we were at escorting young people around Europe!'

This carried on for a few years, during which time the students' parents often commented: 'This sounds great, but when are you going to organize something for us?'

In 1972 they gave it a try. 'It was a cycling tour of Austria and Bavaria,' recalls Butterfield. 'We printed and distributed 30,000 brochures. And we did not get one single booking.'

Understandably, they carried on lawyering for a while. Then in 1980, they placed 'one tiny ad' for a cycling trip around Burgundy in the *Toronto Globe & Mail*. 'We filled the trip within 24 hours,' says Butterfield. 'I think it was an idea whose time had come.' People had become aware of the importance of having an active lifestyle. 'I never really had a specific audience in mind; I just thought that a great way to see the world was by bike. It's the perfect pace, somewhere between walking and driving.'

The following year, they organized three trips. And the year after that, 15. More than double the year after that.

'In five years we had gone from one annual trip to 70. No one else was doing this, so once the American press picked up on it we got a big following.

Americans loved our trips. It felt much healthier than driving a car; they were outside and connected to what was going on around them.'

And because these travellers felt so much more 'alive and alert', as Butterfield puts it, suppliers like restaurants and hotels were getting a much more enthusiastic response. Dealing with B&R's customers was not a task, but a delight.

'We were the first company to tap into the notion of high-end outdoor tours. Not over-the-top, but deluxe, sophisticated.' For the first decade they had the market to themselves. 'But by 2000 there were probably a hundred or even two hundred competitors.'

Butterfield & Robinson, though, had two crucial things going for it: a solid heritage and a database of loyal customers. 'No matter how good your product is, it's very difficult to establish a brand from scratch in a growing market. We had so much press at the beginning because the idea was new.' Today B&R is simply the reference. 'We have a staff of 70 and trips around the world.'

The company no longer advertises. Communication is through press coverage, word of mouth, a well-designed website and a luxurious annual catalogue. 'The catalogue is a statement of quality,' says Butterfield. 'When you see how beautiful it is, you immediately get an idea of the care we put into our trips.'

In fact, he cites 'meticulousness' as one of the mainstays of the company's success. 'We pre-trip everything. Even if we've done the Burgundy tour about 200 times in the past 10 years, we send trip planners in advance.'

Fair enough – when you're paying up to US$7,000 for your vacation, you don't expect any slip-ups. But nor do you expect a homogeneous packaged experience, so B&R travellers aren't obliged to travel in a huddle. Once they have the daily route map, they can pretty much take things at their own pace, meeting up with their fellow travellers for dinner. Vans are on hand to race to their assistance if they get in trouble along the way.

Butterfield notes that fully customized trips are growing in popularity. B&R collaborates on the itinerary and books the accommodation, but after that the travellers are on their own. Or so it appears – in fact the company has representatives on the ground to help out whenever required. It's a form of travel that is rather disparagingly referred to as 'soft adventure', but the combination of challenge and comfort is an attractive one.

Butterfield is undismayed by competition in this and other areas, but he certainly isn't apathetic. 'I don't want to be the biggest – but I do want to be the best. And we're at the top of our game, for sure.'

Truffle hunting with the experts

In 2003, Charlie Scott noted that while online was 'exploding' in the world of travel, it wasn't necessarily helping people. 'They were just drowning in a sea of options,' he says. 'If I asked you to find the best hotel in Iceland, you could probably go online and do that within a few minutes. But if I asked you to find the guide in Reykjavik who tells the best stories, that may take you a little longer, and you still won't be certain you've got the right guy.'

Trufflepig – the company Scott founded with two colleagues – could find you the right guy.

Scott is an acquaintance of George Butterfield and an alumnus of Butterfield & Robinson. He has something in common with Juan Trippe, the founder of Pan Am, in that he chose travel over the banking sector. 'After school in Canada I came very close to becoming an investment banker,' he says. 'But after one particular interview I thought: "This is not going to feel very good if they actually give me a job." So instead I ended up working as a parking valet at a hotel in Vancouver, while saving up money to travel.'

On the suggestion of a friend he got in touch with Butterfield & Robinson, and in the autumn of 1994 found himself guiding bicycle trips in France. This was the start of a nomadic existence in which he would guide bike trips in the summer, ski in the winter, and branch out for research trips on behalf of B&R in Morocco and India. 'I became totally hooked on this alternative lifestyle. Once I became part of the business of travel, I knew I couldn't do anything that other people might describe as "normal" – but what I'd say was "boring".'

In 2003, Scott realized that there was a growing need for what he describes as 'pure custom travel'. 'At that stage, most tour companies were still basing a large part of their business on scheduled, brochure-driven group trips. Custom was maybe 15 or 20 per cent of their business. Meanwhile, I was speaking to people who'd say, "This trip sounds great, but I can't go in June" or "The destination is cool, but I don't wanna travel with people I don't know".'

Hence Trufflepig: a purely bespoke, high-end travel company. 'The idea was that we'd be an enabler that helps you find these amazing things that are very difficult to unearth.'

Scott and his co-founders would travel extensively, research destinations and then 'basically wait for the phone to ring'. There was no such thing as a typical client. 'One might say, "I wanna go to New Zealand to watch birds, and I love hiking and food." And based on our knowledge we would put the trip together for them.'

Trufflepig called itself a 'trip planning company', because it was neither a tour operator nor a travel agent. 'We had a bit of media coverage, but it was almost exclusively word of mouth and repeat business,' Scott adds. 'We would develop a relationship with people.'

He describes the keys to the business as 'knowledge and service'. 'We had no hotels, no boats, no tangible products – what we had was knowhow and the ability to deliver it. The thing that you absolutely cannot find online is the expertise that will match your interests to the ingredients of your trip.'

Scott believes people are willing to pay for expertise; indeed, Trufflepig introduced a 'trip planning fee' on top of the main ingredients of its vacations. This was determined by the length and complexity of the trip. 'It was a way of reminding customers that the kind of service we provided came with a cost.'

Scott believes such fees may become critical for travel organizers due to decreasing commission from conventional suppliers like hotels and airlines. He adds: 'But generally speaking people got it. One customer said to us, "You know why I travel with you guys? Because I don't want to blow a day." It's not a question of money – it's a question of making sure that the two-week vacation that your customer is going to take is perfect, with not a single bad day. We were that insurance.'

Scott suggests that, if you are a particular type of travel consultant, dealing with a niche group of customers paying US$20,000 or more for a trip, you don't even need a social media presence – or for that matter a website:

All you need to build a company are a handful of good client relationships. If you want to build a brand, however, you do need an online presence. But you need to get it right. The kind of language you use, the photos you use, the design – all of those are hugely important. At Trufflepig we spent a lot of time working out how to convey our sensibility. One thing we had in our favour in terms of branding was a really sticky name.

Scott sold his interest in Trufflepig to his partners in 2014, partly because he had an itch to travel with his family and find out 'what the next big thing was'. At the time of writing he's working as an independent travel consultant under the brand name Ditoui:

One thing I'm interested in is finding out is how to offer the kind of services we specialized in at Trufflepig to a more mid-market customer. I don't necessarily see it as my purpose in life to take rich people on vacation. I'm happy to introduce someone to the best hotel in Paris – but I also get a kick out of bringing people to the most amazing tapas bar in Barcelona, where they may not spend more than 10 bucks. What I'm proud of is connecting people to what they love.

Cultivating cultural travellers

'I've just done a trip to Paris,' says Florian Wupperfeld, founder of Leading Culture Destinations. 'An art safari.'

Perhaps that one line captures the singularity of Wupperfeld's company. Most visitors to cities spend an afternoon or two at a museum or a gallery, but for LCD's cultural explorers, that's the entire point of their trip. The London-based organization is designed, Wupperfeld says, for 'travellers who see arts and culture as an integral part of their lifestyle'. In some ways, it's a 21st-century throwback to the cultural curiosity that motivated the very first Grand Tourists.

And these tourists are very grand indeed: on Wupperfeld's Paris trip a group of 12 stayed in a hotel with rooms decorated by the fashion house Margiela, visited the Louis Vuitton gallery above the store on the Champs-Elysées, spent time in the private homes of prominent art collectors, enjoyed private fittings at cutting-edge fashion boutiques and dined in the city's most experimental restaurants.

Wupperfeld studied film production at UCLA before a stint as a DJ led unexpectedly into the marketing field. Working with Mercedes on the launch of the Smart car in 1997, he produced a compilation CD that was placed in the glove compartments of the first 200,000 cars to be sold ('A musical journey from Russian ballet and French movie soundtracks to electronic jazz and salsa'). In his next experience he helped BMW develop a culture strategy: 'They realized even earlier than Mercedes that Formula One, "performance" and all the rest of it appeals to men, but not particularly to women. Culture works for both.' Hence the brand's partnership with the Frieze art fair in London, among other initiatives.

After that, he worked for seven years with the Soho House Group – a collection of exclusive members' clubs for people in the creative industries – where he was creative and media director. This essentially meant ensuring the loyalty and connectivity of members, in person and via social platforms, a website and a magazine. He also launched the Berlin outpost of Soho House, he says, with a dash of modesty, 'because I was the German in the group'.

His next venture was CultureLabel.com, an online store selling objects 'curated' from the gift shops of prestigious galleries and museums. Not souvenir tat, he emphasizes, but exclusive homeware, jewellery and limited edition prints. 'In gift shops there are only 20 great products – the rest is garbage,' explains. 'The site just brings you the great stuff.'

Having sold that business in 2014, he founded the REMIX summits, which bring technology companies together with museum directors. 'Most museum directors think that cultural consumption has to do with buying a ticket to a museum and seeing a show, but today 90 per cent happens on your mobile and online.' REMIX helps museums and other institutions explore and benefit from the intersection between technology and the arts.

Leading Culture Destinations weaves together various strands of these disparate experiences. 'It's really about the fact that museums are transforming from places of pure cultural pilgrimage into social hubs. So in Paris you don't go to the Palais de Tokyo [a contemporary art space] just to see a show any more, you go to have lunch or dinner.'

Another example is the Whitney Museum of American Art in New York, which re-opened in a new location in May 2015. Conceived by starry Italian architect Renzo Piano, the building – which resembles a beached container ship – is located in the Meatpacking District and comes with its own hashtag: #NewWhitney. This was attached to more than 6,000 Instagram pictures in the first four days after launch. Inside the museum, visitors who want to snap photos with their phones are not admonished by security staff, but actively encouraged – turning them into the museum's PR team. You can hang out in the airy bookstore, lunch at the trendy restaurant (it's called Untitled) or shop Whitney handbags designed by Max Mara. Curbed.com called it 'the most social museum ever' (4 May 2015).

'Actually the idea of "exit through the gift shop" doesn't apply any more,' says Wupperfeld:

> It's more 'enter through the restaurant and exit through the exhibition'. The customer journey has changed. Add to this the fact that many countries are investing in museums because they see culture as one of their main nation branding tools – from Singapore to Abu Dhabi – and I thought that what Leading Hotels of the World are doing, six degrees to the right, I could do with Leading Culture Destinations.

LCD is a blend of online magazine, Michelin-style guide to the world's most fascinating cultural hubs, and travel company selling unique experiences. One example is a road trip to Marfa, Texas. Couples are flown to Los Angeles, where they pick up the keys to a Mustang and drive to Marfa, famed for its art galleries. They are accompanied by a top-flight photographer who shoots pictures of their trip and transforms the captured images into 12 signed prints. The trip and classy holiday snaps come at a cost of £49,000.

'This is a luxury travel business. What I do is not haute couture – it's haute culture.'

Alongside these activities, Wupperfeld launched the LCD Awards, designed to 'shine a light' on the world's leading cultural attractions, which need foot traffic and funding. 'Take the Aspen Art Museum in Colorado – amazing place, but somewhat drowning in cool architectural magazines without drawing the attention of the mainstream. That's because editors either don't have it on their radar, or the hotels pay more money to be in their magazines. Governments are spending a fortune on these museums, but they have to activate them.'

Customers for LCD's trips tend to come, he says, via word of mouth. Thanks to his years working for Soho House, he is a formidable networker:

> If you ask [fashion designer] Haider Ackermann, whom I know, where the customers for his haute couture dresses come from, he'll also tell you it's word of mouth. That's logical, because it's a very niche audience. Like my trips, everything is hand-crafted. To find the real jewels, you have to be very well informed. When I did my Paris art safari with a group of 12, I had a five-week pre-production period working with two people to ensure that every aspect of the three-day trip was perfect. That's what my customers are paying for.

Gift packages in the hotel room on arrival, chauffeur-driven cars, private rooms in top restaurants where the chef pops out to say hello – it's about as far from mass tourism as can be imagined. In a world where everyone can go anywhere, travellers will pay for the new, the exclusive and the hidden.

Tour highlights

- Travel agents have suffered in the digital era, but they have three things on their side: brand familiarity, the human touch – and data.
- They can use data 'horizontally' to determine travel habits among specific groups of customers.
- Many have closed their physical presences to become online businesses, building customer relations through social media.
- But others have swung in the opposite direction to take a more personalized, service-based approach.
- In a digital world, human expertise is a valuable asset. Exclusive tour operators and bespoke trip planners with on-the-ground knowledge are sought after.
- Service fees may become crucial in an environment of shrinking margins. But the service must be discernible to the customer.

The world between two covers

16

'A good guidebook is still fantastic value for money.'

A café on a beach in Goa, southern India. Actually, café is too grandiose a word for it – this is a shack, which looks as if it has sprung organically from the sand in an ad hoc arrangement of driftwood and dried palm leaves. The proprietor, if one can ever really own such a place, cooks up searing fish curries – kingfish, pomfret, occasionally prawns – with a big pan and a butane stove out the back. Cold Kingfisher beers and Cokes are conjured from a rapidly liquefying ice bucket. We've been warned off the mineral water, because the bottles are sometimes refilled from the tap, which can result in stomach unpleasantness.

Otherwise, it is a wonderful arrangement. You dive into the rolling Indian Ocean breakers, recline on a towel, refuse offers of handmade rugs, Ganesh statuettes and massages from the strolling hawkers and then, when you're ready, roll up your towel and take your place at a weathered wooden bench to eat lunch.

The warm grey wood of the table in front of me already bears a couple of fading rings left by the moisture trickling from my beer bottle. Beside them is a battered, dog-eared paperback book, already besmirched with greasy finger-marks and smelling faintly of sunblock. Its title is *The Rough Guide to India*.

There have been other guidebooks, of course. The Lonely Planet brand is bigger and more famous. But for a certain generation of British travellers, the Rough Guides were *our* guides. We felt as if they'd been written specifically for us, by people like us.

Which, of course, they had.

Tools for travellers

By the early 19th century, guidebooks had evolved from picaresque travel journals containing a smattering of hints and tips into practical guides. Mariana Starke, whom you may remember from the first chapter, helped visitors to France and Italy grapple with foreign food, accommodation and even bureaucracy with unfussy prose and a useful ratings system based on exclamation marks rather than stars. Her books were published by John Murray, who went on to produce a whole series of highly respected guidebooks.

One early brand name you might be familiar with is Baedeker, if only from the 1908 EM Forster novel (and very popular 1985 Merchant–Ivory film adaption) *A Room With A View*, in which Lucy Honeychurch finds herself 'in Santa Croce with no Baedeker'.

Karl Baedeker was a third-generation German publishing mogul who began publishing travel guides after acquiring a smaller firm that had released a successful guide to the Rhine, *From Mainz to Cologne*. Still in his 20s, Baedeker was hungry for culture and experience: he was said to be fluent in 10 languages. He brought out a revised and repackaged version of the Rhine guide in 1835. This was followed by guides to Holland, Belgium and Switzerland, all prized by users for their infallible advice and beautiful fold-out maps.

Taking his cue from John Murray, Baedeker packaged his guides smartly, in red leather with gilt trimmings. He also adopted Murray's star system for reviews. Necessarily detail-oriented, he researched each guide personally: he was once spotted counting the stairs to the roof of the cathedral in Milan by placing a coin on every twentieth step to ensure accuracy. And while it's hard to imagine toting around these hefty, encyclopaedic tomes today, it's worth remembering that the wealthy tourists who bought them also travelled with a couple of steamer trunks' worth of clothing and accessories.

Baedeker died at the age of 57 – but he had taken the precaution of having three sons, all of whom worked in the business. The eldest, Ernst, published the guide to the Rhine again – this time in English. Other guides were soon translated, spreading Baedeker's renown. The English later had cause to regret this innovation – the Nazis are said to have used the guides to select historic sites for bombing (albeit in a reprisal for the Royal Air Force's bombing of Lübeck and other storied German cities). Thus, Exeter, Bath, Norwich, York and Canterbury were subject to a series of savage raids in the spring of 1942, collectively known as 'The Baedeker Raids'.

This seems to have had little impact on the respectability of the Baedeker name. The Baedeker guides remained in the family until the death of Eva Baedeker in 1984. Vintage Baedekers are highly collectible – and the German publisher MairDumont now publishes brand new guides under the Baedeker imprint. ('Baedeker is back', www.telegraph.co.uk, 22 December 2007.)

So successful were Karl Baedeker's guides – and so pervasive his brand – that he became known retrospectively as 'the father of modern tourism'.

Turning a new page

The story goes that Mark Ellingham was looking for a guide to Greece and couldn't find one that suited him. So he sat down in 1981 and wrote the first Rough Guide. The truth, as even he admits, is slightly more complicated.

'The fact is that I was looking for a job – and couldn't really find one,' he says:

> After my rejection from the BBC shortlist I decided to try my hand at writing travel guides. I'd noticed that there was a huge gap in the market: at that point Lonely Planet only covered Asia, and all the other guidebooks were rather old-fashioned and almost entirely American. They seemed to exist in some parallel universe where French people wore berets and striped shirts. I thought I knew Greece fairly well, so that seemed like a good place to start.

For Ellingham, travel was about 'mixing it up with the locals', as well as taking the history and culture of the country he was visiting seriously. 'At the time I assumed that the people we were writing for had no money at all – which was probably the case. But a couple of years later we realized that all sorts of people were using the books because of the contemporary angle, so we broadened the contents to reflect that.'

It's fair to say, though, that the books reflected the realities of the era: 'This was very much before low-cost flights. Travellers on a budget would take trains or coaches, while others would take rather expensive flights. Most people didn't just go away for the weekend – once you got to a place you'd stay there for two or three weeks.'

Ellingham says 'Rough Guide' was more of a catchphrase than a brand name. To British readers it came over as self-deprecating irony, which was often lost on US audiences. 'I once got a telex from a US distributor saying "'Rough' at best pejorative",' Ellingham recalls. For a while, the guides were published in the United States under the name Real Guides. 'That was a mistake, of course. Once you have a name you should stick with it.'

The initial guide to Greece was followed by guides to Spain and Portugal. More were quickly commissioned, and Ellingham found himself at the hub of a bustling editorial office in South London. 'It grew entirely organically as a business, with the advantage that all the people who ran it started out as writers.' This shone through in the readability of the text and the in-depth insights into art and architecture; you could actually sit down in a corner of a café and escape into a Rough Guide.

It's fair to say that, for their users, Rough Guides became something of a cult. So perhaps it's not surprising that a Rough Guide television show followed. It was brought to life by Janet Street-Porter, the ground-breaking TV producer behind the influential youth-oriented current affairs show *Network 7*. In 1987 she had just been appointed head of youth programming at BBC2 when Ellingham's pitch for a new type of travel show landed on her desk. British travel broadcasts at the time were still stranded in the 1970s, with orange-faced presenters of a certain age sipping Campari in unthreatening locales; they were aimed at holidaymakers, not travellers.

Street-Porter's vision for *Rough Guide* tossed a Molotov cocktail into that cosy scenario. It was hosted by Magenta Devine, a former rock band publicist, along with smoothly spoken Indian journalist Sankha Guha. Whether they were in Amsterdam or Vietnam, Devine wore fabulous outfits and dark glasses, while Guha remained a model of insouciant charm. The Steed and Mrs Peel of travel reporting, they showed a generation how to see the world. All this, naturally, had a positive impact on the guides themselves.

The books were initially published by Routledge, but when the publisher decided to sell, it was forced to consult Ellingham. 'I had a clause in my contract stating that the guides could not be sold without my permission. So I borrowed some money and bought the company myself.'

Penguin took over distribution duties – and in 1995 bought 50 per cent of the company. 'We felt that to become a global name and compete with Lonely Planet, we needed to be part of a bigger group. Plus, everyone who had ever written a book for us got some money.'

By then, the Rough Guides had expanded beyond travel to guide readers through the labyrinths of world music and classical music. 'But our biggest selling guide ever was *The Rough Guide to the Internet*,' says Ellingham, with a laugh. 'It sold 4.5 million copies.'

Ellingham himself was excited by the possibilities of the web and negotiated a deal with technology magazine *Wired*. 'We hatched a plan to publish extracts from the guides online and make money by selling links to hotels,' he recalls. The idea failed. 'We were far too early. Even though *Wired* was based in San Francisco, only about five hotels there had decent websites. We made a reasonable amount of money from banner advertising, but eventually *Wired* decided to concentrate on technology.'

Today, Ellingham admits that the Rough Guides 'never really cracked' the internet – but he's not convinced any of the big brands have. 'People are unwilling to pay for content now. I'd say most guide companies are doing about half the business they did at their peak.'

Penguin acquired the remainder of the company in 2002 and Ellingham quit the business in 2007 'after 25 Rough years'. With a touch of irony, he had become concerned about the growth of air travel – mostly due to budget airlines – and its contribution to climate change. So in 2006 he teamed up with Tony Wheeler, the co-founder of Lonely Planet, to raise awareness of the impact of travel on the environment, using the campaign slogan 'Fly less and stay longer'.

Logically, Ellingham and Wheeler should have been rivals, and the histories of the two brands have parallels. Today owned by NC2 Media, and still said to be the largest guidebook publisher in the world, Lonely Planet began as a kitchen table operation in the home of Maureen and Tony Wheeler. Having 'met on a bench in Regent's Park and married a year later', in 1972 the couple embarked on a honeymoon voyage overland across Europe and Asia to Australia. Inspired by the experience, they sat down and wrote *Across Asia on the Cheap*, which they stapled together and sold to friends. Within a week they'd sold 1,500 copies – and suddenly they were publishers. ('About Lonely Planet', lonelyplanet.com.) The name 'Lonely Planet' came from a misheard lyric: the actual words are 'lovely planet', from a song called Space Captain, recorded by Joe Cocker. Two years later, the couple's second journey led to *Southeast Asia on a Shoestring*.

The series expanded when the couple encouraged other travellers to approach them with ideas for – or preferably fully-completed – guide books. These were rough-and-ready, authentic affairs, culturally attuned to the 1970s hippie trail. But like the Rough Guides, the books soon became more inclusive, maintaining an alternative image but losing their whiff of hashish. By 2007, when BBC Worldwide acquired 75 per cent of the Australian company, it had become, in the words of one reporter at the time, 'travel publishing's Microsoft'. ('Journey's end for the guidebook gurus?', *The Guardian*, 7 October 2007.) A Lonely Planet magazine was launched in 2010, adding to the sense of ubiquity.

Of course, all guidebooks could be criticized for creating mini parallel universes within the countries they cover: a list of sights, cafés and restaurants that their users feel obliged to stick to, leaving other destinations on the fringe. Bolder travellers might prefer to rely on happy accidents, chance discoveries and unexpected meetings. Or today they might wish to mine social networks for tips that correspond more closely to their own tastes. In that respect, guidebooks have lost much of their power to influence the economic fortunes of hospitality providers.

At first, Lonely Planet's BBC experience seemed to indicate that travel guides could flourish in the digital era. By 2011, when the BBC acquired the remainder of the company from the Wheelers, Lonely Planet's digital presence embraced a website with 8.5 million users, as well as 140 different apps for various destinations. But slumping print sales, radical changes in the way consumers navigated the world – 'the mobile social revolution' – the rising value of the Australian dollar and a global recession all began to bite. In 2013, the BBC sold the Lonely Planet brand to NC2 Media, owned by US billionaire and former tobacco magnate Brad Kelley, for £51.5 million (US$77.8 million) – almost £80 million less than it had paid for the company.

At the time, the surprisingly young executive director of NC2 Media, 24-year-old Daniel Houghton, stated:

> The challenge and promise before us is to marry the world's greatest travel information and guidebook company with the limitless potential of 21st-century digital technology... If we can do this, and I believe we can, we can build a business that, while remaining true to the things that made Lonely Planet great in the past, promises to make it even greater in the future.

'US buyer for BBC's book unit on travel', *The New York Times*, 19 March 2013

Agonizing staff cuts and restructuring followed. But apart from the news that the brand had relocated its head office to swish new digs in a former Melbourne brewery – whose spaces are divided into 'zones' recalling New York City, tropical jungles in Borneo, sparse Iceland landscapes and traditional Japanese architecture – messages from the Lonely Planet remained strangely muted. This may confirm Mark Ellingham's intimation that travel guides have a hard time hacking a path through the digital jungle.

Meanwhile, some years after his partnership with his former rival, Ellingham himself remains a strong believer in ethical travel: 'If you're travelling in Europe,' he says, 'take the train.'

These days he runs another small publishing company, Sort of Books, with his wife Natania. This was initially set up to publish an autobiographical travel book by a friend, Chris Stewart. *Driving Over Lemons: An optimist in Andalusia* was a surprise bestseller and a breakthrough for both author and publishing house.

Ellingham also retains an affection for guidebooks, in their non-app, non-internet, paper form. 'A good guidebook is still fantastic value for money. If it leads you to just one hidden away restaurant, and one evening that you'll never forget, that's £12.99 well spent.'

Tour highlights

- Early travel guides were picaresque affairs penned by well-travelled writers, from Michel de Montaigne to Robert Louis Stevenson.

- As the Grand Tour took off in the 18th century, guides began to include practical tips and advice.

- In the 19th century, the German publisher Karl Baedeker became a force in the guidebook business.

- 20th-century guidebooks by a string of US publishers helped travellers feel more secure abroad, but had a certain staidness about them. In 1972, intrepid travellers Tony and Maureen Wheeler sat down to write the first Lonely Planet guide, a chatty alternative.

- Almost a decade later, in the UK, Tony Ellingham created the Rough Guides, which inspired a new generation of budget travellers and a cult TV show.

- Sales of paper guides have slumped in the digital era, although the major brands are battling on with internet and mobile content.

Rise of the 'poshtel'

17

'A type of customer we didn't even know was out there.'

Josh Wyatt was learning to surf in Bali when he came up with a plan. When he wasn't riding the waves, Wyatt worked for a London investment company called Patron Capital, which was looking for opportunities in the hospitality sector. Wyatt had asked for time off 'on my own dime', as he put it, to travel and reflect. When he returned to Patron, he shared his big idea. '[I] said, look, hostels seem really interesting right now, and nobody's exploiting this.'

Right on cue, a company called Generator Hostels came up for sale. Established in 1999, it had only two locations – in London and Berlin – and was family-owned. In 2007, on Wyatt's prompting, Patron bought it and began developing it into a European chain and a coherent brand – with Wyatt as chief strategic officer. ('The Generator game', *Boutique Hotelier*, February 2015.)

For years, youth hostels had been the crash pads of choice for hard-up young tourists. But they were about as glamorous and comfortable as army barracks, without the discipline or the mess hall. Generator and a clutch of rival chains deliver on the gregarious, informal atmosphere of the original hostels – as well as the budget rooms – but score far higher on satisfying the demands of globe-trotting millennials (and those of a similar mindset), such as free Wi-Fi, a bustling bar, a lobby that feels more like a bohemian apartment, private rooms and even en suite bathrooms. No more creeping out into the hallway with a towel to discover that all the showers on your floor are occupied, or stepping into a flood zone when you finally get your turn. Welcome to the 'poshtel' – a hostel with charm.

Along with Generator, a couple of the better known 'poshtel' brands are Meininger and Freehand. The latter's locations in Chicago and Miami feature idiosyncratic design – the lobby of the Chicago Freehand has a Native American feel, with bright prints and even totem poles – destination bars and amenities like swimming pools and ping pong tables. Travellers can access all this for as little as US$30 a night, if they're willing to share a room. Private rooms are a tad below standard hotel prices.

Meininger is a German company that has established a string of hostels across Europe, starting in Berlin in 1999. 'Grandma sewed the curtains, and the founders developed a great concept: their Meininger hotel should offer more than a hostel and be cheaper than a hotel,' the website reads. It positions the brand as 'The urban traveller's home'. ('How it began', www.meininger-hotels.com.)

When he took charge of Generator, Josh Wyatt knew what he wanted to do: he would borrow from the playbook of boutique hotels and offer character, quirkiness and experience at a budget price. By the time of the interview with *Boutique Hotelier*, the chain had expanded to 11 locations across Europe. Design-wise, the beds and the showers were similar throughout the chain, so regular guests would know 'that they'll get the same sleep experience'; but Generator went to town on the façade and the public areas. 'Each building looks unique, which has been purposefully done because we want to create a product for both travellers and locals.'

Connecting with the tribe

What's fascinating is that Wyatt – in common with, I believe, the other entrepreneurs in the 'poshtel' niche – tapped into a market that he barely knew existed, or had at least intuited but did not proactively target. These were the digitally-enhanced global nomads, often working in tech or creative industries, who've cropped up elsewhere in these pages. In short, a tribe. Very often, they're looking for a single room that does not resemble a cell in a hotel that has a cool and sociable atmosphere. Not an easy find in the mainstream hotel market, take my word for it.

'Yes, our core demographic is the 18- to 35-year-old, traveller, backpacker market, but we've seen families and corporate people coming in – the young graphic designer who is in town for a conference, that sort of thing,' said Wyatt during the interview above. 'That type of customer we didn't even know was out there, but we do now.'

This appealing mix of youth, business and creativity has bred an aura of trendiness that Generator has learned to tap into. It 'activates its spaces' with talks, launch parties and fashion shows. When it opened a new hostel in Stockholm in 2016, it deliberately provided more event space – at the expense of 22 guest rooms.

Wyatt said:

The fact that we're actually thinking about doing this is absolutely shocking, because when we first set out to look at creative hostels, or design-led experiences, we didn't actually foresee or think that cool, on-brand corporates would start to look at the hostel space to have an event… But that's the real story today. Companies like Uber and Urban Outfitters reach out to us now to launch a new event or tie-in at Generator.

'Generator Hostels' leaders explain the rise of hostels for business travellers', www.skift.com, 29 February 2016

A stronger emphasis on events is likely to grow more common in the poshtel niche, especially as millennial travellers are lured away by the sharing economy – as we're about to see. Design-led hostels need the right guests to legitimize their air of coolness, but the discounted rooms could be balanced by big-bucks corporate events in their public spaces.

In any case, Wyatt believes most mainstream hotels waste money on amenities that many guests don't care about. He told Skift: 'The reason why we can charge less than a hotel room is that when you walk into the hostel, you don't have a bellman. You don't have a concierge. There's probably 10 other operational touch points that are reduced. Then you go in the room… we've really stripped down the room to be functional and very comfortable, but not superfluous.'

Wyatt reckons that in a traditional hotel room there are about 10 things you'll never touch. You've probably noticed some of them: the trouser press, the ballpoint pen, the letter-headed paper, the shower cap, the shoe-polishing sponge and so on. Not to mention three-quarters of the stuff in the mini bar. 'That requires housekeeping to check them and inventory them… I'm not saying it's a poorly designed room. It's simply a room that just has stuff that people don't use. That is what effectively forces the owner and the hotelier to drive a higher rate.'

But here's the problem: many younger travellers have discovered that not only can they do without a trouser press and shoe-polishing sponge, but they can actually do without a hotel room. In fact, they prefer to stay in somebody's home.

Tour highlights

- Today's young travellers require free Wi-Fi, a buzzing bar scene, and a cool lobby in which they can tap away on their devices.
- The 'poshtel' combines budget rooms with design consciousness and all the amenities mentioned above.

- Poshtel owners stripped away some of the archaic, superfluous elements of traditional hotels – do you really need a concierge, a porter and a trouser press? – to provide rooms that were functional yet comfortable.
- Poshtel brands like Generator have parlayed their trendy vibe into a corporate event offering for brands that want to benefit from conferred coolness.

Airbnb and the sharing economy 18

'Live anywhere in the world, even if it's just for one night.'

I meet Jonathan Mildenhall, the chief marketing officer of Airbnb, in almost ridiculously glamorous circumstances. We're both attending the Cannes advertising festival, and I've hot-footed it to our rendezvous after watching Gwyneth Paltrow talking about her lifestyle brand, Goop, to an intimate audience of marketing folk. Her presentation took place on a terrace overlooking the beach. The actress-turned-entrepreneur was perched on a stool, framed by the sea, with her hair stirring in a slight breeze. I expected someone to shout 'CUT'.

The meeting with Mildenhall has a slight air of art direction, too. It takes place in the Airbnb flat his team is installed in. The room is beautiful, with high ceilings, moulded cornices, a polished parquet floor and just the right blend of contemporary and antique furniture. Mildenhall later reveals that Gwyneth is also staying in an Airbnb property during her sojourn in Cannes. Both of these examples play into one of the company's marketing challenges: to convince potential customers that the site is not just for budget travellers; that it has properties to suit every taste and bank balance. Airbnb has discreetly spread the message that celebrities such as Mariah Carey, Beyoncé and the soccer star Neymar have all stayed in luxury apartments listed on its site.

To say that Airbnb has shaken up the travel industry is an understatement. In theory its offer is simple: it's an online marketplace that allows people to rent out their own homes, either in part or entirely, to travellers on a short-term basis. In practice, since its launch in 2008 it has changed the way people think about travel and plucked millions of tourists out of hotel rooms. One travel industry journalist told me: 'If a hotelier tells you they're not worried about Airbnb, they're lying.'

The company started modestly as AirBed & Breakfast, when industrial designers Brian Chesky and Joe Gebbia realized they could cover part of the rent on their shared San Francisco loft by accommodating travellers in their living room, via a trio of airbeds. The pair were prompted by the fact that there was a dearth of accommodation in the city during the annual conference organized by the Industrial Designers' Society of America.

Their promotional article on the design site Core77 read:

> For 'an affordable alternative to hotels in the city', imagine yourself in a fellow design industry person's home, fresh awake from a snooze on the ol' air mattress, chatting about the day's upcoming events over Pop Tarts and OJ… And so was born AirBed & Breakfast, where 'guests' receive a home-cooked breakfast (not necessarily Pop Tarts, but hey, we can't guarantee anything) and designer type hosts who know their way around town.

'AirBed & Breakfast for Connecting '07', www.core77.com, 10 October 2007

Realizing they were onto something, Chesky and Gebbia – with the help of a third associate, technical architect Nathan Blecharczyk – officially launched AirBedandbreakfast.com in October 2008, shortening it to Airbnb the following spring. At the time of writing the original article could still be found online – except that now it links through to the massive Airbnb offering, with two million listings and rising.

Airbnb has evolved into one of those brands that transcend their original purpose to embody a shift in society – in this case the rise of a more mobile, flexible and self-sufficient generation. Mildenhall refers to it as 'a community-driven superbrand'. A breezy and exuberant sort, he talks of the brand with infectious enthusiasm.

He did not always feel that way.

When Mildenhall got the call from Airbnb, he was working at Coca-Cola as 'SVP integrated marketing and design excellence', which in essence meant he helped to lead the strategic and creative marketing agenda across Coca-Cola's brand portfolio. In other words, one of the best marketing jobs in the world. And he had scrapped his way up to that position: as Mildenhall himself has pointed out, he is by no means a traditional US marketing executive. In fact he's English, black, and was brought up on a Leeds council estate by his single mum. After graduating from Manchester Polytechnic (now Manchester Metropolitan University), he became the first ethnic minority (and indeed the first polytechnic) graduate at McCann Erickson in London. During the first part of his career he stepped from one starry British agency to another; immediately before Coca-Cola, he was head of strategy at the pioneering independent shop Mother.

After seven years at Coke, hopping across to a start-up that rented out vacation flats was not really on the cards. Nevertheless, he was intrigued enough to fly to San Francisco to meet Chesky.

'At that point, although I was very curious, I didn't think I wanted a job at Airbnb,' he admits:

I worked at Coca-Cola, and Coca-Cola knows the one thing that really protects the fortunes of a brand is excellence in marketing, storytelling and creativity – Coke puts a premium on those things, they see them as a competitive advantage. I was head of marketing for North America, their biggest market, so I had a big voice, a big team, big results. When I looked at Silicon Valley, I saw a place that created amazing tools that disrupt the way people connect, create, share, converse and learn, but never really invested in branding, with the notable exception of Apple. For every strong brand that comes along, there are hundreds that vanish, consumed by the next big thing. You could almost call Silicon Valley the graveyard of brands.

So his attitude as he sat down opposite Brian Chesky was one of scepticism, to say the least:

I told him: 'Look, Brian, before you interview me, I need to ask you a couple of questions – because to be honest, your response will determine how hard I'm going to work at this interview.' I explained to him that I wasn't interested if this was a vanity CMO hiring, or a sales development drive. I'm interested in building cultural brands: brands that actually mean something; brands that have purpose. So how did he feel about that?

Mildenhall recalls that Chesky took a deep breath and then spoke at him for half an hour. 'It was a 30-minute monologue about his vision for Airbnb, his vision for the community, his vision of creativity – and frankly after just seven minutes of it I'd made the decision that I was going to work for him. Today I see my job as getting inside his head and transforming his vision into a globally recognized brand narrative.'

Airbnb, Mildenhall believes, will be a generation-defining brand – as symbolic as Coca-Cola in the eighties, Nike in the nineties and Apple in the early 2000s. 'All three founders want that for Airbnb, but they also want it to be a multi-generational company; they hope their sons and daughters will work there. So they're not interested in being one of these Silicon Valley companies that rises for a few years and then just disappears.'

Mildenhall was also attracted by the notion that Airbnb can change lives by introducing people to new cultures in the most intimate way, by literally making them feel at home. 'We are a business and a community that is fuelling greater trust and greater humanity.'

Anybody who has watched the TV series *Silicon Valley* will be familiar with the cliché of the tech mogul who believes his technology will make the world a better place, but Mildenhall is all the more convincing for being an outsider. And crucially, for his employers, he's able to convince others too.

Belong anywhere

One of my favourite Airbnb ads is an animated tale from 2014. It begins in Berlin, at the time of the Wall, where two border guards spend years facing one another from opposite sides of the divided city. Eventually, the guard on the Western side leaves Berlin for a new home in Copenhagen, but the memory of the Wall continues to haunt him. Years later, his daughter persuades him to return to a reunified Berlin, where they rent an Airbnb apartment. As they arrive to pick up the keys, the former guard is astonished to be greeted by his opposite number from the East. The key to the apartment turns out to be the key that unshackles the man from his past. 'Belong anywhere,' says the end line.

We're told at the start that the spot is based on a true story, so I ask Mildenhall about it.

'It's incredible, isn't it?' he says:

> These are two people who spent years more or less pointing guns at one another. I was actually told that story shortly after I'd arrived at Airbnb, as an anecdote. I said, 'Wait, who else knows about this? Why aren't we doing anything with it?' This was in June 2014 – and as luck would have it, November 2014 was the 25th anniversary of the fall of the Wall. One of the great things about working for Airbnb is that our community is also a source of stories.

But Mildenhall's first job when he took up his post was to help the company launch its new logo, primarily to symbolize the brand among Asian consumers, who couldn't necessarily decipher the word Airbnb in its distinctive 'bubble script':

> There was a project to come up with a universal symbol of belonging before I arrived, and the new logo was the result. So literally on day one Brian Chesky told me: 'We're launching this in seven weeks and we need a complete campaign – and we need you to figure it out.' He also wanted to make sure the logo could be taken and adapted by the community, so they could make their own versions, which was a technical issue as well as trademark one. And I came from Coca-Cola, where it was all about trademark protection.

The logo, as you may remember, proved controversial – some cheekier commentators compared it to a vagina. 'It sparked the biggest conversation in Airbnb's history to date. The creative community and the design community found it iconic, but there was a social debate about what it actually... represented.' To his credit, he says this with a smile and a twinkle. 'Some people looked at it and thought of women, others looked at it and thought of men. I look at it and think of humanity!'

Mildenhall points out that for a socially-driven company, the debate wasn't a problem. 'For launch day we'd set up a social media room staffed with 18 designers, writers and photographers, all responding to the social media comment, and doing so in a way that felt part of the community and not part of the corporate culture. Given where I'd come from, I was a bit nervous about how much I could lean in to the conversation, but Brian told me, 'Don't worry, really lean into it – I want this conversation to last a week.' It was crucial because people saw that we weren't going to shy away from the issue: if our community wanted to talk about the logo in a fun, provocative way, we were going to give them the fuel for that.'

He observes that the brand has a history of confronting 'uncomfortable truths'. In 2014, there were 500,000 homes on the site – still an enormous amount relative to its humble beginnings, but nothing compared to what it would become – and it was still perceived as something of an outlier by the hospitality industry. Enter Mildenhall:

> At that stage, staying in a stranger's home was still seen as kind of weird behaviour. Some people were a little bit freaked out by the concept. So we sat down and decided that unless we confronted that uncomfortable truth, it would follow us around all the time. So the opening line of our first multi-market TV campaign – where the single female traveller is narrating her own thoughts – is: 'Dear stranger, when I first booked this trip, my friends thought I was crazy. Why would you stay in someone else's home?' I still think that's one of the most provocative lines in advertising. We actually wanted people to have a conversation about whether this behaviour was weird or not.

The campaign was measurably successful, says Mildenhall. 'It had a visible impact on site traffic, booking and new homes. Within a year, we'd doubled the business and brand awareness had gone through the roof. Now we've become part of the travel establishment.'

Don't go there, live there

It's fair to say that for millennial travellers – and increasingly for families too – renting an Airbnb home has become the new normal. The platform's rapid growth has alarmed city authorities and created a grey economy that they have struggled to deal with. The press is full of stories of entrepreneurs who've bought two or three or more properties to rent out on Airbnb. In Paris – its most popular city – Airbnb fell foul of tax regulations until it agreed to collect taxes from hosts and remit them to local authorities. Similar solutions have been reached in other cities. There's also a whole sub-category of Airbnb remora who offer cleaning and concierge services to hosts and their guests. The snowball is rolling now and it's not going to stop – but the company has trodden a carefully diplomatic path in its dealings with city hall.

'Our approach is to work with the cities, all over the world,' says Mildenhall:

> It's constant management, because almost every city has a different position on Airbnb and the context is always changing. Some welcome us because they understand what we do for their citizens and the local economy; others have laws that were written 200 years ago that are quite draconian in terms of property and taxes, but they want to adapt to this new world, so there is a dialogue. Ultimately, everybody in Airbnb and our community believes that we are a net positive benefit for citizens, because we allow people to experience the reality of a city, to discover different parts of the city, and to bring money into the local economy.

More controversially still, some Airbnb hosts have been accused of racism. The site allows hosts to 'screen' guests, ostensibly to determine whether their apartment and belongings will be respected. At first, an anecdotal bias surfaced via outraged comments on social media, but it gained credence when a study released in early 2016 by Harvard Business School suggested that 'guests with distinctively African–American names' were around 16 per cent less likely to be accepted by hosts than 'identical guests with distinctively white names'. ('More Airbnb customers are complaining about racism', *The Economist*, 27 June 2016.)

In July that year, CEO Brian Chesky responded with a blog post on the site saying that the company had been 'talking more openly about discrimination and bias on our platform, and are currently engaged in a process to prevent it'. He added that he was working with former American Civil Liberties Union official Laura Murphy and former US attorney general Eric Holder to 'review every aspect of the Airbnb platform' and 'help craft a world-class anti-discrimination policy'.

Mildenhall himself, of course, is appalled by the racism claims. 'Anything that challenges the ideology of the company, the humanity of the community, the legitimacy of the business, we take very seriously,' he says.

Airbnb has promoted the idea of 'openness' in its advertising. To rent one of its apartments, it suggests, is to experience the world in a more authentic and enlightened way. At the time I meet Mildenhall, the endline of the brand's campaign is 'Don't go there, live there'. In the opening frame of the TV spot there's a selfie stick, almost as a symbol of everything that's wrong with tourism.

'Modern travel is sick,' Mildenhall states:

> Herds of people are shepherded around cities, all looking at the same museums and monuments and eating in the same neighbourhoods. They don't go to local restaurants, they don't use local businesses, they don't meet local creators – they don't really have a local experience. That's the tension we're pushing against right now. Modern travel is broken, and why would you want to be a tourist in a place when you can actually live there? We believe we're the only brand that can genuinely deliver that experience. You're staying in a home, you've got a local host, a local coffee shop, a local restaurant... everything about what we do is helping travellers have an authentic local experience.

The campaign, like its predecessors, was made by the Los Angeles outpost of the global advertising agency TBWA. Mildenhall mentions that he contacted several 'iconic' agencies when he arrived at Airbnb, but some of them declined to pitch for the account; they didn't believe the nascent brand had either the budget or the commitment required for creating great advertising. 'Now, of course, a lot of them are calling me saying, "Oh. You were serious. You had the resources and the backing after all. Can we work for you?" But no – TBWA believed in the business and believed in me, and they did by far the best work at pitch.'

One day somebody will conduct a survey on how many ideas are born in cars plodding through traffic. 'Don't go there, stay there' is a good example. Mildenhall says he was in the back of a car in Shanghai with Brian Chesky while they were researching the Chinese market. Mildenhall mentioned that he saw his angle for the Chinese campaign as 'travel like a local'. In response, Chesky asked him how many places he'd lived. 'Five,' he replied. Then Chesky asked him how many places he'd travelled to. 'I don't know – maybe 60?' Chesky replied: 'I think it's a shame that you've visited 60 countries, but you say you've only lived in five places. I think with Airbnb, because of our homes and our host community, we can promise people that they can live anywhere in the world, even if it's just for one night.'

Mildenhall says he immediately took out his phone and texted the agency. 'Love this line – what are we going to make of it?'

The result was a campaign that contrasted images of tourist buses and guides with people cooking and relaxing in their new 'homes' before strolling the city streets with the confidence of locals.

Travelling for 'bleisure'

While Airbnb has largely achieved its goal of moving beyond its core millennial market into families – and is making inroads into the luxury segment – it still has work to do in the business travel sector. But Mildenhall believes all the signs are positive.

'I think some of the loneliest travellers in the world are people travelling on business,' he says. 'Because they don't actually stay in places that allow them to connect with the local community.'

They do, however, stay in places that enable them to get a shirt pressed and grab breakfast from the buffet before dashing out of the door to a meeting – not amenities one associates with Airbnb.

'We are now certifying certain places as "business travel ready",' counters Mildenhall. 'They must have all the immediate conveniences and services that a business traveller requires.' These include 24-hour check-in, a guarantee that the accommodation will be used exclusively by the traveller, the ability to wash and iron clothing, room to work – and of course great Wi-Fi. In addition, Airbnb has done deals with business travel services such as American Express and Carlson Wagonlit to help incorporate its accommodation into the services they offer road warriors. 'We're also seeing a massive growth in – although I don't really like this term – the "bleisure" market.'

As you may have guessed, this is 'business/leisure' – people who travel on business but deliberately choose to arrive at the end of the week, so they can spend the weekend in the city.

'People are being a little more calculating about how they travel; so they're not always on the road, because they make time for cultural experiences. That's a big growth area in travel and an opportunity for us. After all, why just work there when you can live there?'

Before and after Airbnb

History will show that there was a pre- and post-Airbnb travel industry. Obviously, rental apartments existed before Airbnb came along – but its innovation was to allow homeowners to profit from space that might otherwise have remained vacant. It also required a certain spirit of adventure. Its digital forebear in that respect was CouchSurfing, a hospitality service created by Casey Fenton, a computer programmer.

Fenton had the idea when he was planning a trip to Iceland in 1999. He'd managed to find a cheap plane ticket, but the idea of staying in a hotel gave him a pain in his slender wallet. So he sent an e-mail to 1,500 students – spammed them, basically – asking if any of them could give him a place to stay, if only on the couch. 'The result was a new network of friends who offered to show him the "real" Reykjavik. After spending a weekend immersed in the culture of the area, Fenton walked away with disdain for the typical sanitized tourist experience.' ('How CouchSurfing got its start, and landed VC millions', *Entrepreneur*, 9 December 2011.)

Inspired, Fenton began developing his site, which launched in 2004 as a donation-funded non-profit with a similar world-changing mission to that of Airbnb: creating immersive 'local' experiences and connecting people across the globe. Interestingly, in an interview with *The New Yorker*, Fenton revealed a classic escape motivation for his own travels. 'As a boy growing up in Brownfield, Maine, he'd become fascinated by the concept of free will, cherishing the hope that someday he would have the existential where-withal to escape his home town and explore the world.' Fenton tells the interviewer that, almost as soon as he'd left high school, he began 'buying tickets that would take me as far away as I could go'. ('You're welcome', *The New Yorker*, 16 April 2012.)

Perhaps there's a lesson here for parents: if you want your kids to become globe-trotting explorers, make sure they grow up in a boring place. Install them in an exciting locale too early and they might find it harder to leave.

CouchSurfing remained a non-profit until 2011, when tax requirements – and lack of cash – forced it to apply for B-Corporation status, designed for companies that have 'socially-responsible missions'. Some of the community grumbled, but you can't run a business – even a socially-responsible, horizon-broadening one – on fresh air. These days CouchSurfing operates as a regular for-profit company and has a community of 12 million members.

The article in *The New Yorker* also mentioned the very intriguing Servas, founded in 1949 and 'generally regarded as the earliest hospitality exchange'. The article states that – guess what? – Servas was created 'as a means of promoting world harmony'. The organization still exists, with about 135,000 members, and a quick click on its site provides the backstory. Its original name was 'Peacebuilders', and it was initiated in Denmark by Bob Luitweiler, an American conscientious objector, and friends. 'They were deeply concerned about world peace and wanted to prevent a catastrophe like World War II from ever happening again,' the site explains. 'Their aim was to work actively for peace… and institute a work study travel system that would make it possible for people of various nations to make visits to each other's homes. To accomplish these aims a network was established of people who shared these goals and who would offer free hospitality for like-minded people.' ('Who we are', www.servas.org.) It sounds as though CouchSurfing and Airbnb have beat generation grandparents.

As well as feeling threatened by the sharing economy, hotel groups are learning from it. They're designing lobbies that feel like living rooms and hotels in which each room offers a unique experience. Local artists, designers and even chefs have been conscripted to add an authentic neighbourhood feel.

In a separate development, sites have sprung up that allow visitors to a city to 'eat with a local' – go to their home one evening for a delicious home-cooked meal – rather than spending the same amount, or more, at a regular restaurant. VizEat, EatWith, MyTable… like all great parties, the sharing economy has moved into the kitchen.

Airbnb's Jonathan Mildenhall is not surprised:

> There's a demand for individual experiences, not just in the travel industry but in bars, restaurants, museums, you name it. Experiences, rather than possessions, have become the new markers of success. The notion of owning an iconic pen, an iconic watch, an iconic car – that doesn't seem to synch with, in particular, the millennial mindset. They are much more about collecting experiences that are personal to them. They don't want to experience a great city like Barcelona and stay in a hotel that's devoid of any kind of originality and personality. We're seeing this whole shift from commoditization to individual, personal experiences – and that can only be good for the traveller.

Tour highlights

- Airbnb got its start in 2007 when two flatmates in San Francisco realized they could cover part of the rent on their loft by renting out their living room – and a couple of airbeds – during one of the city's most popular conferences.

- The platform enjoyed a quantum leap in 2014 when it launched its first multi-market TV advertising campaign, 'Belong anywhere'. Listings on the platform doubled within a year.

- Airbnb positions itself as a force for good because it connects travellers with local communities and enables them to experience different cultures closer to hand.

- But it has also created a grey economy and a sub-category of entrepreneurs who are feeding off its success.

- The hospitality industry as a whole has taken note of Airbnb's rise. Hotel groups have introduced similar models and begun creating 'unique experiences' for travellers.

- Meanwhile, the 'sharing economy' has moved into other hospitality niches such as food – with sites that enable travellers to eat at local homes.

The only way is ethics

19

'The destructive hand of visitors.'

Travel is desirable, but it is not necessarily harmless. There have been moments, in India or Zanzibar – while I'm giving boiled sweets and cheap biros to school children, or money to beggars – when I've wondered if I really have any business being in these places, and what impact my actions will have on them. And this twinge of guilt is minor compared to the carbon footprint left by the flight that brought me there.

The aviation industry accounts for roughly 2 per cent of global greenhouse gas emissions annually, according to the Air Transport Action Group (ATAG), or 781 million tonnes of CO_2 (www.atag.org). Some airlines offer passengers carbon offset schemes, and a deal to cap emissions across the industry by 2020 is in the air as I write, subject to negotiations between governments, airlines and environmental groups. But ATAG estimates that this will come at a cost of US$1.3 trillion to the industry, as it is forced to buy 12,000 fuel-efficient aircraft.

As you've heard, veteran travellers such as Mark Ellingham and Tony Wheeler, founders of immensely popular travel guides, began to question their comportment in the face of climate change. According to the United Nations World Tourism Organization, more than 1.1 billion tourists zip around the world every year (UNWTO Tourism Highlights 2016, e-unwto.org). As an article in *The Guardian* pointed out a couple of years ago 'empty wilderness is not what most [of them] will find at their destinations'. ('Wanderlust and the environment: can we afford to keep travelling?', *The Guardian,* 6 October 2014.)

What they will find – apart from other tourists – is 'the destructive hand of previous visitors'. It adds that 'tourism is responsible for one third of all the waste generated in the Mexican Caribbean, for instance'. Across the globe, beaches are ravaged, garbage spills into the sea, local populations are corrupted, women and children are abused by the tourism-boosted sex trade. Then there's the question of pumping tourist cash into dubious regimes.

Should we travel to Indonesia, currently engaged in a murderous war on drugs? What about Myanmar (Burma), which has made great progress but whose regime is still 'firmly tilted to the military junta', in the words of Tourism Concern. ('Responsible travel in Myanmar', www.tourismconcern. org.uk, 13 February 2015.)

In fact Tourism Concern – first mentioned in an earlier section on cruise ships – is a useful resource when weighing the ethical dimensions of a trip. The charity was established in 1988 to campaign for tourism which is 'ethical, fair and a positive experience for both travellers and the people and places they visit'. Entirely independent of the tourism industry, it publishes regular reports on its website, as well as its Ethical Travel Guide. This is particularly useful, as it's often difficult to tell whether a tour operator is genuinely 'ethical', or simply using the concept as a marketing tool.

And then there are the travellers who want to do good – but are in fact doing exactly the opposite.

Voluntourism

One of the most illuminating stories about a volunteering trip (or 'positive impact' vacation, or 'voluntourism') involves a young woman who went to Tanzania to build a school. Early every morning the volunteers would start work, occasionally making a few disdainful remarks about the locals, who went on sleeping. But towards the end of her trip, the woman discovered something both ironic and heart-breaking. Each day, after her team had finished building a wall and left for the evening, the locals would come and tear it down. Whereupon they would build it again – expertly, this time.

The anecdote on the website World Travel Guide is attributed to Mark Watson, executive director of Tourism Concern. It appears in an article by Jack Palfrey, who goes on to suggest that volunteering has been popularized 'by its inclusion on the archetypal gap-year agenda and regarded as another tick on the CV'. Such is the demand for spots, writes Palfrey, that hundreds of commercial organizations have sprung up, charging fees that go straight into their pockets while they 'send volunteers on unsatisfying, purpose-built placements'. ('Does voluntourism do more harm than good?', www.worldtravelguide.net, accessed 16 September 2016.)

Tourism Concern itself points out that 'many of the volunteering placements being offered by commercial operators are little more than expensive holidays' and adds that 'many volunteers have misplaced idealism, misconceived attitudes and unrealistic expectations of what they can offer local communities'.

It suggests that they would be better off volunteering for legitimate organizations back home, 'where they will receive proper training, support and supervision – without the need to pay a tour operator for the privilege'.

Some of the effects of voluntourism are very serious indeed. You don't have to look very far on the internet to stumble across stories of fake Cambodian orphanages set up to cater for volunteers duped by scam NGOs. Parents are either persuaded that their children will be better off in one of these institutions – or bribed. In 2014 *The Telegraph* reported: 'The Cambodian city of Siem Riep, with a population of 100,000, is now home to roughly 35 orphanages. And according to activist group Orphanages No… 75 per cent of children living in Cambodian orphanages are not orphans.' ('Gap years: voluntourism – who are you helping?', *The Daily Telegraph,* 14 August 2014.)

There are, of course, perfectly legitimate non-profit volunteering organizations, such as People And Places, which dates back to 2005 and matches people with genuine skills – teachers, nurses, social workers – to suitable projects. Co-founder Sallie Grayson, also quoted in the article above, offers a useful rule of thumb for judging whether your contribution will be useful, or ethical. 'Volunteers should ask themselves, "Do I have the skills to do this job?... Would I be allowed to go and hug a baby at an orphanage in my own country?" And we know what the answer is… Why should we be allowed to go and use economically poor communities as our playthings?'

Tourism Concern also provides a number of tips for would-be volunteers. It urges them to take a close look at the organization they're thinking of volunteering for (charity, NGO, profit-making?), its record within the local community and independent evaluations of its legitimacy. It suggests that they get in touch with previous volunteers via social media, to learn about their experiences.

Those who are keen to fly to a far-off destination and dig wells should also question their own motivation. Personally I suspect that the appeal of voluntourism is more about what it does for the traveller than the community concerned. Ultimately, as with most forms of tourism, the underlying goal is to feel good.

Virtual tourism

So what can we do to feed our craving for travel, while minimizing our impact on the environment? One of the more outlandish suggestions is virtual travel. If travel agents like Thomas Cook can use VR headsets to give customers a taste of a destination, why bother boarding the plane at all? Of course, a virtual experience is no replacement for breathing in the spices of the Khan el-Khalili bazaar in Cairo, or eating fresh seafood in a little taverna overlooking the beach in Crete; but it may protect some of the world's endangered beauty spots from further damage: the Galapagos Islands, for example, or the game reserves of the Maasai Mara.

An organization called YouVisit offers virtual tours, although founder Abi Mandelbaum suggests that these are primarily to 'give people a preview and an understanding of what they would experience if they went physically'. The problem lies in that word 'preview'. In the end, a VR tour is likely to encourage travellers to sign up for the real thing. YouVisit has found that '13 per cent of people who take a VR tour of a destination have their interest piqued enough to take the next step in the process of planning an actual trip'. ('How virtual tourism will enhance real-world travel', www.mashable.com, 22 April 2016.)

An alternative suggestion, then. The truth is, we don't need to get on a plane to experience other cultures. In cities, particularly, you can take a bus to the exotic. In London you can find elements of China, the Caribbean, India, Pakistan, the Middle East... I could go on. New York has Chinatown and Little Italy, just for starters. Paris has its own Chinese quarter too, and several slices of Africa. Beyond the city, I'm willing to bet that, wherever you live, there are inspiring destinations only a train ride or two away.

Of course we will always want to take off now and then, but the occasional 'staycation' shouldn't be too much of a hardship. If we want to travel ethically, the best option is to explore closer to home.

Tour highlights

- Travel has a negative impact on the environment – not least during the flight, as air travel counts for two per cent of annual greenhouse emissions globally.

- Beauty spots that were once inaccessible are now overrun with tourists, who bring with them noise, litter, over-consumption and disrespect for local cultures.

- Travellers who want to 'do good' through volunteering are also being exploited by for-profit scam operations.

- Those who want to travel ethically are urged to consult organizations like Tourism Concern, cut back on flying and – if only once in a while – take domestic vacations.

The final frontier

20

'Space is hard.'

Mojave Desert, 31 October 2014. Shortly after 10am, the Kern County sheriff's office got a call: an aircraft had crashed around 20 miles south-east of the city of Mojave. When the wreckage was photographed from the air, the remains of the aircraft looked like a broken white bird in the beige vastness of the desert. Except that it was not exactly an aircraft: it was a rocket plane built by the aerospace company Scaled Composites for Virgin Galactic, Richard Branson's space tourism initiative.

The plane closely resembled a previous craft, SpaceShipOne, with which Scaled Composites had won a manned spaceflight competition in 2004 called the Ansari X Prize (funded by entrepreneurs Amir and Anousheh Ansari). The winning project had been backed by another billionaire, Microsoft co-founder Paul Allen. Shortly afterwards, Branson's Virgin Galactic became a major Scaled Composites customer.

On the morning of the accident, the SpaceShipTwo craft left Mojave Air and Space Port at 9.18am, hitching a ride on its larger WhiteKnightTwo carrier. At 50,000 feet the carrier dropped its charge and SpaceShipTwo's rockets fired.

Between 60 and 90 seconds later, disaster struck.

Stuart Witt, the spaceport's director, said: 'I knew something was wrong. I didn't know what. It wasn't obvious at first.' The radio reported an anomaly. 'And we waited.' ('Virgin Galactic's SpaceShipTwo crashes in new setback for commercial spaceflight', *The New York Times*, 31 October 2014.)

Inside the plane, pilot Peter Siebold was experiencing a rapid chain of catastrophic events. First the craft pitched up violently and he felt crippling G-forces. Next, 'a loud bang' was followed by cabin depressurization. In the background he could hear a sound like paper fluttering in the wind, 'which he believed was the sound of pieces of the cabin coming apart'. Suddenly he was outside the plane and 'at high altitude, above the haze layer'. Apparently still strapped to his seat, he managed to unbuckle his seatbelt and assume a free-fall position. Then he passed out. 'The next thing he remembered was a "sudden jolt" when the parachute opened and feeling as though he had been asleep.' The chute had deployed automatically. He told the official investigation team that the opening of the parachute was 'gentlemanly… it was not harsh'. ('A detailed account of Pete Siebold's survival in the SpaceShipTwo crash', www.parabolicarc.com.)

Peter Siebold survived the accident. Co-pilot Michael Alsbury was killed. The full details of the crash would not emerge until eight months later, when the National Transportation Safety Board (NTSB) in the United States concluded its investigation. The NTSB determined the cause of the in-flight disintegration as 'the co-pilot's premature unlocking of the spaceship's feather system'. (NTSB press release, 28 July 2015.)

So what does that mean? Imagine SpaceShipTwo igniting its rockets and hurtling towards the edge of space. Just before it reaches the zenith of its ascent, its twin tails are rotated into an upright position – or 'feathered', a little like the tail of a peacock – deliberately causing drag to ensure a smooth and stable re-entry. This is supposed to take place at a point when the thinner atmosphere makes the manoeuvre safe. Instead, the investigation found that the co-pilot engaged the feathering system too early, and the force of the air roaring around the craft caused it to break up.

But the NTSB report also said that Scaled Composites failed to adequately 'consider and protect against' such a miscalculation. 'NTSB Chairman Christopher A Hart emphasized that consideration of human factors, which was not emphasized in the design, safety assessment and operation of SpaceShipTwo's feather system, is critical to safe manned spaceflight to mitigate the potential consequences of human error.' (NTSB press release, as above.)

Even in the immediate aftermath of the crash, it looked unlikely that Virgin would give up on space. At a news conference after the tragedy, Virgin Galactic CEO George Whitesides said in a shaken voice, 'Space is hard… and today was a tough day.' But he added: 'The future in many ways rests on hard days like this, but we believe we owe it to the folks who were flying these vehicles, as well as the folks who've been working so hard on them, to understand this and move forward.' ('Will Virgin SpaceShipTwo crash set back space tourism?', www.bbc.com/news, 31 October 2014.)

Virgin founder Richard Branson was of a similar sentiment. 'In testing the boundaries of human capabilities and technologies, we are standing on the shoulders of giants. Yesterday, we fell short. We will now comprehensively assess the results of the crash and are determined to learn from this and move forward together as a company.' ('Space community united to learn from tragedy, then move forward,' www.virgin.com, 1 November 2014.)

Less than two years later, on 19 February 2016, at a press conference in a Mojave Space Port hangar, Virgin rolled out its new SpaceShipTwo, named Unity. Among the technical advances on its predecessor, the 'feathering system' could now only be engaged in the optimal conditions. Richard Branson himself was in the Land Rover that hauled the craft from behind a giant curtain. Was this Branson the showman? Or Branson the curious schoolboy, keen to experiment with the newest toys? Or rather, Branson the indefatigable explorer, forever pushing boundaries? Perhaps all of the above.

But one thing's for sure: when it comes to the race for space tourism, Branson is not alone.

The new space race

In terms of passenger numbers, Russia is winning the space tourism game. It took the first paying customer into space in 2001, when Dennis Tito, a US engineer – a very wealthy US engineer – paid a reported US$20 million to visit the International Space Station. He blasted off on 28 April aboard a Soyuz spacecraft, although the trip was brokered by a US company called Space Adventures, based in Virginia.

Space Adventures was co-founded in 1998 by Eric C Anderson, a maths prodigy who became hooked on the idea of spaceflight as a child. Later he studied aerospace engineering at Virginia University, still with his eyes on the stars. In 1995 he was one of only a handful of undergraduates chosen to take part in the NASA Academy's summer programme. He went on to become lead engineer and business development lead for aerospace software firm Analytical Graphics, and has 'held various consulting and research positions with NASA' (www.spaceadventures.com/about us). As well as arranging hundreds of zero-gravity flights, Space Adventures has sent eight paying guests to the International Space Station.

Ten years after becoming the world's first space tourist, Dennis Tito reminisced about the experience. Like Anderson, who made his dream come true, he'd been a space enthusiast since his youth. And although he made his fortune in finance, he'd worked as an engineer at NASA's Jet Propulsion Laboratory. In 2000 he was due to turn 60, so he figured his spaceflight was 'now or never'. While the Russians agreed to take him on a Soyuz flight, his old employers at NASA advised them against the idea, stating that the training period would be insufficient. Tito assumed his age was a problem too.

'If you're older, heart attacks happen, strokes happen, whatever,' he told the website Space.com. 'And what are they going to do, transport a corpse back to Earth? That would be very embarrassing for them, and traumatic.' ('First space tourist: how a US billionaire bought a ticket to orbit,' www. space.com, 27 April 2011.)

Long story short, Tito made his flight, enjoyed a six-day sojourn on the space station, and returned to land safely in Kazakhstan. Needless to say, he was entirely satisfied with the experience. 'The thing I have taken away from it is a sense of completeness for my life – that everything else I do in life would be a bonus.'

Space Adventures president Tom Shelley told Space.com that he believed Tito's flight made space tourism look feasible. 'That was the first real milestone and demonstrated to a lot of people that there was a market for private citizens to go to space.'

So who are the other commercial space explorers? You may have heard of SpaceX, shorthand for the Space Exploration Technologies Corporation, founded in 2002 by Elon Musk, one of the entrepreneurs behind the PayPal system and CEO of pioneering electric vehicle company Tesla Motors. Musk's primary goal is not, like Branson's, to transport tourists into space, but to develop reusable rockets that make space travel less costly. In 2006 it won a contract from NASA to transport cargo to the International Space Station. Even so, you'll be pleased to learn, Musk's project sprang from a dream: that of eventually colonizing Mars. He's spoken of this ambition many times. At a conference in California, for instance, in the summer of 2016, he 'explained that the road toward the Red Planet and to other destinations in the solar system will be paved with the development of reusable rocket technology because space becomes more accessible when travel costs are reduced'. ('Elon Musk charts path to colonizing Mars within a decade,' www.observer.com, 6 July 2016.)

Musk's plans ran into a setback on 1 September of that same year when a SpaceX rocket exploded on the launch pad. Nobody was hurt, but the rocket's cargo – an Israeli-owned communication satellite – was destroyed, and the media speculated that despite the company's 'solid safety record', the accident would raise questions about its rapid rise 'by offering lower costs and promising accelerated launch schedules' for commercial clients wanting to send satellites into space. ('SpaceX explosion reverberates across space, satellite and telecom industries', *The New York Times*, 4 September 2016.)

Another participant in the space race is Jeff Bezos, founder of Amazon. com, whose Blue Origin project is focused on orbital spaceflight for tourists. Passengers will sit inside a capsule, New Shepard, and be boosted into space by a reusable rocket, which will then break away and return to Earth. According to the Blue Origin website, the capsule will then give its passengers 'unparalleled views' of space and the Earth (our 'blue origin') thanks to 'the largest windows in spaceflight history'. They'll experience weightlessness until a signal warns them to return to their seats and strap themselves in. Then the capsule will re-enter the atmosphere and drop gently to Earth using a mixture of thrusters and parachutes.

But that's not all: Blue Origin's vision is of 'millions of people living and working in space'. It's going to get crowded out there.

Let's not forget space hotels. Robert Bigelow is working on those. The US billionaire – born and raised in Las Vegas, Nevada, with a rangy and weathered cowboy look about him – already owns an earthbound hotel chain called Budget Suites of America. He's also the founder of Bigelow Aerospace and a firm believer in life on other worlds. But before we get that far, he wants to give humans a taste of life in outer space.

Bigelow's model is an inflatable habitation – something like a giant rotund tent – called the Bigelow Expandable Activity Module, or BEAM. It's far less ridiculous than it sounds, and is based on NASA technology. In its deflated form it's about the size of a refrigerator, which makes it easy to loft into space on a SpaceX rocket, for example. Once it arrives at the International Space Station, 'a robotic arm would reach into the arriving SpaceX Dragon capsule, grab the BEAM and attach it to the station's Tranquility node. Astronauts would then send a command releasing compressed air into the BEAM'. ('Can billionaire Robert Bigelow create a life for humans in space?', *Popular Science*, 8 April 2016.) The air would then inflate the BEAM into a space of '10.5 feet wide and 565 feet cubed', about the size of 'an eight-person tent or a studio apartment in Manhattan'. Naturally, it's made of material that is impenetrable to space debris and 'micrometeorites', which can really ruin your space vacation if the 2013 film *Gravity* is anything to go by.

The theory is that several of these modules – or their more sophisticated successors – could be linked to form a floating space station, or even a habitation on the surface of the moon. Bigelow himself told *Popular Science* that BEAM was 'a first step... towards a permanent habitation on the lunar surface'. He emphasized that his project was 'not a stunt – and neither are our moon plans'.

Hotel tycoons, the article points out, often see real estate opportunities in unexpected places, 'and there is no real estate more compelling to Bigelow than the moon'. He might just be the Conrad Hilton of outer space.

Designing space

When NASA was designing the first space suits, I'm not sure aesthetic considerations were a high priority. NASA doesn't equal natty. But where space tourism is concerned, looks do seem to matter. French designer Philippe Starck was 'consulting art director' for Virgin Galactic at the outset and came up with some early designs for its space suits, as well as working on 'space luggage' co-created with Louis Vuitton. The suit designs were unveiled at an exhibition devoted to space travel in Vuitton's flagship store on the Champs-Elysées in 2007. ('Take me to your designer', *The New York Times*, 10 May 2007.)

These days, Virgin Galactic's flights are conducted from Spaceport America – where SpaceX is a fellow tenant. Completed in 2012, the spaceport's location is laden with accidental symbolism: the Journada del Muerto ('route of the dead man') desert in New Mexico, not far from a place called Truth or Consequences. Since the spaceport was created and is partly funded by the State, and income has been lower than expected – due to the slow birth of the space tourism sector – it has attracted some controversy, with occasional calls for it to be sold. But diversification into guided tours, film shoots and speedway racing – in which the runways become tracks – have edged it closer to self-support.

Virgin Galactic has its own facility at the site, the unpretentiously-named Gateway to Space. The low yet suitably awe-inspiring building was designed by the UK's Foster & Partners: it looks like an alien butterfly settled on the desert floor. But what about the space suits? In January 2016 Virgin Galactic announced that the fashion brand Y-3 – a collaboration between Adidas and the Japanese designer Yohji Yamamoto – would be designing 'a full range of garments' for its passengers and ground crew. Space will be stylish, after all.

The subject of space tourism is so – forgive me – outlandish that it's difficult to stop a tone of levity from creeping in when one writes about it. But as the opening paragraphs make very clear, this is a journey fraught with danger. The promotional language used by the space tourism companies orbits this idea at a safe distance; it attempts to assure its niche audience of hyper-rich customers that they have 'the right stuff' – the souls of astronauts. Take these lines from the Blue Origin website: 'Having crossed over the Kármán Line into space, you will have earned your astronaut wings… You'll also belong to an exclusive Blue Origin alumni network – a community of modern space pioneers.'

Yes, space is hard – and you may question the wisdom of trying to turn it into a tourist attraction. You may even find something distasteful about the idea of billionaires building space rockets as playthings. But what if every technological advance had been left to the engineers, to the scientists? The rest of us might still be standing on the shore, gazing out to sea. I believe there is a direct line between Georges Nagelmackers of the Orient Express, Isambard Kingdom Brunel of the steamship *Great Western*, Juan Trippe of Pan Am and the likes of Richard Branson and Elon Musk. They are not purely motivated by a business opportunity – there are far easier ways of making money. They are dreamers who want to see how far they can push us.

Space is tourism's final frontier. Until, that is, somebody invents a time machine.

Tour highlights

- Space tourism began to look possible in 2001 when the US organization Space Adventures brokered a US$20 million deal with Russia to send a private citizen to the International Space Station aboard a Soyuz craft.

- Tesla's Elon Musk, Amazon's Jeff Bezos and Virgin's Richard Branson have launched commercial spaceflight ventures.

- Characteristically, Branson's Virgin Galactic is the most heavily publicized and branded.

- The promotional language of space tourism suggests that customers will enter the pantheon of space exploration – by turning them into astronauts for the price of a ticket, it promises to make their childhood dreams come true.

- Despite setbacks and tragedy, it seems unlikely that the space tourism pioneers will step back from their ultimate goal; the allure of space seems to outweigh common sense or practical concerns.

- Regular commercial spaceflights for paying passengers are close to becoming a reality – and a space hotel could follow.

Conclusion

'A site may be able to keep track of your habits, but it will never know who you are.'

'Chaos,' my new friend Jerôme told me, when I asked him to summarize the contemporary travel industry. 'But chaos I can benefit from.'

Jerôme Balandraud runs a small travel agency called Les Planeteurs in the charming Batignolles neighbourhood of Paris. The area has everything you could want from a Parisian *quartier*: tranquil tree-lined streets, handsome limestone buildings with peeling shutters and wrought-iron balconies, quaint cafés and bustling bistros – even a park with a duck pond and a carousel.

I discovered Les Planeteurs by accident, just a few weeks before I was due to put the finishing touches to this book. As I strolled past on my way elsewhere, my eye was caught by the smart charcoal-grey shop frontage, with a logo in the form of an Eiffel Tower encircled by a globe, the bright red scooter parked outside and the suggestion of mid-century modern furniture within. So I walked through the door and met Jerôme. A few days later, I was back to interview him for these pages.

He's an all-round travel expert – he started out at a booking call-centre for a network of travel agents, then ran a Paris franchise of Thomas Cook for 10 years – but saw an opportunity in the digital era. 'When I was running Thomas Cook, the fact that we were a franchise gave me a certain amount of flexibility – I could adapt to the needs of my clients, rather than obliging them to accept a standard offering. In the end I had a personal network of loyal customers, so I realized that I could create something for myself.'

He points out that while some travellers are satisfied with a vacation bought from a brochure, and others find what they need on the internet, a third – and considerable – group demand one-to-one advice and bespoke trips. 'For the same price as a traditional travel agent, I can practically deliver a concierge service. I have several mobile phones and I'm always there for people.'

Jerôme sees the internet as a mine of ideas. 'Information exists on the internet, but in a raw form – like uncut diamonds. Plus there's too much of it; a lot of people just don't have time to sift through it all. And because I'm a licensed tour operator I have access to professional booking sites that they can't go to. I can gather pieces from here and there and weave them into the vacation a customer wants.'

An algorithm, he points out, will never replace a personal, human relationship. 'A site may be able to keep track of your habits, but it will never know who you are. I know my customers personally: their family, their tastes, the kind of places they like. Small hotel? No problem. Apartment? Sure. I'll tailor your perfect trip.'

He draws a comparison with the technological advances in the music world. 'There was a time when you needed two or three different synthesizers and a couple of other instruments to build a track. But now you can do it with one piece of software, on your laptop. That's similar to how I compose a trip for my clients.'

At first Jerôme ran his operation from home, but then he realized that he needed a physical presence:

> The most ironic thing about the digital era is that it has given people the desire to see something concrete, something they can trust. They're sometimes paying thousands of euros for a trip that will take place more than a year later. A lot of them have had bad experiences before. So they need to have confidence in you. Plus I wanted to work in a neighbourhood again, where I could get to know people. A proportion of my customers come from this area. They walk past and drop in, just like you did.

Jerôme admits that booking online is often cheaper than using his services, but his customers accept that. 'Obviously a lot of people are looking for a bargain, it's a natural human urge. But if you're willing to pay a thousand euros instead of nine hundred, you get someone who you can pepper with questions and who will spend time crafting your personal voyage, just for you.'

I note aloud that Jerôme has his brand identity all worked out, from his smart logo to the Japanese trinkets on the agency's shelves and the vintage arcade game in the corner. 'But it's all really me,' he protests. 'You're looking at my personality – I could never reproduce this on an industrial scale.'

One of the things that surprised me when researching this book – call me naïve – was the extent to which most aspects of the travel business are simply about filling space as efficiently as possible: hotel rooms, apartments, aeroplane seats, cruise liner cabins and so on. Rather as the fashion industry uses what it often refers to as 'the dream' – a vaporous blend of glamour, self-actualization and status – to add value to chain-produced clothing and accessories, the escape industry uses the lures of relaxation, discovery and adventure to shift inventory.

Jerôme says: 'The travel industry in the digital era has become a dog-eat-dog world, creating a sort of turbulence in which customers often find themselves battered and directionless.'

Their salvation, Jerôme is convinced, lies in unique individuals with the ability to create memorable journeys.

The primacy of 'experience'

If you do a search to identify the most frequently used words in this book, 'experience' will come close to the top. A number of travel experts spoke to me of 'the experience economy' – and they're convinced that it will become even more important to their business in the future.

Indeed, the luxury and fashion industries – which use intangible values to sell material goods – are worried about the competition. Speaking at a conference in Shanghai, Shaun Rein, founder of the China Market Research Group, noted that spending among Chinese luxury consumers was shifting from products to experiences. 'The new luxury is not buying a branded bag, it's swimming with dolphins, hiking mountains, visiting far-flung amazing places – and then sharing the images on your phone.' ('Is fashion ready for the experience economy?', *The Business of Fashion*, 5 March 2016.)

As noted above, 'experiences' would seem to be best created – or curated – by people like Jerôme at Les Planeteurs. Travel agents are scrambling to reposition themselves as a blend of coach, consultant and concierge. But 'big data' is out there, and it is increasingly being used by travel brands to track our behaviour, identify our preferences and propose bespoke services. When we are on a journey, our phones know exactly where we are – and to a certain extent, the travel brands we use at each stage of the journey know that too. Is this creepy? Or is it an advantage? Let me know next time you arrive at customs and your hotel texts you offering a free ride.

The hunger for experience has caused turmoil in the hotel sector. There's no doubt that the big hotel groups take Airbnb and the sharing economy very seriously indeed. As leisure and even business travellers tire of 'cookie cutter' décor, the hotel giants are responding with distinctive design and a more diversified offering. As we've seen, they're also fighting back against online travel agents by rewarding customers who book directly through their own sites. Meanwhile, the fusion of advertising and entertainment into 'branded content' has encouraged them to experiment with emotive online videos: experience expressed as story. Social media channels and messaging services have given them the chance to further deepen their relationship with guests by engaging in conversations. 'Connected' hotels have brought tablet devices and apps into guest rooms, where they can be used for everything from temperature control to ordering room service.

Airlines seem to be getting left behind by the experiential trend. Airports – although they can't seem to do much about interminable lines at security – have attempted to soothe travellers' frayed nerves with upgraded shopping and dining opportunities, as well as soft play areas and spa facilities. But the flying experience, especially in economy, struggles to rise above average and more frequently hovers around wretched. An organization called Skytrax has ranked the world's airlines since 1999, awarding them a star rating of one to five based on passenger feedback. At the time of writing only eight airlines out of more than 280 surveyed boasted five stars – see www.airlineequality.com for details – so let's challenge them here and now to do better. Sterling service, seat comfort, multiple meal options and extensive in-flight entertainment seem to be the keys to passengers' hearts – joined more recently by mobile device connectivity – implying that there is still plenty of room for innovation.

As somebody who regularly allows himself to be enticed by the unreliable promise of travel, the flight is most often the moment I wished I'd stayed at home. But I will never learn.

The urge to escape

Just as Pan Am was a beautiful failure, its founder Juan Trippe's rosy vision of the future largely failed to materialize. If you recall, Trippe believed that mass tourism would have a positive impact on humankind, that the tourist 'charged with curiosity, enthusiasm and goodwill, who can roam the four corners of the world' would meet 'in friendship and understanding the people of other nations and races'. Other travel pioneers have expressed similar hopes.

Foreign travel is more accessible today than it has ever been. Cheap flights can be bought, rooms reserved, cars hired – all from our phones, without leaving our seats, between two sips of coffee. We can immerse ourselves in foreign cultures, taste unfamiliar food, see things in a single weekend that the original grand tourists took months to reach.

Has all that made us more open as human beings? Look around you. Turn on the news. Nations are tearing themselves apart, conflicts are grinding on, religions are clashing. Wars have given rise to a tide of refugees who have been forced to escape in the most literal sense. Our response, by and large, has been to push for tighter border controls. Has mass travel turned us all into tolerant, broadminded, cosmopolitan citizens of the world?

Hardly. Which prompts me to conclude that the true visionary of the travel business was also one of the first: Thomas Cook. He understood that, for a great many of us, the real purpose of leisure travel is to distract ourselves. To leave our quotidian worries behind, to break the routine, to gaze upon another landscape, to try on a new identity. We may not become better people, but we might become better versions of ourselves. Tanned, relaxed, fulfilled – free.

I won't attempt here to stray too far onto the territory of the philosopher Alain de Botton, who examines the myriad emotional responses to travel in his delightful (2002) book *The Art of Travel* – but his thoughts on the power of the holiday brochure seem relevant at this point. He describes being seduced, in the depths of a miserable English winter, by one particular brochure's images of 'palm trees… on a sandy beach fringed by a turquoise sea'. He notes: 'Those responsible for the brochure had darkly intuited how easily their readers might be turned into prey by photographs whose power insulted the intelligence and contravened any notions of free will: over-exposed photographs of palm trees, clear skies and white beaches.'

Thomas Cook was the first to wield the seductive power of the brochure – and versions of his approach can still be seen on the websites and social media feeds of hotel and travel brands, as well as in some of the better-composed photographs on Airbnb. The urge to edit and embellish the travel experience has been internalized by travellers themselves, who post extravagantly beautiful, often retouched, images of their vacations on social platforms. There has always been a dimension of showing off to travelling – the good story to tell at the bar or during the dinner party – but now we brag in real time.

De Botton travels to Barbados and discovers, of course, that there is far more to his destination than a single stereotyped image; in fact, there is discomfort and bad taste aplenty. Even when he finally gets to sit on a para-disiacal beach, he is distracted by a sore throat and work-related worries. You can never escape yourself – or as he puts it: 'I had inadvertently brought myself with me to the island.'

Nevertheless, the urge to get away is powerful. It fills thousands of flights a day, turns over billions of dollars, creates countless jobs. Even business travellers, who have the technology at their fingertips that would enable them to conduct international meetings from the office, find excuses to leave. A screen is no replacement for a handshake, they will tell you. Which is probably true. But it's an equally poor replacement for an exotic meal in a restaurant far from home. Business travellers may look like serious people in sensible clothing – but in their minds, I'm convinced, many of them are globe-trotting adventurers.

We will continue to travel, across this world, perhaps to others. But we will never be entirely satisfied, and every time we return to our own four walls, our last trip will leave us wanting more.

Costly for us, but very good news for the escape industry.

BIBLIOGRAPHY

Black, Jeremy (2003) *The British Abroad: The Grand Tour in the eighteenth century*, The History Press, Stroud, Gloucestershire

Bluffield, Robert (2009) *Imperial Airways: The birth of the British airline industry 1914–1940*, Ian Allen Publishing, Hersham, Surrey

Clémente-Ruiz, Aurélie and Carayon, Agnès (2014) *Il Était Une Fois l'Orient Express* (exhibition catalogue), Éditions Snoeck, Ghent

Conrad III, Barnaby (2013) *Pan Am: An aviation legend*, Council Oak Books, San Francisco, CA

De Botton, Alain (2014) *The Art of Travel*, Penguin, London

Dickinson, Robert and Vladimir, Andy (1997) *Selling the Sea: An inside look at the cruise industry*, John Wiley & Sons, New York

Eglin, Roger and Ritchie, Berry (1980) *Fly Me, I'm Freddie*, George Weidenfeld and Nicholson Limited, London

Fox, Stephen (2004) *The Ocean Railway*, Harper Perennial, London

Garin, Kristoffer A (2005) *Devils on the Deep Blue Sea*, Viking, New York

Gubler, Fritz (2008) *Great, Grand and Famous Hotels*, Great, Grand & Famous Pty Ltd, Crows Nest, New South Wales

Hamilton, Jill (2005) *Thomas Cook: The holiday maker*, Sutton Publishing Limited, Stroud, Gloucestershire

Hibbert, Christopher (1969) *The Grand Tour*, George Weidenfeld and Nicolson Limited, London

Hilton, Conrad K (1957) *Be My Guest*, Prentice Hall Press, New Jersey

Larson, Erik (2015) *Dead Wake: The last crossing of the Lusitania*, Crown Publishers, New York

Marriott, JW 'Bill' (2013) *Without Reservations: How a family root beer stand grew into a global hotel company*, Luxury Custom Publishing, San Diego, CA

Mazzeo, Tilar J (2014) *The Hotel on Place Vendôme*, Harper Perennial, New York

Reilly, Thomas (1997) *Jannus, An American Flier*, University Press of Florida, Gainesville, FL

Rheem, Carroll (2012) *Empowering Inspiration: The future of travel search*, Phocuswright, Sherman, CT

Seba, Anne (2009) *The Exiled Collector: William Bankes and the making of an English country house*, The Dovecote Press, Wimbourne Minster, Dorset

Toporek, Adam (2015) *Be Your Customer's Hero: Real-world tips and techniques for the service front lines*, AMACOM, New York

Tungate, Mark (2009) *Luxury World: The past, present and future of luxury brands*, Kogan Page, London

Watkin, David and D'Ormesson, Jean (introduction) *et al* (1984) *Grand Hotel: The Golden Age of Palace Hotels: An architectural and social history*, Chartwell Books Inc, New Jersey

Withey, Lynne (1997) *Grand Tours and Cook's Tours: A history of leisure travel 1750 to 1915*, Aurum Press, London

INDEX

Note: The index is arranged in alphabetical, word-by-word order. Numbers in headings, 'Mc' and 'St' are filed as spelt out in full; acronyms are filed as written; the prefix 'al' is ignored in filing order.

CPSIA information can be obtained
at www.ICGtesting.com
Printed in the USA
LVOW13s2105151117
556395LV00016B/195/P